45 CONTEMPORARY POEMS

The Creative Process

Edited by

Alberta T. Turner

Cleveland State University

Longman

New York & London

Longman English and Humanities Series
Series Editor: Lee Jacobus
University of Connecticut, Storrs

45 Contemporary Poems
The Creative Process

Longman Inc., 1560 Broadway, New York, N.Y. 10036
Associated companies, branches, and representatives
throughout the world.

Developmental Editor: Gordon T. Anderson
Editorial Supervisor: Jennifer C. Barber
Interior Designer: Thomas Bacher
Production Manufacturing: Ferne Y. Kawahara/Karen Lumley
Composition: The Composing Room of Michigan
Printing and Binding: Haddon Craftsmen

Library of Congress Cataloging in Publication Data
Main entry under title:
45 contemporary poems.
   (Longman English and humanities series)
   1. Poetry, Modern—20th century—History and
criticism.   2. Poetry, Modern—20th century.
I. Turner, Alberta T.   II. Title: 45 contemporary
poems.   III. Series.
PN1271.F64   1985   809.1'04   84–11272

ISBN 0–582–28443–0

Manufactured in the United States of America
Printing: 9 8 7 6 5 4 3 2 1   Year: 92 91 90 89 88 87 86 85

CONTENTS

*

ACKNOWLEDGMENTS

*

"Syringa" from *Houseboat Days* by John Ashbery. Copyright © 1977 by John Ashbery. Reprinted by permission from Viking Penguin, Inc.

"Variations on the Word *Sleep*" from *True Stories.* Copyright © 1981 by Margaret Atwood.

From *Before Sleep* by Philip Booth. Copyright © 1980 by Philip Booth. Reprinted by permission of Viking Penguin Inc.

"From Stone to Thorn" from *Winterfold* by George Mackay Brown. Reprinted by permission of The Hogarth Press.

"Mourning Doves" by Jared Carter from *The Devil's Millhopper*, Vol. 7, Number 2, Fall 1982. Reprinted by permission of *The Devil's Millhopper*.

"For My Mother: Genevieve Jules Creeley" from *The Collected Poems of Robert Creeley.* Copyright © 1982 by The Regents of the University of California, reprinted by permission of the University of California Press.

"Deborah Burning a Doll Made of House-Wood," from *Puella* by James Dickey. Copyright © 1982 by James Dickey. Reprinted by permission of Doubleday & Company, Inc.

"Elizabeth's War with the Christmas Bear: 1601," Copyright © 1977 by Norman Dubie from the book *The City of Olesha Fruit* by Norman Dubie. Reprinted by permission of the author.

"The Wounded Breakfast" by Russell Edson. Reprinted by permission of the author.

"Yes, What?" by Robert Francis. Reprinted from *Robert Francis: Collected Poems, 1936–1976* (University of Massachusetts Press, 1976), Copyright © 1976 by Robert Francis.

Stuart Friebert, "The Metal Fox." Reprinted from *Uncertain Health.* Copyright © 1979 by Stuart Friebert. Reprinted by permission of Woolmer/Brotherson Ltd.

"The Eye in the Rock" Copyright © 1982 by John Haines. Reprinted from *News From the Glacier: Selected Poems 1960–1980* by permission of Wesleyan University Press.

"Names of Horses" by Donald Hall, reprinted by permission; Copyright © 1977, The New York Magazine.

"Landfill" by Michael Harper. Reprinted by permission of the author.

"The Gypsy and the Man in the Black Hat," by Stratis Haviaras. English translation by Ruth Whitman. Copyright © 1972 by Stratis Haviaras. Reprinted by permission of the author.

"Collision," from *Interferon or On Theater* by Miroslav Holub, *Field Translation Series #7.* Copyright © 1982 by Oberlin College. Reprinted by permission of the Editor.

"Crow on the Beach" from *Crow: From the Life and Songs of the Crow* by Ted Hughes. Copyright © 1971 by Ted Hughes. Reprinted by permission of Harper & Row, Publishers, Inc.

"The Candles Draw Well After All," by Laura Jensen from *Field*, No. 15, Fall, 1976. Copyright © 1976 Oberlin College. Reprinted by permission of the Editor.

"Bus Stop," Copyright © 1966 by Donald Justice. Reprinted from *Night Light* by permission of Wesleyan University Press.

Reprinted from *From One Life to Another* by Shirley Kaufman by permission of the University of Pittsburgh Press. © 1979 by Shirley Kaufman.

"Potato Pie," by Abba Kovner. Translation by Shirley Kaufman with Nurit Orchan from *The Jerusalem Quarterly*, No. 24, Summer 1982, pp. 55–56. Reprinted by permission of the Managing Editor.

Philip Levine, "Angel Butcher" in *They Feed They Lion.* Copyright © 1972 by Philip Levine. Reprinted with the permission of Atheneum Publishers.

"Farmers" from *Sunday* by Thomas Lux. Copyright © 1979 by Thomas Lux. Reprinted by permission of Houghton Mifflin Company.

"Breath" from *A World of Difference* by Heather McHugh. Copyright © 1981 by Heather McHugh. Reprinted by permission of Houghton Mifflin Company.

"Collapsars" Copyright © 1973 by Sandra McPherson. From *Radiation* by Sandra McPherson, published by the Ecco Press in 1973. Reprinted by permission.

"Less than Sixpence" from *In and Out of the Apple* by John Mole. Reprinted by permission of Martin Secker & Warburg Limited.

"Biglietto d'Ingresso," by Carol Muske. Reprinted by permission of the author.

"On Being Asked for a Peace Poem," from *Gnomes of Occasions*, by Howard Nemerov. Copyright © 1973. Reprinted by permission of the author.

"After Whistler," by Stanley Plumly. Reprinted by permission of the author.

"The Coldest Year of Grace" by Giovanni Raboni. English translation by Stuart Friebert and Vinio Rossi. Copyright © 1985 by Stuart Friebert and Vinio Rossi. This poem appears by permission of Wesleyan University Press and is the title peom from *The Coldest Year of Grace*.

"Elegy," from *The Shore* by David St. John. Copyright © 1980 by David St. John. Reprinted by permission of Houghton Mifflin Company.

"Making Chicago" Copyright © 1980 by Dennis Schmitz. From *String* by Dennis Schmitz, published by The Ecco Press in 1980. Reprinted by permission.

"The Child" by Jon Silkin. From *Selected Poems* by Jon Silkin, published by Routledge & Kegan Paul. Reprinted by permission.

"Classic Ballroom Dances" Copyright © 1980 by Charles Simic. From *Classic Ballroom Dances*, published by George Braziller, Inc. in 1980. Reprinted by permission.

"Chocolates" from *Caviare at the Funeral* by Louis Simpson. Copyright © 1980 by Louis Simpson. Reprinted by permission of Franklin Watts, Inc.

"In the House of the Judge" from *In the House of the Judge* by Dave Smith. Copyright © 1982 by Dave Smith. Originally appeared in *The New Yorker* and reprinted by permission of Harper & Row, Publishers, Inc.

Gary Snyder, "Regarding Wave." Copyright © 1968 by Gary Snyder. First printed in *Poetry*, March 1968. Reprinted by permission of New Directions Publishing Corporation.

"Yellow Cars" from *A Glass Face in the Rain* by William Stafford. Copyright © 1982 by William Stafford. Reprinted by permission of Harper & Row, Publishers, Inc.

"For Night to Come" from *The Red Coal* by Gerald Stern. Copyright © 1981 by Gerald Stern. Reprinted by permission of Houghton Mifflin Company.

Mark Strand, "Where Are the Waters of Childhood" in *The Late Hour*. Copyright © 1978 by Mark Strand. Reprinted with the permission of Atheneum Publishers, Inc.

"December 21st" from *The Messenger* by Jean Valentine. Copyright © 1974, 1975, 1976, 1977, 1978, 1979 by Jean Valentine. Reprinted by permission of Farrar, Straus and Giroux, Inc.

Copyright © 1972 by Richard Wilbur. Reprinted from his volume *The Mindreader* by permission of Harcourt Brace Jovanovich, Inc.

"Night Light," from *Household Tales of Moon and Water*, Copyright © 1982 by Nancy Willard. Reprinted by permission of Harcourt Brace Jovanovich, Inc.

From "Becoming a Writer" in *Angel in the Parlor*, Copyright © 1983 by Nancy Willard. Reprinted by permission of Harcourt Brace Jovanovich, Inc.

"Nightdream" Copyright © 1973 by Charles Wright. Reprinted from *Hard Freight* by permission of Wesleyan University Press. "Nightdream" first appeared in *Poetry*.

"October Couplets," by David Young. Copyright © 1984 by David Young. Reprinted by permission of the author. First appeared in *Ohio Journal*, Volume 8, no. 1, Fall-Winter 1983–84.

INTRODUCTION

*

This book is the indirect result of a mistake. Many years ago I read an elegy by Stephen Spender which ended on the line, "And left the vivid air *signed* with their honour." I misread it, "*singed* with their honour." Magnificent, I thought, I wish I'd written that! I've repeated that mistake many times, misread or misinterpreted what someone said or wrote just enough to overcomplicate or oversimplify or twist it to make it better or worse or just quite different. Without meaning to, I tend to cast what I read or hear into forms that I want or expect to find. Knowing that I am not unique and that readers and writers both need to be aware of this tendency in order to exercise restraint, I felt it would be wise to examine poems in process and give other poets and students of poetry a chance to compare their own understanding of a poem with that of its author and their own observation of its craftsmanship with the author's awareness of it—a little like walking into the kitchen and talking to the cook to see if you smell what you think you smell, whether his taste buds react the same way yours do to turmeric or thyme, and if you like it, to see what tools or spices you might use in your own kitchen. This is not idle curiosity. It is apprenticeship; you are a cook too. Nor is it idle curiosity for poets, student poets, or serious readers of poetry to ask a poet why and how a poem they admire got written. Only a loving humility cares enough to ask.

To satisfy this need, I selected a group of the best contemporary poems written in (or translated into) English, poems that represented a range of the subjects, tones, points of view and techniques that young poets and students of poetry are likely to read in college literature courses or Masters of Fine Arts programs. I then sent specific questions on each poem to its author, questions which I hoped would tempt the poets to talk about how the poems started and how they developed. As the poets talked, I hoped to learn, directly or indirectly, something about how they wished their poems to be read, something about their theories of poetic technique, and perhaps even something about what they thought poems were for.

Since I had chosen these poems before I framed the questions, they reflect an outsider's reading, often tilted away from the poet's expectations. The result is dialogue, a chance for the editor to misread and be corrected by the authors, a chance for the authors to discover things about their poems they had been unaware of, and a chance for the reader to perceive how much of a poem's emphasis, tone, and even theme are contributed by a reader and how a second reader, like himself, may further modify a poem in reading it. For example, when I questioned George Mackay Brown, "What determined your choice of the alternating long-line, short-line stanza form? Is it to suggest the rhythm of a halting step?" He answered, "This

1

has not struck me; but I think you've got it right." When I thought I detected satire in Louis Simpson's "Chocolates," he disagreed, "Superficially it may appear that I am poking fun at the kind of people who would go to see a famous author, but readers who feel superior to these visitors are missing the point." And when I said of Robert Creeley's "To My Mother," "A close look suggests a long and careful editing," he replied, "in fact, no. The poem has no 'careful' editing whatsoever."

The poets reacted to my questions as one would expect men and women of widely different temperaments to react. Some enjoyed being scholars of their own work and gave full details—autobiographical, critical, and theoretic; others felt uncomfortable, saying that they could not truthfully tell how the poems developed. A good many had forgotten what determined their choices on such technical matters as sound, rhythm, and line breaks. Several had destroyed their worksheets as soon as their poems were finished. And Randall Jarrell's statement that a poem is one way of forgetting how you wrote it was quoted more than once.

On the nature of the poetic process, these poets agree with the contributors to this book's predecessor, *50 Contemporary Poets: The Creative Process* (Longman, 1977), "that poets cannot *create* poems, they can only edit them; that the precise moment when the emotional reaction to experience is going to fuse experience into an artifact of words cannot be planned or predicted but only invited, induced; that too much intellectual manipulation may stop the process of creation; that the greatest part of craftsmanship is recognizing what has happened *after* it has happened."

In editing, likewise, they tend to trust emotion over intellect. They distrust rhetorical tricks, stating, for example, a preference for literal details that imply metaphor rather than identification of both tenor and vehicle. They prefer revising the sound and rhythm of emotion, bodily movement, and accident, rather than initially filling a prescribed form. Most spend much time editing, but not all. Thomas Lux says, "Nothing after the first draft or two of a poem happens by accident," but Creeley published his first draft almost exactly as it came.

One emphasis I had not expected, nor specifically asked about, was the poets' sense of mission. In their discussions I perceive a drift among American poets toward a position long held by European poets, a drift from the recent emphasis on poetry that explores the inner universe to poetry that confronts the outer. Though the *given* is still respected as the initial impetus of a poem, an early consciousness of theme and movement is often identified and claimed, perhaps even selected in advance. Stylistically, there seems to be less emphasis on indirection, more willingness to assert and interpret. Not that these poets, either in their poems or discussions, seem to want a revolution in poetics, more like a settling of individual guesses and experiments into comfortable convictions and habits without self-consciousness. The result is often a synthesis of deep image and confessional poetry with public poetry, a reacceptance of the poet as teacher and prophet. Not surprising, really, since poets, like the rest of us in the 1980s are increasingly concerned with the end of the world.

A comparison of two essays by John Haines illustrates poetry's growing concern with meaning or vision. In his essay on "At White River" (*50 Contemporary Poets*),

Haines pays the usual tribute to mystery and gift: "I need to concede a considerable area to what I don't know and can't know. Only to understand in a way I do not quite understand." Then he questions the worth of writing poems: "I wonder if the expenditure of time and energy, the space it seems to demand in my life is really justified"; then answers, "It does seem that the effort to be exact, to render an honest account, means something . . . in terms of life generally."

This suggested need for a moral purpose in poetry has become a full assertion in his essay on "The Eye in the Rock" (*45 Contemporary Poems*). He still considers the poem "a gift," as "found by us in the act of living," but if it is found for "egotistical aggrandizement . . . it is the literary equivalent of that material exploitation that in one way or another is wasting so much of the life of this planet." He describes his vision in this poem as an act of responsibility toward the race and its history: "In our time we must think our way back through many centuries in order to regain a kind of understanding in place of what was once intuitive." And he is surprised to find that he has used the term *we* instead of *I* in the poem, "as if 'we' were the natural self."

Even poets writing in a playful mood and denying serious intent, like Edson, Francis, and Nemerov, note poetry's need for significance and mission. Edson: "The poem must earn its reality by being true." Francis, while claiming he wrote "Yes, What?" just for the love of words, is eager to insure that the social attitude the words imply should not be misinterpreted. And Nemerov, who, in "On Being Asked for a Peace Poem," pokes fun directly at the self-importance of poets and the vanity of thinking they have any predictable or controllable influence on world events, ends by quoting, "'We work in the dark—we do what we can—we give what we have. Our doubt is our passion and our passion is our task.'" Most in this book affirm the task. Levine: "I hoped that my reader would be horrified that one being could do this to another being." Raboni: "The only possible narrative today is no longer a story of great epic truths, but a story of truths that are banal, microscopic, and almost elusive." He sees his poetry as a counter to the threat against "the fragility of all that which ought to be saved and which the hardness and cold of history menace." Even those who contribute poems of personal epiphany, like Stern or Kaufman or Muske, accept the importance of these epiphanies to themselves only when they become shared, universal experience. Says Stern: "I hope that what I did will help the reader re-enter his own sweet place, and stop his shaking." Gary Snyder addresses the question of poetry's purpose most directly when he identifies the function of "The Song of the Taste" as grace before meat: "Eating is truly a sacrament. How to accomplish this? We can start by saying Grace. Grace is the first and last poem, the few words we say to clear our hearts and teach our children and welcome the guest, all at the same time. To say a good grace you must be conscious of what you're doing . . . ."

In sum, *45 Contemporary Poems* sustains and expands the work of its predecessor, *50 Contemporary Poets*. It is a rich source for current attitudes toward and theories about the poetic process. Its contributors reemphasize a widespread reverence for the gift of raw material from the subconscious mind, a distaste for paraphrase, and a distrust of conscious rhetoric and critical omniscience—all expressed with considerable rhetorical and critical skill. In addition, this collection shows an increasing seriousness, a tightening of control, an impatience with self-indulgence, a closer examination of purpose, and a firmer commitment. It substantially increases our source material for determining what specific poets think they are doing in specific poems and comparing their interpretations with what the critics, the readers, and the poems themselves suggest that they are doing. It gives grounds for tentative generalizations about how poems start and how they grow. And it suggests what poets in the 1980s think poetry is for.

Alberta Turner

JOHN ASHBERY

*

Syringa

Orpheus liked the glad personal quality
Of the things beneath the sky. Of course, Eurydice was a part
Of this. Then one day, everything changed. He rends
Rocks into fissures with lament. Gullies, hummocks
Can't withstand it. The sky shudders from one horizon
To the other, almost ready to give up wholeness.
Then Apollo quietly told him: "Leave it all on earth.
Your lute, what point? Why pick at a dull pavan few care to
Follow, except a few birds of dusty feather,
Not vivid performances of the past." But why not?
All other things must change too.
The seasons are no longer what they once were,
But it is the nature of things to be seen only once,
As they happen along, bumping into other things, getting
   along
Somehow. That's where Orpheus made his mistake.
Of course Eurydice vanished into the shade;
She would have even if he hadn't turned around.
No use standing there like a gray stone toga as the whole
   wheel
Of recorded history flashes past, struck dumb, unable to
   utter an intelligent
Comment on the most thought-provoking element in its
   train.
Only love stays on the brain, and something these people,
These other ones, call life. Singing accurately
So that the notes mount straight up out of the well of
Dim noon and rival the tiny, sparkling yellow flowers
Growing around the brink of the quarry, encapsulates
The different weights of the things.
                                          But it isn't enough
To just go on singing. Orpheus realized this
And didn't mind so much about his reward being in heaven

5

After the Bacchantes had torn him apart, driven
Half out of their minds by his music, what it was doing to
    them.
Some say it was for his treatment of Eurydice.
But probably the music had more to do with it, and
The way music passes, emblematic
Of life and how you cannot isolate a note of it
And say it is good or bad. You must
Wait till it's over. "The end crowns all,"
Meaning also that the "tableau"
Is wrong. For although memories, of a season, for example,
Melt into a single snapshot, one cannot guard, treasure
That stalled moment. It too is flowing, fleeting;
It is a picture of flowing, scenery, though living, mortal,
Over which an abstract action is laid out in blunt,
Harsh strokes. And to ask more than this
Is to become the tossing reeds of that slow,
Powerful stream, the trailing grasses
Playfully tugged at, but to participate in the action
No more than this. Then in the lowering gentian sky
Electric twitches are faintly apparent first, then burst forth
Into a shower of fixed, cream-colored flares. The horses
Have each seen a share of the truth, though each thinks,
"I'm a maverick. Nothing of this is happening to me,
Though I can understand the language of birds, and
The itinerary of the lights caught in the storm is fully
    apparent to me.
Their jousting ends in music much
As trees move more easily in the wind after a summer storm
And is happening in lacy shadows of shore-trees, now, day
    after day."

But how late to be regretting all this, even
Bearing in mind that regrets are always late, too late!
To which Orpheus, a bluish cloud with white contours,
Replies that these are of course not regrets at all,
Merely a careful, scholarly setting down of
Unquestioned facts, a record of pebbles along the way.
And no matter how all this disappeared,
Or got where it was going, it is no longer
Material for a poem. Its subject
Matters too much, and not enough, standing there helplessly
While the poem streaked by, its tail afire, a bad
Comet screaming hate and disaster, but so turned inward

That the meaning, good or other, can never
Become known. The singer thinks
Constructively, builds up his chant in progressive stages
Like a skyscraper, but at the last minute turns away.
The song is engulfed in an instant in blackness
Which must in turn flood the whole continent
With blackness, for it cannot see. The singer
Must then pass out of sight, not even relieved
Of the evil burthen of the words. Stellification
Is for the few, and comes about much later
When all record of these people and their lives
Has disappeared into libraries, onto microfilm.
A few are still interested in them. "But what about
So-and-so?" is still asked on occasion. But they lie
Frozen and out of touch until an arbitrary chorus
Speaks of a totally different incident with a similar name
In whose tale are hidden syllables
Of what happened so long before that
In some small town, one indifferent summer.

1. *This poem, like many earlier poems of yours, is concerned with the nature of experi-ence, and sees it as the incomplete and shifting perception of a continual flux. Orpheus, considered by the Greeks to be the greatest poet before Homer, is frantic because his music cannot finally make Eurydice immortal, as classical poetic theory says it will; but the poem's speaker offers him a different interpretation of the nature and function of the art. Could you comment, with specific reference to this poem, on how your own poetic theory differs from Orpheus' "mistake?"*

2. *A reader new to the poem and its subject might need to ask the following:*
   a. *Is the "abstract action" "laid out in blunt, / Harsh strokes" the nearest a poem can come to guarding the "stalled moment"?*
   b. *Do the horses who see "a share of the truth" and the trees that "move more easily" after the storm stand for poets and the extent to which their art can participate in experience?*
   c. *Where does Orpheus' reply (Line 4 of the poem's second part) end, and where does the poem's speaker resume? Or does Orpheus in the form of "a bluish cloud with white contours" now share the speaker's view, so that they both speak the rest of the poem?*
   d. *Does the description of the poem as a "bad comet" "so turned inward / that the meaning, good or other, can never / Become known" apply to all forms of art? All periods of poetry?*
   e. *Does the "blackness" which engulfs the "song" refer to the writer's participation, which has now ended, or the reader's or both?*

   f. The "arbitrary chorus" (ourselves reading Homer or Ashbery in future centuries) will preserve what is left of the poet and his work only indirectly, inadvertently, and thus inaccurately. Is this remote effect what is referred to by "But it isn't enough / To just go on singing" earlier in the poem?

   g. The poem's speaker seems to regard this remote effect with neither sorrow nor joy, yet the fact that in "Syringa" he has considered it so long and thoughtfully suggests deep concern. Could you comment on the extent and duration and, perhaps, reason for this concern?

3. *Readers interested in how the poem came to take its present form might ask the following:*

   a. What determined your selection of the Syrinx myth (in the title) and one of the less well known aspects of the Orpheus myth for this poem?

   b. Could you comment on your reasons for choosing the syntax, diction, rhythm, and sound of serious, educated conversation—what Horace or Jonson would have known as the epistolary *or* plain style?

   c. The element of playfulness that appears in most of your poems is apparent in this one chiefly in colloquial phrases and unexpected images ("the poem streaked by, its tail afire;" "That stalled moment;" the horse that says, "I'm a maverick;" "birds of a dusty feather") contrasted to conspicuously formal ones ("Stellification / Is for the few," "music . . . emblematic of life," "the 'tableau' / Is wrong"). Is this done deliberately to keep poets and their readers from taking poetics too seriously, or is it a modification of classical "decorum" to create a new decorum?

   d. How many and what sorts of revisions did the poem undergo and over what period? If you saved the worksheets, could we see a copy?

4. *What readers did you especially have in mind for this poem? How have readers reacted to it?*

5. *What additional or different questions would you have liked me to ask?*

Dear Alberta Turner,

   I'm sorry but I'm afraid I'm unable to deal with your questions. Not that they are bad or irrelevant questions. Quite the contrary—they make perfect sense, and are no doubt the sort of questions that readers of my poetry would like to see answered. And I suppose I could manufacture answers which would make sense and give the reader the impression that his understanding of my poetry had been improved. The problem is that these would be fake answers. I really have no idea why I write, or what I am doing when I am doing it. I write what comes to me and hope that somebody will be able to make something of it. I have no ''poetic

theory.'' The reason I wrote a poem about Orpheus was that
as I was preparing to sit down and write some poetry I
slipped a record on my turntable which happened to be
Monteverdi's ''Orfeo,'' and I thought, well, why not? A
hackneyed subject no doubt, but perhaps as good as many an
other. So much, I fear, for Orpheus, poetic theory, and the
nature of experience. As for the title, it has nothing to
do with the Syrinx myth. Had I wished to allude to that I
would have named the poem ''Syrinx.'' Syringa is an old-
fashioned flowering bush that might well be growing in the
back yards of people who lived in ''some small town, one
indifferent summer.'' If there is any theme to the poem it
probably has to do with that last line and memories of my
own childhood. But a poem first presents itself to me as a
somehow specific blank space which I then proceed to people
with objects, events, and characters. For me they do not
have any symbolic meaning outside the boundaries of the
poem, and therefore I guess my poetry is ''self-
reflexive,'' a term which causes the bosoms of critics to
swell with holy indignation these days. But that's what I
do, and I can't help it. The poem that streaked by is just a
poem which happened to make a comet-like appearance in this
poem. The horses are just some horses that happened to be
talking, and so on. To pretend otherwise and to try to
supply a broader meaning where none exists would be to
bring a false enlightenment to the reader. I'm afraid that
doesn't help with his (or your) problems, but I firmly
believe that the only way to ''understand'' (whatever that
means) poetry is by reading it.

   I'm truly sorry to have kept you waiting so long, and I
apologize again for not dealing with your well-intentioned
questions. I'm avoiding them not from laziness or
unwillingness to shed light on my poetry, but from a
conviction that this can only be done within the poem.
Poetry, I think, is already criticism—criticism of life—
and further criticism must take the form of another poem or
else be forced to operate at a fatal distance from the
subject.

                                        Sincerely yours,

                                        John Ashbery

JOHN ASHBERY grew up in rural New York State, was educated at Harvard and Columbia Universities, wrote art criticism for the Paris *Herald Tribune,* served as executive editor of *Art News,* N.Y., and now lives in New York City and teaches at Brooklyn College. Between 1956 and 1981 he published three plays, a novel, and nine books of poems. His *Self-Portrait in a Convex Mirror,* 1975, won the Pulitzer Prize, the National Book Award, and the National Book Critics Circle Award. His most recent book of poems is *A Wave,* 1984.

MARGARET ATWOOD

*

Variation on the Word Sleep

I would like to watch you sleeping,
which may not happen.
I would like to watch you,
sleeping. I would like to sleep
with you, to enter
your sleep as its smooth dark wave
slides over my head

and walk with you through that lucent
wavering forest of bluegreen leaves
with its watery sun & three moons
towards the cave where you must descend,
towards your worst fear

I would like to give you the silver
branch, the small white flower, the one
word that will protect you
from the grief at the center
of your dream, from the grief
at the center. I would like to follow
you up the long stairway
again & become
the boat that would row you back
carefully, a flame
in two cupped hands
to where your body lies
beside me, and you enter
it as easily as breathing in

I would like to be the air
that inhabits you for a moment
only. I would like to be that unnoticed
& that necessary.

In answer to a question I did not ask, but which needs asking, Margaret Atwood describes the writing of "Variation on the Word Sleep" as "the most desirable kind of poem-composing experience"—a "seamlessness."

The embarassing truth is that I usually can't remember very much at all about how I came to write a particular poem. The process itself is so involving for me that it excludes objective knowledge of itself; if there is a memory of it, it is more like a body memory—the way you "remember" how you ride a bicycle or paddle a canoe—than a "mind" memory, which would involve being able to describe to someone else how you do it. How do you "tell" someone the act of balancing? So this commentary of mine is of necessity a reconstruction; it uses, by and large, the same clues available to any critic—those contained in the poem itself—plus some special knowledge of mine about related but external matters. Only I know, for instance, what books I had read at the time of composition, which parts of them were important to me, and so forth.

"Variation on the Word *Sleep* " was for me the most desirable kind of poem-composing experience—and here immediately I come face to face with the inadequacy of terminology, because what are we to call it? "The Poetic Process?" "Writing a Poem" it isn't, quite; poems for me are written down rather than written, and I expect this is true for many poets. The page itself may be a place where the poem is worked on or worked over, but certainly the poem itself begins as something heard, and the finished poem-on-the-page is only a kind of score for the voice, whether poet's or reader's; an inner voice, usually, but the poem is always in some sense heard and spoken.

In any case, this event—the appearance and notation of the poem—was the most desirable kind because it was swift. The poem took form almost exactly as it now appears, with the exception of some fiddling about with the ends of lines. This 'seamlessness' by no means is a guarantee of a good poem, and usually I revise much more, but I couldn't think of anything I wanted to add to this one, or any other way I wished to see, hear or say things. As with much of my poem-making, I didn't pay a lot of external critical attention to 'influence' and 'symbolism' while I was actually composing, but looking at the poem afterwards I could see that this is in fact a very 'literary' poem in terms of its influences and sources. I don't think that's necessarily a bad thing; all it means is that the imaginative creations of others have become real to you.

It's a journey poem, in which the 'you' goes downwards, accompanied by a guide who is the speaker. (All in the subjunctive: the journey isn't one that has taken place or is taking place, but is wished for.) The concept of sleep as a place, subterranean or underwater—I think I may first have encountered that in Keats, though we always speak of people under anaesthesia as having "gone under," and we think of sleep as down ("deep sleep"). The leaves of the under-water forest come from my own experiences of diving in the tropics, but the three moons are definitely from Blake.

The silver branch and the white flower—the flower is the protective one in the story of Odysseus and Circe, the silver branch is a variation on Aeneus' descent to the underworld; yes I took Latin, but also had to study Greek and Roman mythology as a student of English literature. There's also "The Twelve Dancing Princesses," or, in Grimm's, "The Shoes That Were Danced to Pieces," and other fairy tales in which the underground realm contains trees made of silver, gold and jewels; I think my branch is silver rather than gold because this is a world ruled by the moon rather than the sun, or that's what I would say anyway if I were doing an exegesis. What the sleeper gains as a result of the journey may have something to do with it also: not knowledge of the future, or an encounter with the dead, but—it seems—something much more like an encounter with the sleeper's own central emotions. That's the first mention of 'grief'; the second implies that the grief is not merely personal, but is much more akin to *lacrimae rerum*, 'the tears of things,' a phrase which many translators, including those in our inkspotted Latin class, have struggled with.

The stairway and the boat—the center of the underground is below even the surface of the underground river or lake. The antecedents of the boat are many and obvious; in the poem, the boat and the guide become one. The boat also is the shape made when you place your hands together to hold water or a small candle; the soul as a flame or candle appears in many places, most notably in the Grimm's tale called "Godfather Death," in which the souls of everyone living are kept in the form of candles in a large cave. The sleeper's soul—which has been making the journey—slides back into the body in the penultimate stanza.

The last stanza seems to make a jump, but I think it continued from the concept of "soul"; if it is a flame, it is also, traditionally, a "breath," and at death it leaves the body in this form. So the speaker's wish to be air is also a wish for union with the "living" part of the person being spoken to.

This exposition makes the composition of this poem appear to be a much more deliberate thing than it was. As I've said, I didn't pay a lot of attention to where I was "getting" these images at the time. I think imagery of this kind—when you've lived with it long enough—becomes simply a way of speaking, another language, if you like. This is by no means my only "underground journey" poem, and more often than not the journeys are much less pleasant. But it's the one I like best so far. I don't think, by the way, that a reader of the poem has to have on hand all or indeed much of the above. It's a love poem, and it ought to communicate very simply on its own terms.

MARGARET ATWOOD was born in Ottawa, Canada, in 1939; was educated at the University of Toronto and Radcliffe College, Harvard University; and lives in Toronto. She has published eleven books of poems, the latest of which is *True Stories*, 1981, and seven works of fiction, including *Surfacing*, 1973, *Life*

Before Man, 1979, and, most recently, *Murder in the Dark,* 1983. She has also published children's books and books of criticism. Her work has been recognized internationally by such awards as the Governor General's Award (Canada), a Guggenheim Fellowship, and the Welsh Arts Council International Writer's Prize.

PHILIP BOOTH

✳

Eaton's Boatyard

To make do, making a living:
                              to throw away nothing,
practically nothing, nothing that may
come in handy:
                      within an inertia of caked paintcans,
frozen C-clamps, blown strips of tarp, and
pulling-boat molds,
                to be able to find,
for whatever it's worth,
                    what has to be there:
the requisite tool
                in this culch there's no end to:
the drawshave buried in potwarp,
chain, and manila jibsheets,
                    or, under the bench,
the piece that already may fit
                    the idea it begins
to shape up:
              not to be put off by split rudders,
stripped outboards, half
a gasket, and nailsick garboards:
                    to forget for good
all the old year's losses,
              save for
what needs be retrieved:
              a life given to
how today feels:
           to make of what's here
what has to be made
to make do.

1. *The poem starts to make a statement about what is needed "to make do, making a living" in the context of a boatman's life. For more than a page it details the kinds of choices to be made ("to throw away nothing . . . that may come in handy," "to be able to find/. . . what has to be there," "to make of what's here / what has to be made," "To find the piece that already may fit") from a detailed jumble of wornout or random or misfit bits of boat-building stuff. The poem, though it ends with a period, does not put a verb to the long list of infinitive subjects, much as the builder of a boat or a poem or a life never completes the job of choosing and making and remaking with whatever materials happen to be within reach. Was this syntax calculated to make the reader expand the meaning and again expand it in this fashion? Have your readers tended to expand it as far as you want them to? Farther?*

No, the syntax was in no way "calculated"; I discovered in the process of writing, revision after revision, how constantly the implications expanded. And, I would hope, deepened. How deeply a reader cares to look into the poem depends, I guess, on how well my syntax presents my sense of relationships. Early in *Before Sleep*, a poem called "Words for the Room" speaks my inclination toward "infinitives, relative objects." In all possible senses.

2. *As a reader who spent many summers of my youth sailing an old gaff-rigged, ex-clam boat off Nova Scotia, I recognize the different kinds of necessity and the condition of many of the objects in "Eaton's Boatyard." Our sails, too, were patched and our ropes much spliced. I don't recognize culch, pulling-boat molds, potwarp, but I do most of the others. Would it make a difference, do you think, to the impact of the poem if I recognized none of them? If the boatyard were an auto repair shop? A gardener's tool shed?*

This poem began long before I began to write it. It's a distant relative of a poem of mine called "Cleaning Out the Garage," and an even earlier poem called "Jake's Wharf," a wharf that was, in my boyhood, next door to Eaton's Boatyard. The poem descends more directly from another early poem called "Builder," which is about the grandfather of the boy who gave me one of this poem's prime words. The boy was about thirteen, I was maybe forty, still hanging around the waterfront, when I heard him yell to his father, Alonzo Eaton, "Dad, *when*'re you going to clean up this *christly* culch?" I missed the ultimate word the first time he yelled, but I got him quieted to say it again. And when I got back home to an unabridged dictionary, there it was: a word so old that Cabot or Champlain may have imported it to my home coast, a word I trust is as self-explanatory in the context of the poem as it was when the boy first yelled it.

"Culch" may be, in the poem, more self-evident than "potwarp" (the kind of rope that attaches a lobsterman's buoy to his trap far below it), or "pulling-boat molds" (the wooden patterns around which old Maine rowboats were built), but I've tried, all through the poem, to build around such terms a sufficient context for whatever reader may share my delight (with Hopkins) in "áll trádes, their gear and tackle and trim."

3. *Your book* Before Sleep, *in which this poem appears, contains a wide variety of poetic forms, a number of which seem to be selected for the sake of their visual effect. Is this poem's appearance on the page selected for that reason?*

No. Except as white space around dark print is a kind of visual notation even in sheet music, I don't think of my poems as being an eyeful. Not least as I hear line-ends as being variously inflexed, I feel the lineation in *Before Sleep* as being notational: as being one part of indicating hesitancies, holds, surges, in the overall score of the poem. I mean to help attune readers to how the poem wants to be heard.

4. *What determined your rhythms and sound repetitions?*

My ear. After years of practicing traditional English meters, and then moving to the roughened voice of accentual verse, I've here turned back toward what I early heard in Hopkins and, even earlier, in jazz: the offbeat working against the drumfoot. These influences, in ways I'm not sure I want to understand, work in me now as rhythms of my body language driving the poem to find its own music.

5. *If the poem is also a description of how you work at your own craft of poetry, how would you identify the throwing away of "practically nothing," the "culch," the disorder of the shop, the way the piece that already fits "begins to shape up" the idea, the "old year's losses"?*

Yes. I think, after the fact, that the poem *is* about the inevitable process of giving one's life, or one's poem, to what comes of feeling down into the materials at hand. Even in the culch of Eaton's Boatyard or the apparent chaos of being alive, nothing is ever lost. The problem of what to make of what's here (where else, after all?) is always, for me, a matter of piecing together what presents itself with "what needs be retrieved" in order to make sense of what's present.

6. *What started the poem? What revisions did it go through, in what order, over what period? If you have saved the worksheets, may I see a copy?*

I knew for years that there was a poem in Eaton's Boatyard. But only when a friend from (improbably) Paris made me a present of her unread (she said "unreadable") copy of *The Savage Mind* did I find Levi-Straus making his own distinction between the bravely planned world of the Engineer and the "devious means" of the person he calls "the 'bricoleur.'" Once I'd read his marvellous first chapter (and, indeed, found the rest of the book beyond me), I had only to retrieve the word "culch" before I found myself writing the present poem.

The draft sheets are far from me now, in a library. The poem as it has come to be completed has displaced those drafts in my mind. I'd guess that there are twenty to thirty draft sheets (fairly typical for me, given a poem of this length and complexity); my draftsheets are themselves a measure of process, of incrementally imagining "the piece that already may fit / the idea it begins / to shape up," of listening and listening to how words build to normative (and variant) lines, of how lines break to integrate (and vary) triadic forms, of how the pace of the poem is itself a measure of "what has to be made" to do justice to the materials: to bring feeling into such meaning, and meaning into such feeling, as the materials implicitly offer. The poem itself is what I have made "to make do."

PHILIP BOOTH is three times a grandfather, and the author of six books of poetry, all published by The Viking Press. He is by birth and inclination a northern New Englander; he lives and writes in Maine.

GEORGE MACKAY BROWN

*

From Stone to Thorn

Condemnation
The winter jar of honey and grain
Is a Lenten urn.

Cross
Lord, it is time. Take our yoke
And sunwards turn.

First Fall
To drudge in furrows till you drop
Is to be born

Mother of God
Out of the mild mothering hill
And the chaste burn.

Simon
God-begun, the barley rack
By man is borne.

Veronica
Foldings of women. Your harrow sweat
Darkens her yarn.

Second Fall
Sower-and-Seed, one flesh, you fling
From stone to thorn.

Women of Jerusalem
You are bound for the Kingdom of Death. The enfolded
Women mourn.

Third Fall
Scythes are sharpened to bring you down,
King Barleycorn.

The Stripping
Flails creak. Golden coat
From kernel is torn.

Crucifixion
The fruitful stones thunder around,
Quern on quern.

Death
The last black hunger rages through you
With hoof and horn.

Pietà
Mother, fold him from those furrows,
Your broken bairn.

Sepulchre
Shepherd, angel, king are kneeling, look,
In the door of the barn.

Dear Alberta,
    Thank you for your letter and list of questions on my
poem ''From Stone to Thorn.''
    Perhaps I should try to clarify my thoughts on the poem
before answering the questions. (It is quite a while since
I wrote it. I always think of it with affection, because I
had an almighty struggle with it; and it seems as it stands
to distil all my thoughts about life and time that appear
in more scattered form elsewhere in my writings).
    Every little couplet parallels one of the 14 Stations of
the Cross that are so familiar to Catholics, through being
depicted on the walls of most Catholic churches. They
represent the ''death-going'' of Christ from Pilate's
judgement hall to the stone tomb in the garden.
    The life that is most familiar to Orcadians is farming,
with all its ritual (though to the farmer they seem
natural) stations throughout the turning year. Thus, Lent
is the time before ploughing when the stores in the
cupboard are at their lowest ebb (1).

  2. Ploughing the field: first action in the getting of
     bread.

3. The perennial burden of land work—the farmer must labour till death. It is ''man's lot.''
4. The sustaining ''feminine principle'' that upholds and sweetens life and labour.
5. God has ordained the elements: he leaves man to make full and wise use of them. . . . In the *Stations*, Simon helps Christ (God) to carry the cross.
6. Again, the perpetual pity and kindness of women. . . . Veronica, at Station VI, wipes the face of Christ of its ''harrow—sweat.''
7. Wrestle with the hard cruel acres. . . . Christ falls for the second time. But in the field the corn has taken root.
8. Death is at the end of all labour, all work and planning whatsoever (in every sphere of life). Again the perpetual springs of women's solace and kindness are there to help: . . . The women of Jerusalem weep for Christ as he goes on to Golgotha.
   And we are to imagine all the time, of course, that the corn is growing higher and riper towards harvest. ''I am the Bread of Life,'' Christ had said.
9. The corn is cut. Christ endures his third fall.
10. The kernel and chaff are separated by flails in the barns. Christ is stripped on the mount of Calvary.
11. The corn is ground at the mill. Christ suffers the agony of a protracted dying.
12. What was cornstalks is now meal and malt. Christ dies: ''the bulls compass him round'' (as in the 22nd Psalm).
13. Brewing and baking, the women's work at the end of summer. The mother of God enfolds the 5 wounds of her son.
    It is the mystery of new life out of death.
    The Bread of Heaven is offered and accepted on our altars.
14. Winter again. The nourishment won by the farmer is in the barn, life for the long winter to come. In the churches the Bread never fails.
    It is in mid—Winter that the Nativity occurs. The wheel comes full cycle from death to birth.
    This is the paradox and triumph of Christianity ''The wheel turns and is still'' . . .

I do hope the above explains most of what you want to know.

I'll look again at the list of questions to see if I can usefully elucidate more. But the above is a gist of the poem.

With best wishes,

George Mackay Brown

George Mackay Brown

P.S. Alas, I don't now have the many successive rewritings of the poem. They were many and long; and as I mentioned to you I had a harder struggle with <u>From Stone to Thorn</u> than with any other poem. Perhaps for that reason I like it best. He or she who doesn't like the idea of painfully working through my many—<u>too</u> many—books, may take comfort from the fact that here, in 28 brief lines, is all I really want to say.

1. *For me this poem is both a mourning and a celebration of mankind's wholeness. It weaves the myth, history, psychology, physiology, and geology of every human life into a cloth as seamless as that of a rock or a fish. Man's transcendence becomes as much a part of his nature as his failings, and both as much a part of earth's nature as the seasons, analogous to other traditions of death and renewal, such as those of Dionysius and the Fisher King. The result is not so much the incarnation of holiness as the holiness of incarnation. Is this the way you hope the poem will be read? Would you be willing for a reader to infer that in a sense every life is the life of Christ?*

It has that Potential.

2. *The prayers at the 14 Stations of the Cross are familiar to Catholics but not equally familiar to all contemporary readers. How would it affect the meaning and tone of the poem if some readers did not know the name and sequence of all 14 stations as used by the church? Whom did you perceive as your readers?*

As many as possible. (If the 14 stations are obscure, it is a simple enough matter to find what they are.)

3. *Are the details of the agricultural year, as portrayed in the poem, true of Biblical agriculture, of Orkney agriculture of Christ's time, of current Orkney agriculture? Were the Orkney people then or are they now Catholics?*

Of Orkney agriculture as it was a century ago. With tractors and machines, much of the *great meaning* is lost.

4. *The structure of the poem seems to be circular: from late winter to winter again (once around the seasons) and from Lent to Christmas (once around the life of Christ). Yet the traditional Stations of the Cross emphasize Christ's death. Why did you make them into a Christmas wreath ending in a Christmas card?*

Because Good Friday looks forward to Easter Sunday: and every year ends and begins with Christmas.

5. *What determined your choice of the alternating long-line, short-line stanza form? Is it to suggest the rhythm of a halting step?*

This has not struck me; but I think you've got it right.

6. *What determined your repeated slant rhyme on* urn, born, yarn, quern, bairn? *Am I perhaps hearing more slant rhyme than is there?*

No, there are 14 "slant" rhymes. I was quite proud of having managed to manipulate so many!

7. *The poem is the first in a series called* Stations of the Cross. *Does it correspond to the traditional first station in relation to the rest of the series?*

No: each is complete in itself.

8. *The title of this section of the series is the second line of stanza seven. Is this title selected as a key to the poem's tone—a way of saying that most human sowing is wasted, that as you reap you sow; as you sow you reap?*

It could be. The composer Peter Maxwell Davies wrote music to the poem, and gave it its present title, which I like, and have kept.

9. *What triggered the poem, started you writing it? How many revisions did it go through, of what kind, over what period of time? If you have saved the rough drafts, may I see a copy of them?*

I thought of a simple church in Rackwick, Hoy, and how a medieval artist might have wanted to relate the work of peasants to Christ's Passion.

GEORGE MACKAY BROWN was born in the Orkney Islands, Scotland, where he still lives and writes. He attended Stromness Academy and Edinburgh University. He has published six books of poems, five books of short stories, two novels, a long play, four books on Orkney, and three books of children's stories. *Three Plays* (in one volume) and a new novel are his most recent publications.

JARED CARTER

*

Mourning Doves

That all my life I have listened to the calls
of mourning doves, have heard them hidden far back
under the eaves, or perched among sycamore branches—
their five still notes sometimes lost in the wind—
and not known how to answer: this I confess,
lying here now, on a summer morning, in a dark room
no less lit by the sound of their soft calling

than by your breathing. And though you might dream
that I lie stretched beside you, I am alone again,
and a child, hearing these same dim voices drifting
high outside my window, explaining to myself how
these are the cries of the newly dead, in the dawn light,
rising toward heaven. Only that, and a child's need
to make up stories on falling asleep, or waking.

And though you might speak, out of that dream, or form
some forbidden word on your lips, my response
would be no more than the music two of them can make—
matching their notes in time, setting up harmonies
that are clear, and pure, and accidental even
to their own reckoning, since all of their singing
is circular, and comes back to the same stillness.

It is back to that place they are calling us now,
and it is out of not knowing that I brush away
strands of hair from your face, and begin to kiss
your eyes, your lips—that I might take sleep
from your mouth into mine, that we might dream invention,
and you hear my confession, and I your answering,
like a song traded back and forth in the morning light.

Mourning Doves

That all my life I have listened to the calls
Of mourning doves, have heard them hidden back
Under the eaves, or perched among the willows—
Their five still notes sometimes lost in the wind—
And not known how to answer: this I confess,
Lying here now, on a summer morning, in a dark room
No less lit by the sound of their soft calling

Than by your breathing. And though you might dream
That I lie stretched beside you, I am alone again,
And a child, hearing these same dim voices drifting
High outside my window, explaining to myself how
~~How~~ these are the whispers of ~~the departing dead~~, angels, in the dawn light
Rising toward heaven. Only that, and a child's need
To make up stories on falling asleep, or waking.

And though you might speak, out of a dream, or form
Some forgotten word on your lips, my response
C~~W~~ould be no more than the ~~sound of~~ music two of them make,
Matching their notes in time, setting up harmonies
That are clear, and pure, and accidental even
To their own reckoning, since all of their singing
Is circular, and comes back to the same stillness.

It is back to that place they are calling us now,
And it is out of not knowing that I brush away
Strands of hair from your face, and begin to kiss
Your eyes, your lips—that I might take sleep
From your mouth into mine, that we might dream invention,
And you hear my confession, and I your answering,
Like a song traded back and forth in the darkness.
                                          light of dawn
                                            morning light.

                              Monday 17 May 1982
                              11 A.M. – 3 P.M.

1. *This poem is a declaration of love so full and so intense that the speaker wants to take his loved one into him wholly, even her sleep and her dream, all the way back to his*

childhood. Is that because the doves mean to him, now, as then, a mystery and a
transcendence and a comfort? A transformation of the unknowable and unanswerable
into the familiar and the harmonious? A change of aloneness into a ritual sharing, all
the more comforting because it is expected and repeated and sung and interchanged
between two? And because love, as described here, is all that can give an adult this
comfort and can be exchanged only in this half-dream, half-ritual way?

Half-dream, half-ritual—yes, that says it very nicely. Yet I'm not convinced
the persona wishes to take the beloved "into him wholly"; nor do I think the
poem suggests that love is *all* that can give comfort, or that it can be exchanged
only in this way. On such matters the poem is descriptive rather than prescrip-
tive: this is what is happening to this particular couple, not what should or
could happen to someone else.

But in the main these questions provide useful ways of looking at the poem.
I should explain here that even though I wrote it, my ability to interpret it is not
much greater than that of the average reader—and probably far less than that
of the serious critic or student of literature. The poem pleases me, as do most
poems I admire, because I cannot quite get to the bottom of it. In other words,
I'm in the curious position of having created something I cannot entirely explain. Such indeterminacy may not always be one's goal in writing verse, but it
is an attractive quality to stumble onto now and then. Aimlessness, in the
several senses of the word, seems to me an important precondition if poetry is to
flourish.

2. *In the age of Plath, Sexton, and Lowell this poem is singularly unnarcissistic, retaining*
   its privacy, replacing personal details with more general and abstract words, yet losing
   none of its intensity and individuality. Were you consciously writing a nonconfessional
   poem—a love poem more in the tradition of Wordsworth and Keats?

When I begin to write I am not certain that I intend *not* to do something—
that is, not to use a particular form, or not to accept the conventions of a
particular style. Rather, it is a surrendering of all intention except to be recep-
tive. I become aware simultaneously of what will work and what will not work
and try to choose what will best serve "the interests of the poem."

Confessional poetry by its very nature risks the charge of narcissism, but the
best of it, written by poets such as those you mention, manages to transcend the
merely personal. Clearly I was attempting to do this, but then this inductive
strategy—moving from the particular toward the universal—is fundamental to
most imaginative writing. Between my poem and Lowell's "To Speak of Woe
that Is in Marriage," for example, or Plath's "Blue Moles," the essential difference is not one of style or strategy but of attitude and tone. These are brilliant
poems, but neither is particularly hopeful or encouraging on the subject of
physical love. Nor should we expect them to be. What each poet says rings true,
and that is sufficient.

My poem sprang from a contrasting situation, one not of isolation and despair, but of connectedness and intimacy. Keats and Wordsworth are plausible influences, as is the Tennyson of "Now Sleeps the Crimson Petal," a remarkably sensual poem. But for models I suspect I must have gone back much farther, to Shakespeare's "Take, Oh, Take Those Lips Away," for example, and especially to Wyatt's "They Flee from Me." These are consummate lyrics. I memorized both of them as an undergraduate and have drawn sustenance from them ever since. I don't think I was consciously trying to imitate either one in writing "Mourning Doves," but I am sure they are very much a part of the way I look at love and physical longing. I suppose you might say they got into my blood, and from there into my poetry.

3. What is lost to the reader who has never heard a mourning dove?

It's a difficult question. After thinking about it I find I am of two minds. Let me explain by going back for a moment to the early 1960s, when the Vietnam War was just beginning, and when I was drafted, and the Army, with its inscrutable logic, sent me to France for two years. I lived off post and my first wife and I had an apartment in the village of By-Thomery, which is on the Seine, and also at the edge of the Forest of Fontainebleau, which is the third largest forest in France. We had a lovely time there. In the summer we could walk out into the forest along the paths and there would be cuckoos calling to one another in the trees.

It was a wonderful sound. The more I listened to it the more I began to feel sorry for those who had heard only cuckoo clocks but never the real thing. I thought, too, of the cuckoo as it appears in various poems—in Shakespeare's "When Daisies Pied," for example, or even earlier, in a poem that stands at the beginning of English poetry, "The Cuckoo Song." Hearing the cuckoos gave me a renewed interest in such poems, one which seems to have lasted all these years. So that's one side of the argument: it could in some instances be helpful to have heard the call of this or that bird mentioned in a particular poem.

Yet this puts us in a quandary. Where does one draw the line? Is it essential to have heard a nightingale or a skylark in order to appreciate Keats or Shelley? The problem is complicated by the fact that traditionally we have a shorthand for some of these creatures. The nightingale, we are told, goes "jug-jug." But does this make any sense either? And does it bring us any closer to an understanding of nightingales or of poems that refer to them? I doubt it. If a nightingale really sounded like that, would anyone have written about it? (Thomas Nashe, incidentally, has a poem in which he quotes four different birds as they greet the spring: cuckoo, nightingale, lapwing, and owl. According to Nashe they sound like this: "Cuckoo, jug-jug, pu-we, to-witta-woo!")

I have a few more observations about the mourning dove's call, and its relation to my poem, but I'll save them for the questions that follow. Here I would simply state my belief that ultimately the power of poetry depends more on association than on imitation, on evocation rather than literal reproduction. Not the thing itself, but its presence—much as the cuckoos in the Forest of

Fontainebleau, even as they were calling to each other, stayed hidden among the leaves.

4. *I first heard the doves when my daughter was born, and I often mistook their call for her low-pitched cries. For me they became associated with both meanings of mourning/morning. Your poem of celebration almost removes the idea of mournfulness established by the poem's title. Did you intend that it should, i.e., were you consciously "working" that pun?*

Yes, I think I had always been aware of the contrasts of mourning/morning, and the mysteriousness of this bird for a number of readers. The mourning dove is widely spread across the Middle West and the Great Plains, yet many Americans are completely unfamiliar with it and claim they have never heard such a creature. Of course they have—midwesterners hear mourning doves all the time, in good weather, but some of them have not learned to identify the call.

When I recite the poem during poetry readings I usually preface it by doing my mourning dove imitation, which is one of two I can do (the other being a cardinal). Invariably, after a reading, someone will come up to say that he or she has always known the call but did not know the name of the bird making it. Others will say, too, that, like the persona in the poem, they made up their own explanations for the sound the mourning dove makes. And they frequently have very personal associations with the call. Still others will share bits of folklore about the bird. In Nebraska, for example, it is called a "raincrow," and its song is said to predict rain. Finally, there are those who want to know whether the spelling is "mourning" or "morning."

I seem to have played on this uncertainty in the poem, but rather than attempting to make a pun, I think I was simply trying to allow for some additional ambiguity—to work both sides of the street. The implications of "mourning" are not entirely eliminated; "the newly dead" in line 12 are "rising toward heaven" in the following line. And yet the poem takes place in the morning, a time traditionally symbolic of youth, beginning, and renewal.

5. *The word* traded, *with its connotation of commerce, seems unusual in the context of the last line. Why did you choose it?*

Here the question would seem to be not why I chose it, but rather once I hit upon it during the heat of composition, why did I allow it to stand? The successive worksheets show that I stuck with "traded" from the first, but that I had a difficult time deciding how that same line should end. Was the song being traded back and forth in the darkness? in the light? the trees? the dawn? While I was tinkering with these alternatives, I think I kept "traded" because it works, rhythmically, and because the connotation you mention—commerce—seems to me to be rather far down the list. Several more vivid usages come to mind, as when we trade compliments, or insults, or letters or baseball cards. When musicians rehearse they trade riffs or melodies; in everyday conversation we lead and follow, give and take. This was the sense of "traded" I hoped would be understood and the reason why I decided to keep it in the poem.

6. *The form of the poem—its long lines, long sentences, long stanzas, the running over of stanza 1 into stanza 2, the repeated use of ing words and words ending in vowels or soft consonant sounds, both at the ends of lines and within them—creates a sustained hum suggestive of the sound of the doves, and of the dreaming, stretching, and breathing of sleepers just beginning to wake. How much of this congruence of sound, structure, and mood was happy accident, how much conscious craft?*

The answer lies within the congruence itself—again, the poem, rather than what I might say about it. I do find writing to be a "happy" process, to use your term, and much of it is a process of discovery, as distinguished from the craft one later applies to the impulse, and the factual knowledge one brings to it. But I don't see any of this as "accident," to use another of your terms; though it might lack direction initially, it brims over with purpose, with seeking.

In one sense everything I write is intentional. And yet in another, since it happens in a trance, a kind of daydreaming on paper, I'm not accountable for any of it, am I? Whatever is there flowed through me on its way from somewhere else. And I'm far more concerned with where it's going than where it's been.

Having made such disclaimers, I can look back through the finished poem and agree that, yes, it does seem to possess the characteristics you describe, and these in turn suggest the activities taking place within the poem. If I could sum it up, I would say there is a languorous quality about these stanzas. I have a dictionary at hand which explains that one of the meanings of "languor" is "an air of soft or wistful tenderness." Before that frightens you away let me add that "languor" is related to "languish," which has the connotation of something which is "slow, lingering." A reviewer discussing my first book said that some of my poems—"Gathering Fireflies," for example—possess a kind of "tolling sound," and I suspect this quality is also characteristic of "Mourning Doves." We come back to your notion of "congruence" again, since this lingering, bell-like progression is very much like the actual sound made by mourning doves. Let me talk about that for a moment.

Earlier I suggested that one need not have heard a mourning dove in order to appreciate the poem. I'll now contradict myself and go on to say that if one *has* heard such a creature, or if one is in a position to go out and listen to one for a while, one might pick up certain awarenesses that could conceivably be of help in interpreting the poem. Just as, I suspect, there is a scholar somewhere who has listened carefully to nightingales and skylarks, and who has brought that knowledge to an examination of the respective poems by Keats and Shelley.

There are five notes in a mourning dove's call and these occur in a low–high/low–low–low pattern, with the first low note at about B below middle C and the single high note at E. It's a perfect fourth, and it becomes a diminished interval when you hear the last three low notes, which are somewhere between

B and B flat. The mourning dove regularly sings these as half or quarter tones, rather in the way that jazz horn players "bend" notes in order to achieve that special blues sound. This improvised bending gives the mourning dove's call its distinctly unresolved quality.

Now all of that simply describes the pitch, but there are many other factors to consider. The first two notes have the greatest intensity, for example; they are followed by a pause, and then the last three notes are decrescendo, sometimes trailing away until you cannot hear them at all. As one might expect from a member of the dove family, the notes are rounded and rather like the flute stop on an organ, barely opened. This is a hushed, solemn sound, with little tremulo or timbre, and its overall effect is haunting and elusive. Correspondingly, this lingering, this slowness which at times seems to fade out altogether, is hinted at in a number of ways by the poem.

In the first half of line 4 the procession of spondees retards the forward motion, and there is an echo of the rhythm of the call in "times-lost/in-the-wind." In the last line of the third stanza "comes back" suggests the low–high part of the call, while "to the same stillness" resembles the trailing off of the low–low–low portion. There are other echoes of the call in the poem. None of these effects is exact, of course. As I pointed out earlier the aim should be evocation rather than mimicry. The poem barely manages to imply the rhythm of the mourning dove's call; the many additional characteristics of that call are left to the imagination. Nevertheless, these rhythms, combined with the other elements you mention—long lines, long sentences (there are only five sentences in the poem)—serve to bring out that languorous quality I sense lurking here and there among the bedclothes.

I use that last word advisedly, because, after all, this is what is happening in the poem, on another level—languorousness in relation to foreplay, to the drawing out of the sexual experience in order to heighten it. This is in itself, of course, a time-binding process.

7. *How did the poem start? How many changes did it undergo? Of what kind, in what sequence, over what period? If you have saved the worksheets, may I see a copy?*

There was a proximate cause and a remote cause. The latter is explained in the opening lines. The mourning dove has always been a personal totem for me. When I was beginning to write I was not sure why it interested me, but I sensed that in time it might become useful material—rather in the way that Rilke describes in *Malte.* I accepted the task of watching and waiting, and I continue to do this, almost every day, for many things, natural and man-made. In the winter, for example, I go out and look at flocks of migrating starlings when they're in the neighborhood; the starling is, for me, an extremely interesting bird. Or, in the fall, I find an Osage orange tree and collect a sack full of the fruit, and bring it back and set the oranges on the railing of my porch, and look at them, and touch them, and think about them, without knowing precisely what I'm doing, or why. You never can tell; something might come of it, sooner or later.

My earlier poems involving mourning doves, undertaken in this manner, were unconvincing, but the writing of them enabled me to store up a considerable amount of observation and lore. One thing I noticed was the curious sound—an aleatory music, really—that two or three of them make when their singing overlaps. It's marvelously arhythmic and atonal. You can hear something resembling the rhythmical complexity when two woodpeckers are working in the same area, but the mourning doves are musical, too, and far more stately.

So that was the remote cause: a longstanding interest in mourning doves. The proximate cause is rather obvious and is described throughout the poem. We were in bed. I had just awakened and it was one of those tremulous mornings when everything is leafy and green and full of light. The curtains were drawn and for some reason we had the day off. We could sleep late, we could do whatever we liked. While I was becoming aware of all this I heard a mourning dove somewhere outside in the trees, and it seemed to be connected with what we would probably be doing within the next ten minutes or so. Again, I didn't realize this in a conscious way. I wish I could say, following Casteneda, that the bird seemed to be speaking to me about that moment, and about all those things which subsequently came out in the poem, but that really wasn't the case.

Previously almost everything I knew about mourning doves was observed phenomena. I had not yet noticed a poetic equivalency, an additional set of phenomena to which I could yoke the bird and its call in a convincing manner. In other words, I had not found the right metaphor. Nor did anything as clear as "Aha, now I have found it!" run through my mind. The manner in which the two sets of phenomena became poetically related was something which later worked itself out as I wrote the poem. At that particular moment I simply *sensed*—and it is far better to use that word than to say that I knew, or I understood, or I figured out, because it was none of those—I sensed there was something similar about the two. About mourning doves and lovemaking. That's all. It was an extremely fleeting impression. I didn't dwell on it and I didn't pursue it at the time because I was, after all, not on the verge of writing a poem but of doing something else, something equally creative and fulfilling.

I was fortunate in having sensed not simply the metaphor itself, but the possibilities of the metaphor—that it would allow me to talk poetically about matters of interest to me, some depending on years of observation, others deriving from the passion and urgency of the moment. The metaphor in itself was nothing, and even the sensing of it was no more significant than, say, Keats walking through the British Museum and suddenly realizing that, yes, there *was* something peculiar about that vase over there in the corner. What counts is what each of us managed to do with the metaphor as we wrote our respective poems. And that is precisely what cannot be explicated by either critic or poet. The how, perhaps; but not the why.

Later, when I sat down at my typewriter (on which I compose directly), it was one of those rare, mysterious poems which appears on the paper almost effortlessly—at least in comparison to the work that sometimes goes into the others. I number worksheets and date successive drafts rather carefully. The version reproduced here is the second draft and the first is preceded by thirteen worksheets in which I developed the four individual stanzas. A notation on this second draft indicates that it took me four hours to reach this point, by which time I had finished the poem in all but a few minor details. For me, that is a very quick study.

8. *How do you view this poem in relation to the rest of your work?*

When I look back over the process of composition just described, and when I read the poem again in the light of the questions you've asked, it occurs to me that this particular poem is a product of a career-long interest of mine in achieving synesthesia in what I write. I seem to have been working at this for a long time.

By synesthesia I simply mean the substituting of one sensory image where another would be more expected in logical or physiological terms—as when we say, for example, that we "see a sound" or "hear a color." In lines 6–8 the "dark room" is "lit" both by the sound of the doves and the woman's breathing. Of course that's impossible; sound doesn't give off light. But this sort of substitution can make for interesting poetry. An earlier poem of mine, "Shaking the Peonies," is almost entirely given over to such substitutions and crossovers between the senses. I do this enough in my writing that I've begun to suspect that I'm slightly synesthetic myself. It's either that, or the fact that on both sides of my family there are a number of painters, draftsmen, musicians, weavers, dancers, and so on, and growing up with them provided an excellent education for a poet attracted to sensory images.

My earliest attempts both in prose and poetry centered on the sense of vision—trying to show what I saw in the physical world. Next came the sounds of words and their interrelationships with the sense of hearing. I would not begin to claim that I mastered any of this, but while I was working with such notions I also became more aware of the relationship between words and the sense of touch. I was fascinated, for example, by the fact that we write with our fingers, where much of the tactile sense is concentrated. Our fingers hold a pen, or press the keys of a typewriter, or—the manner in which I'm writing at this moment—manipulate the keyboard of a word processor. All of this is coordinated by the eye, of course, and sometimes the ear. But there is a relationship between touch and the very texture of words as they appear on the paper or on the screen. One might say, following Bachelard, that there is not only a poetics of space, and a poetics of material substances, but also one of fingertips, of skin. If one is to call upon this in a poem, however, it must be accomplished with words alone.

The last two senses have remained the most elusive, but lately I have become more aware of how certain words and syllables *taste*. We take note of this in our everyday speech when we say, for example, following an unpleasant experience which frequently involves some sort of sharp verbal exchange, "It left a bad taste in my mouth." There is also that peculiar crossover between meaning and the gustatory sense which occurs when you are attempting to remember a word or a phrase or someone's name you have momentarily forgotten. To explain that "it's right on the tip of my tongue" is to acknowledge that you're trying to retrieve it from a long-term storage area in your brain normally reserved for memories of the way things taste. You're looking in the wrong pigeonhole, in other words, although anatomically they're probably very close together. I believe there are words and combinations of words that play on this shunting and that can effect such synesthetic crossovers in a poem. In "Mourning Doves" the persona's admission that he doesn't quite know what's going on is akin to the experience of not quite remembering but at the same time almost *tasting* the word you want. The fifth sense, that of smell, would be quite simple to evoke if one took a direct approach—just throw in a few lilacs or some wisteria—but it may prove to be the most difficult of all if one attempts to achieve it indirectly and relies on crossovers from the other senses.

To sum up, I trust that nothing I've said in response to these questions detracts from the poem itself. As indicated, I'm not really concerned with what it means, or whether it means anything at all. It is ultimately not something written but something meant to be spoken aloud—that is, speech. I wanted it, following Auden's remark, to be memorable. Toward this end I've always been encouraged by Housman's comment about Shakespeare's lyricism—how in the songs he sometimes poured out his loveliest poetry in saying nothing. Housman quotes "Take, Oh, Take Those Lips Away" in full. "That is nonsense," he observes, "but it is ravishing poetry."

Not much contemporary poetry is admired on the basis of its being thought "ravishing." That criterion has certainly gone out of fashion. Which means that one of these days it will just as certainly come back in. Yet even that is not what intrigues me about Housman's comment, since there will always be changes in fashion. Rather, it is that if one accepts his dichotomy, one can assume that it may be as much an accomplishment to write a beautiful poem as it is to write a meaningful one.

JARED CARTER was born in Elwood, Indiana, in 1939 and now lives in Indianapolis. He attended Yale University and Goddard College and has taught at Purdue University and Indiana University East. His first book of poems, *Work, for the Night Is Coming*, was given the Walt Whitman Award for 1980 and the Great Lakes Colleges Association poetry award for 1981–82. He has received fellowships from the Guggenheim Foundation and from the National Endowment for the Arts.

ROBERT CREELEY

*

For My Mother: Genevieve Jules Creeley

April 8, 1887–October 7, 1972

Tender, semi-
articulate flickers
of your

presence, all
those years
past

now, eighty-
five, impossible to
count them

one by one, like
addition, sub-
traction, missing

not one. The last
curled up, in
on yourself,

position you take
in the bed, hair
wisped up

on your head, a
top knot, body
skeletal, eyes

closed against,
it must be,
further disturbance—

breathing a skim
of time, lightly
kicks the intervals—

days, days and
years of it,
work, changes,

sweet flesh caught
at the edges,
dignity's faded

dilemma. It
is *your* life, oh
no one's

forgotten anything
ever. They want
to make you

happy when
they remember. Walk
a little, get

up, now, die
safely,
easily, into

singleness, too
tired with it
to keep

on and on.
Waves break at
the darkness

under the road, sounds
in the faint
night's softness. Look

at them, catching
the light, white
edge as they turn—

always again
and again. Dead
one, two,

three hours—
all these minutes
pass. Is it,

was it, ever
you alone
again, how

long you kept
at it, your
pride, your

lovely, confusing
discretion. Mother, I
love you—for

whatever that
means,
meant—more

than I know, body
gave me my
own, generous,

inexorable place
of you. I feel
the mouth's sluggish-

ness, slips on
turns of things
said, to you,

too soon, too late,
wants to
go back to beginning,

smells of the hospital
room, the doctor
she responds

to now, the
order—get me
there. "Death's

let you out—"
comes true,
this, that,

endlessly circular
life, and we
came back

to see you one
last
time, this

time? Your head
shuddered,
it seemed, your

eyes wanted,
I thought,
to see

who it was.
I am here,
and will follow.

1. *One first notices the poem's tone: its quietness and strong tenderness, lack of self-pity and respect for privacy and dignity. This poem, one feels, was not written in front of a mirror; it is wholly honest. Although it has the same three elements as classical commemorative verse: grief, praise, and consolation, it lacks the traditional hyperbole. Tenderness and respect stand for praise; regret, even relief, stand for grief; and acceptance for consolation ("I am here, / and will follow"). Is this understatement in any way a conscious answer to expectations usually associated with the genre?*

2. *When urged to be concrete, my students often say, "A generalization or an abstract term says more to more people than a unique, concrete detail." Would you comment on your fairly large proportion of abstract versus concrete terms in this poem? For example, "dignity's faded dilemma" or "lovely confusing discretion" in contrast to "hair / wisped up" or "Your head / shuddered."*

3. *At a time when many poets prefer to use methods of indirection, such as irony, persona, dramatic scene, metaphor, even surrealism, you use relatively few of these devices, but tend to speak directly, "Mother, I / love you" or "eyes / closed against, / it*

must be, /further disturbance—." Is this because you feel that the other devices are too self-consciously rhetorical to convey sincerity?

4. Like most of your other poems, this one is very compressed. The sentences are so elliptical and so divided by the punctuation of line and stanza breaks that sometimes the same one may be read in two different ways at once, and both are essential to the meaning, i.e., *"It/is your life, oh/no one's//forgotten anything/ever,"* in which no one's can be both a possessive and a contraction. Would you talk a bit about the principles that determined this technique?

5. The very short lines, a preponderance of one-syllable words, and frequence of punctuation give the poem a spondaic rhythm, suggestive of labored breathing. And when I have heard you read your poems aloud, I have noticed that you made a marked pause at each line end, even when the line end was unpunctuated; whereas most other poets I've heard tend to disregard line-end breaks in favor of syntactical breaks. Could you comment on the principles which determined the rhythm of this poem?

6. Most of the poem's sound echoes seem to be slant and at least partly internal (alone, again, long in stanzas 22 and 23, or let, out, that in stanza 32). Are these congruities determined automatically by meaning and ear, or are they consciously sought, or both?

7. Though the poem gives the immediate effect of inevitability, a close look suggests a long and careful editing. Do you recall when the poem began and how many and what kinds of revisions it underwent? If you have kept the worksheets, could I see a copy?

(Note: The following is the partial text of a taped commentary by Robert Creeley, in answer to the questions, May 7, 1983.)

I've been trying to think about this poem and what one might say. It's crucial for me, simply that it *had* to be enough. My mother was a very significant person in my life and I wanted to write something in an absolutely unequivocal respect of that fact. Looking at the date of the actual writing, I see that I wrote it eight days after her death: October 15, 1972. I felt I had written it immediately, but possibly, probably, the ability to do that was affected by shock and other obvious circumstances. In any case, this poem had to "make it," like they say. I felt that if ever I was called upon to be a poet, if I *could* practice whatever virtues or accomplishments that that responsibility requires, now was the time.

After my father's death in 1930, when I was four years old and my sister, Helen, was eight, my mother was our sole support. She returned to public health nursing and worked at that occupation until, I think, she was sixty-seven—always in New England and for a long time in the Actons (I was raised in West Acton, Massachusetts, primarily, although born in Arlington, Mass.)

She was also a nurse in Melrose—that's where she finished—and then on Mount Desert Island, up in Maine, as well.

She was a very just woman, certainly not stern, rather shy. I think she felt a great deal of responsibility toward me, the youngest child, and also the sole boy. Apparently I had been a great pleasure to my father, and this she both remembered and respected. In any case, as the poem says, we did not speak easily, although we loved each other without question. We were simply, in an old fashioned sense, quite shy. The poem itself was written actually in one sitting, as I recall. The notebook pages show remarkably little change in what is, I'm quite sure, the first draft. In fact, all that is changed is some misspelling apparently in the third from the last stanza: "Your head shuddered." I've corrected that. And in the very last stanza: "who it was./I am here,/and will follow." I had first, seemingly, wanted *am* italicized, to be given that particular stress, and subsequently must have decided against it.

Apropos the *feeling* in the writing, the measure, the way it is in that respect put together, I think I can say quite simply what my modes of procedure are either in this poem or in any. Once there's a determined sense of rhythm clear to me or accessible to me, I follow it in much the same way that a musician might or someone following a particular rhythm in some activity—skipping rope, for example, or dancing. Once the rhythm in any respect is determined, clear to me, I follow it. So that in this poem, once that "Tender, semi-" pattern of emphases or stresses is clear, that becomes the measure effectually for the continuing poem. Because the emotional field, let's say, was in no way resolved. I still had remarkably various feelings, most of them sad indeed, about my mother's having now died. I wanted both to delay and summarize at the same time what had happened. I didn't want, in some clear sense, to *have* to say what was the obvious fact of her now being dead. I wanted to both understand it and state it in a way that would let *me* accept its reality in a manner that would also be an unequivocal respect of her having *lived*. In any case, that truncated or curiously delayed pattern of statement is decisive throughout the poem in my own sense of it. For example, "Tender, semi-/articulate flickers/of your//presence, all/those years/past//now, eighty-/five, impossible to/count them//one by one, like/addition, sub-/traction, missing//not one. The last/curled up, in/on yourself,//position . . ." That whole manner of rhythm, or that *mode* of rhythm, is constantly avoiding any particular term of closure. In fact, looking at the poem, one sees that the terminals and/or the conclusions of statement are far more frequently met with in the middle of a line, rarely at the end. In other words, there is a great determination *not* to conclude, to keep the terms open and continuing both in the sense of the qualification that the statement is attempting but equally in the rehearsal of the physical and emotional facts which obtain.

I don't know that I understood explicitly what I had to say, or in what way I *wanted* to say it previous to the writing. My strongest impulse, or most determined feeling, was one of wanting to respect her life, wanting to make a clear acknowledgment of it, wanting even more to state my own dependence and information from and on it. So I was avoiding anything that would be too encapsulating. At the same time, the one determining fact is, bleakly and simply, that my mother's dead—that's the literal case. There is, therefore, some wish not to gloss that, or to euphemize it, but to *rehearse* it, to come back to it particularly, again and again and again. In fact, the poem's "time" is the rehearsal of my last sad visit to her as she was then dying in the Marin County Hospital in San Anselmo, just north of San Francisco.

There is an attempt, on the one hand, to make report, or to qualify the whole dear person, e.g., "dignity's faded//dilemma," or "lovely, confusing//discretion." These are qualifications of my mother that are of necessity generalizations; they're both my own sense of her, which makes them in that respect generalization. They're also attempts to summarize what was the sense of the relation we seemingly had, and what, more particularly, was the *feeling* I had of her in contrast to the *specific* person, the look of her then and there in the hospital, which was "hair//wisped up" or, factually, that she was now in coma and dying: "Your head/shuddered." There was a racking of the body as it attempted to keep going. Someone's dying is painful, often, and one comes to an almost automatic situation of *physical* act, so that the heart continues to beat or the body continues to breath, let's say, but in a very stuttering, awkward, harsh and hardly managed activity. So I wanted that, frankly, to be clear also. I didn't want to euphemize the actual sense of her physical state.

I was also talking to *her* in the poem, in some true way. For example, when I came to say things such as, "Mother, I/love you—for//whatever that/means," I was rehearsing again for myself something I had certainly said to her but could only now hope that she had heard in quite the way that I meant it—that it had been clear to her that I loved her. As ever, there's always the sad fact that we may not make known to those we love quite what that is for us during that chance we have or that time we have in which to say it. So, I'm rehearsing, I daresay, for myself in this poem what feelings I hoped she understood me to have.

Throughout the various poems and circumstances of writing that I've been involved with, I must say that the continual measure of any activity in writing, whether my own or anyone else's, is finally the emotions that are made articulate in that writing—the intensity and interest they have for me, humanly speaking. I do believe Ezra Pound's contention that "only emotion endures." The rest, frankly, fades so quickly. I'm fascinated, obviously, at times by intellectual possibilities or by that kind of intellectual play, let's say, of mind-tripping that one finds variously in such people as John Donne, or Wallace Stevens, or e. e. cummings. But finally it's the intensity of the emotion that seems to me most valuable. Poetry, for example, seems to me, of all the arts, that which can reach most particularly and intensively into the circumstance of being specifically human—if only because it makes use of a singularly human agency, the words we have as common factor and inheritance. We and they are entirely human. No matter that other species may have a "speech," the fact is that our human speech is particular to ourselves as human and engenders all of the complexities of that state, if we take it seriously. In any case, the emotions that can be made articulate in poetry have always seemed to me the most valuable of its qualities. So that in this poem, as in any other I've written, the attempt to make emotion articulate is really my most sincere and committed determination. Whether or not I succeed, of course, is something else.

For years now, I've been generously given the respect of having been able to write in a consciously determined and skillful manner. I learned a lot as a younger poet from music, actually, and from one of the most common and accessible situations in music, I suppose, that persons in this country might have, i.e., jazz. It was nothing culturally inaccessible, at least not for someone like myself growing up in New England. At times I was the white kid, etc., but that didn't finally prove much limit. In any case, I could hear very clearly in jazz structures of emphasis and delay, duration, stress, all of that kind of patterning, very, very easily. And I found the same kinds of playfulness and resolution in jazz that I didn't really find the equivalent for in the poetry of that same time— I'm thinking of the 40s or the 30s. Also, the fact that it was a *common* possibility made me feel much more secure with it, whereas, at times, the models in poetry argued cultural distinctions and habits and possibilities and privileges which I didn't, in my own case, quite share, or certainly didn't feel confident with. So in any case, the manner of line, let's say, that's characteristic of me is probably more taken from jazz musicians such as Charlie Parker or Miles Davis, certainly in his early compositions and performance, than from any poet other than, say possibly, William Carlos Williams. Williams was a great and sustaining inspiration for me always. I think that without question his influence was absolutely significant.

The characteristic of compression that this poem has is something that I simply feel very comfortable with. I have a far harder time being rhetorically expansive—far, far harder. I was always suspicious of rhetorical hyping, let's say. It was like putting on the dog—I just didn't feel at all easy with it. Poets of my respect would not usually be involved with such rhetoric. Coleridge was certainly capable of interesting rhetoric; Shakespeare, Donne, again certainly so. But poets I really felt utterly at home with were those like Herrick, or again, Williams. I felt very at home with Coleridge, actually, as a younger reader. His way of thinking was extremely close to my own—at least I felt it so. Poems like "Frost at Midnight" I really had immediate affection for. I also liked, for example, almost the rhetorically flat or deliberate diction of a poem like the "Rhyme of the Ancient Mariner"—that really delighted me—it still does. It's an obvious "tour de force."

Thinking of jazz again, and the characteristically short lines, the preponderance of monosyllabic words, and the frequency of punctuation—these were all modes of statement I probably got, as I say, more from jazz, that kind of staccato phrasing, or overlapped phrasing—where the periodicity, of the melodic line, let's say, is working both backwards and forwards at one and the same time. The *duration* is what's important rather than the "direction of the

rhythm" within the duration or unit of time. This habit has become so characteristic of my writing at this point, being fifty-seven, that I don't remember, in
fact, where it came from.

I can, however, say something a little more particular about the line endings and the use I make of them. I've always used the end of a line as a pivot, or
a situation of slight pause, so as to give me the feel of the unit the line constitutes. That is, I do feel each line is of a particular duration or a measure,
more accurately, of the rhythms that constitute the poem's frame or coherence.
I've never understood, in fact, how one could read through line endings without
some kind of audible pausing or acknowledgment, because I would fail to
understand why have them if they aren't particularly used. If they're only an
automatic counting, as in the case of syllabics, for example, I don't myself get
much use out of them as a poet. So I've always used the line ending as a pause—
as a place of pausing to indicate the measure, the unit of measure, that I am
using to set the rhythm. I think I began doing this very particularly, really
because I was back then misreading poems of William Carlos Williams, and I
understood his use of the line ending to be equivalent to mine, which in fact it
really wasn't. It's only in the later poems, beginning with the material recorded
by Caedmon, for one instance, that you'll hear him using line endings in a way
parallel to myself. The poems that we have recordings for previous to that—the
Library of Congress material or the National Council of Teachers of English
record—have none of this characteristic pausing that's true of the last
recording.

The echoing, seemingly accidental rhyming, that's also present in the poem,
is again quite characteristic of my manner. When very much younger and
having occasional opportunity to read publicly, I would be nonplussed by a
frequent question as to why I never used rhyme. And I thought I used rhyme
insistently and unremittingly! And I *did* in fact. If you'll look at the early poems
in my *Collected Poems, 1945–1975*, you'll see indeed that rhyming is insistent in
their composition. But very often it's a rhyming that's assonantal, or "half-
rhyming," as we used to say. Sounds like "alone," "again," "long," "let," "out,"
"that," etc.—they aren't full rhymes; they aren't rhymings that have to do with
full and entirely similar vowel or consonantal agreements. I love half-rhyming,
the echoing rhyme, as opposed to the full rhyme, which for me tends to stop the
movement all too emphatically. And if that isn't necessarily what one wants,
then one has to think of some other means of letting the movement continue.
These sound patterns are not, I should make clear, determined by some very
specific consciousness. Again, they are a habit. I've always felt that the simplest
way to put the situation of writing, such as I've known it, would be to say it's
equivalent to someone's driving a car or to skiing or to surfing—any one of
those three possible activities would be in some ways commensurate, analogous
to the sense of writing that's been most familiar to me. I know how to do
something and in the demand of its now being there to be done, I may not be
literally conscious of all that I do. But I have so particularly its habit, that I *do* it
in some knowledge that precedes any necessary consciousness of what I'm in

fact truly doing. I practiced it a lot. I practice in the same way that someone practices playing tennis or golf, or again, skiing or surfing, or driving. I don't know my entire disposition intellectually when I make a turn with the car, but I certainly (hopefully!) have the "consciousness" to manage it. In like sense, when I'm writing, I may not know specifically that "let" and "out" are echoing one another as a pattern of vowels and consonants, but I certainly have that resource, in my own abilities now as a poet, to be able to do it without thinking twice, in fact. Therefore, although the poem does give possibly "the immediate effect of inevitability"—a phrase I take from Professor Turner, who had generously said, "the poem gives the immediate effect of inevitability, a close look suggests a long and careful editing"—in fact, no, the poem has no "careful editing" whatsoever! I think the scholar or the critic kind enough to pay attention to my work will be immensely disappointed if that's what she or he expects. I "edit" almost not at all. This poem is a classic instance. As I say, there isn't a single word changed from the beginning to the end. There isn't a line altered. The form is set after the first three lines. There isn't a change in a single word except for that apparent misspelling of "shuddered." I may have said initially "your head/shudders" and then shifted it to "your head/shuddered." I think I was probably worried a bit about those "d, d" sounds—"your hea*d*/shuddere*d*, it seeme*d*." But then it *is* that way, it is that final, it is that slowing, it is that deliberation now necessary—"your head/shuddered,/it seemed, your//eyes wanted,/I thought,/to see//who it was./I am here,/and will follow." No, there's nothing changed. I think I must have wanted it to be absolutely, unequivocally clear that *I am here*, both in the sense of being present, sadly, to bear witness to this terrifying moment of my mother's death, but too, that I am also human on earth and I will therefore *follow* her in that death as will all persons now alive.

ROBERT CREELEY was born in 1926 and grew up in New England. He attended Harvard College and received his M.A. from the University of New Mexico. He has taught at a number of colleges and universities, among them Black Mountain College (he edited *The Black Mountain Review*, 1954–1957), University of New Mexico, University of British Columbia, San Francisco State College, and the State University of New York at Buffalo, where he is presently David Gray Professor of Poetry and Letters. He has published many books of poetry, prose and criticism, among them *Collected Poems, 1945–1975*, *The Collected Prose* (1984), *Later*, *Mirrors*, and *A Quick Graph*. His awards include two Guggenheim Fellowships, a Rockefeller Grant in writing, an NEA Fellowship, and the Shelley Memorial Award.

JAMES DICKEY

*

Deborah Burning a Doll Made of House-Wood

I know, I know it was necessary
for us to have things of this kind,
which acquiesced in everything

RAINER MARIA RILKE

I set you level,
Your eyes like the twin beasts of a wall.

As a child I believed I had grown you,
And I hummed as I mixed the blind nails
Of this house with the light wood of Heaven—
The rootless trees there—falling in love
With carpenters—their painted, pure clothes, their flawless
Bagginess, their God-balanced bubbles, their levels.
I am leaving: I have freed the shelves

So that you may burn cleanly, in sheer degrees
Of domestic ascent, unfolding
Boards one after the other, like a fireman
His rungs out of Hell
                    or some holocaust
                                        whelmed and climbing:

You only now, alone in the stepped, stripped closet, staring
Out onto me, with the guaranteed kiss
Off-flaking, involvedly smiling,
Cradling and throning,
With the eyes of a wall and two creatures:

Ungainly   unbroken   hungering
For me, braving and bearing:
Themed, intolerable, born and unborn child
Of this house—of table and floorboard and cupboard,
Of stranger and hammering virgin—
At the flash-point of makeup I shadow
My own eyes with house-paint, learning
From yours, and the shelves of Heaven-wood

           take fire from the roots

Of earth, dust bodies into smoke
The planks of your pulverized high-chair,
Paint blazes on the eyelids

Of the living in all colors, bestowing the power to see
Pure loss, and see it
With infinite force, with sun-force:

          you gesture

Limply, with unspeakable aliveness,
Through the kindling of a child's
Squared mess of an indoor wood-yard

         and I level

Stay level

    and kneel and disappear slowly

Into Time, as you, with sun-center force, take up the house
In Hell-roaring steps, a Heaven-beaming holocaust

Of slats

    and burn   burn off

Just once, for good.

In "*The G.I. Can of Beets, The Fox in the Wave, and The Hammer Over Open Ground*" (Night Hurdling) *you distinguish between "magic-language" poets (like Hopkins, Stevens, Berryman, Mallarmé, Valéry, and the surrealists), who depend on the suggestions of words themselves ("sufficiency of language") to give meaning to a poem, without the control of logic, narrative or theme, and the "literalist" poets (like Homer, Frost, Robinson, Hardy, Larkin, and Jarrell), who use "plain words" in a "statement of conditions," creating "a clear pane of glass that does not call attention to itself, but gives clearly and cleanly on a circumstance." Though allowing that both practices tend to overlap, you classify yourself as a literalist, but admit a strong attraction toward word-magic, so long as it is not used without authorial control. You would like to use it as Dylan Thomas used "the freedom, the risk of the merely arbitrary, the range of his mind and imagination over everything available to him, everything he could reach or conjure up, submitted them to thematic law, and placed them within his imposed formal limits." Using word-magic in this controlled way, you hope to make "metaphors I have never yet been able to achieve, bound into one poetic situation, one scene, one event after the other, as I have usually been."*

1. *"Deborah Burning a Doll," first published in 1981, is close enough in date to "The G.I. Can of Beets" to embody its critical values. Do you believe that it does?*

Yes, I do believe that it does, but perhaps not to the extent that I would like, or to the extent that is possible.

2. *Were the poem's theme, tone, narrative, and position in the book* Puella's *sequence clear in your mind before you started to write it?*

No; these things were discovered during the word-play. When *Puella* was first conceived, there was a possible question of publishing the poem with a series of photographs. One of these concerned a doll, and, since *Puella* is about puberty, a poem about saying a kind of ritual farewell to childhood and its allegiances seemed a good place to begin. Without the photographs it seemed equally good.

3. *Did you use Thomas's technique of allowing "one image to breed another?"*

No; though I am by no means entirely sure I understand what Thomas intended, my own practice was to let the words build the images, and through many reworkings, to come down to a single image, a single action. It seems to me that in the practice of surrealism the juxtaposition of objects and entities takes place according to whims—or "laws"—which are spur-of-the-moment, catch-as-catch-can formulations; they are Yeats's vision of the roulette ball coming to rest on the number; who is to say that the number and the ball coming to it are not, as Yeats thought, magical? The same with words and images; the important thing is what they release.

4. *In the context of the poem, the literal facts of doll, wood, house, shelves, nails, carpenters, levels, etc. and finally fire are combined into such an unrealistic (sur-realistic) situation that it could never be confused with actual arson, but becomes a metaphor for a rather furious coming of age, something like Thomas's green fuse. Is this one of the "metaphors I have never been able to achieve"?*

As to whether or not this poem constitutes one of the "metaphors I have never been able to achieve," I don't have this feeling about it as much as I do some of the other portions of *Puella*. The poem is, as is said, "a metaphor for a rather furious coming of age," and the feverish hallucinatory cast is part of the fury, or at least so I intended.

5. *Is this a new feature of your work, or has the temptation to try the risk of the "absolute freedom" been taking hold gradually on your poems?*

So far as I am able to tell, the *Puella* poems come closest to what has been an evolving idea of mine—some of it taking shape during sleep and in the unconscious, no doubt—that has arisen out of a growing dislike of the versified-anecdote approach to the conceiving and writing of poetry. I felt that too many of my poems depended with undue short-sightedness on the events, locales, and actions depicted in them. One remembered the incidents more than the language in which they were related, and, though that is a legitimate and sometimes accurate aim for some kinds of poetry, it is not the only possible one. My lines were not as memorable, word for word, as I would have liked them to be. In *Puella* I made a directed attempt to change this, and to give the initiative to the words themselves, and follow where they went, toward whatever associational wholes might arise from them, implementing them as I could, as they emerged.

JAMES DICKEY was born in Atlanta, Georgia, graduated with both a B.A. and an M.A. from Vanderbilt University, served in the Air Force in World War II and the Korean War, worked six years as an advertising executive, and since 1962 has been writing poetry full time. He is currently Carolina Professor and Poet-in-Residence at the University of South Carolina. He has won the National Book Award and the Melville Cane Award and served as poetry consultant to the Library of Congress. Between 1960 and 1982 he published eleven books of poems, the most recent of which is *Puella,* 1982, from which "Deborah Burning a Doll Made of House Wood" is taken.

NORMAN DUBIE

*

Elizabeth's War with the Christmas Bear: 1601

For Paul Zimmer

The bears are kept by hundreds within fences, are fed cracked
Eggs; the weakest are
Slaughtered and fed to the others after being scented
With the blood of deer brought to the pastures by Elizabeth's
Men—the blood spills from deep pails with bottoms of slate.

The balding Queen had bear-gardens in London and in the country.
The bear is baited: the nostrils
Are blown full with pepper, the Irish wolf dogs
Are starved, then, emptied, made crazy with fermented barley;

And the bear's hind leg is chained to a stake, the bear
Is blinded and whipped, kneeling in his own blood and slaver, he is
Almost instantly worried by the dogs. At the very moment that
Elizabeth took Essex's head, a giant brown bear
Stood in the gardens with dogs hanging from his fur . . .
He took away the sun, took
A wolfhound in his mouth and tossed it into
The white lap of Elizabeth I—arrows and staves rained

On his chest, and standing, he, then, stood even taller, seeing
Into the Queen's private boxes—he grinned into her battered eggshell face.
Another volley of arrows and poles, and opening his mouth he showered
Blood all over Elizabeth and her Privy Council.

The very next evening, a cool evening, the Queen demanded
13 bears and the justice of 113 dogs: She slept
All that Sunday night and much of the next morning.
Some said she was guilty of *this* and *that*.
The Protestant Queen gave the defeated bear

A grave in a Catholic cemetery. The marker said:
Peter, a Solstice Bear, a gift of the Tsarevitch to Elizabeth.

After a long winter she had the grave opened. The bear's skeleton
Was cleared with lye, she placed it at her bedside.
Put a candle inside behind the sockets of the eyes, and, then
She spoke to it:

You were a Christmas bear—behind your eyes
I see the walls of a snow cave where you are a cub still smelling
Of your mother's blood which has dried in your hair; you have
Troubled a Queen who was afraid when seated in *shade* which, standing,
You had created! A Queen who often wakes with a dream of you at night—
Now, you'll stand by my bed in your long white bones; alone, you
Will frighten away at night all visions of bear, and all day
You will be in this cold room—your constant grin,
You'll stand in the long, white prodigy of your bones, and you are,
Every inch of you, a terrible vision, not bear, but virgin!

1. *This poem is an especially successful example of a sub-genre you have perfected and made popular among those poets who want to achieve the immediacy of the confessional poem without its merely autobiographical details. In this case you use an event in the life of Elizabeth I and, toward the end, have her speak in her own voice to make your point. To what extent are the event and the words in which it is described from a historical source? Are Elizabeth's words to the bear hers, yours, or a mixture?*

2. *What difference does "For Paul Zimmer" make to the meaning and tone of the poem? For you? For readers who know Paul? For readers who do not?*

3. *As the poem is written, Elizabeth and the bear are represented as grotesquely alike. Both are fierce, brutal, and cruel. The surface difference is that the bear is that way because of need, Elizabeth because of will. Yet we have a second thought. Perhaps her savagery is the result of need too—a desperate self-defense. Essex represents the dominant male principle that Elizabeth spent all her life outwitting. Just this once, at the time she "took Essex's head" and just before it died, the bear stood up and overshadowed her. It had been blinded, but she thought it saw into her private box. Her retribution is also its retribution: it can no longer cast a shade, but only light; it cannot attack, only protect. Its grin is forced, fixed; yet the very fact of its towering over her is a vision a virgin can't bear. The incident has become not merely a grotesque example of Renaissance cruelty, but an example of the universal fear of woman for man and of mankind for raw nature. Did you plan that the poem's meaning would escape its historical context in this way?*

4. How did the poem start? How did it develop?

I'll answer some of the little questions first. The dedication is important; Paul is a sort of bear of a man in his way, but I really don't want the dedication discussed. The writing of this poem is a curious matter, and I'll tell you the simple truth about it, but you may not want to speak of it in your anthology. I wrote the poem totally blotto. A friend had visited and we drank late into the night. He had mentioned the diary of a Virginian squatter in which there was a brief account of a bear baiting. My friend left and I had another large scotch and then pulled out the typewriter—I never knew why I chose Elizabeth I, but just now it occurs to me that it was probably the fact that this obscure squatter was a *Virginian*, this yielding a virgin queen. I don't know. All I set out to do was a little description of the baiting itself. I think I got the poem in one draft; the poem wrote itself in the space of an hour. I passed out, in the well of the typewriter, woke up at dawn and went to bed. That afternoon I looked and saw it was a poem, I crowed. That night I sent it to *The New Yorker*; they accepted it the next week. I had never written a poem drunk before, and haven't since.

The poem is not from any historical source; it is invented. Elizabeth took Essex's head I think in February; this baiting occurs in early summer—I knew that but it hardly mattered.

Now, what does the poem mean? I think you are wrong, in a sense, to say that the poem contains a universal fear of woman for man and of mankind for raw nature—I think Elizabeth is playing a man's game here, I think she is the male principle in conflict with nature, which is the dark female principle in the poem. But then of course you are not wrong—she is a woman opposed by men. (If only she had been a man, then Henry in his quest for a male heir would not have executed her mother, Anne). This is a poem about conflict; the dark and the light sides of our nature—Elizabeth loved Essex; they were divided by a Privy Council and its intrigues against their long affection. There must be some irony to this being a Christmas bear, the virgin mother of the Christmas story, etc. Jesus was born to slaughter, it was his calling; and there's Herod killing all the male newborn far and wide. The reduction of the bear to white bone and candlelight must be tied to a transfiguring through suffering. What Elizabeth began with wars and commerce another queen, Victoria, made absolute—and how the world suffered. This is a poem against a bored, despotic government. It is really a poem about human nature. I'm still touched by her speech to the bear. I feel sorry for Elizabeth and I admire her spunk.

NORMAN DUBIE was born in Barre, Vermont, in April 1945. Mr. Dubie has published twelve books, most recently his *Selected and New Poems* with W. W. Norton. He is a member of the English Department at Arizona State University.

RUSSELL EDSON

*

The Wounded Breakfast

A huge shoe mounts up from the horizon, squealing and grinding forward on small wheels, even as a man sitting to breakfast on his veranda is suddenly engulfed in a great shadow, almost the size of the night.

He looks up and sees a huge shoe ponderously mounting out of the earth.

Up in the unlaced ankle-part an old woman stands at a helm behind the great tongue curled forward; the thick laces dragging like ships' rope on the ground as the huge thing squeals and grinds forward; children everywhere, they look from the shoelace holes, they crowd about the old woman, even as she pilots this huge shoe over the earth . . .

Soon the huge shoe is descending the opposite horizon, a monstrous snail squealing and grinding into the earth . . .

The man turns to his breakfast again, but sees it's been wounded, the yolk of one of his eggs is bleeding . . .

1. *Your poems tend to put two familiar things, not normally found together, side by side so that their union makes them strange—the reader is surprised into seeing them for the first time. Nothing is more familiar than the nursery rhyme of the "Old Woman Who Lived in a Shoe" and the Mother Goose illustration of a very large lace-up shoe with small faces peering out everywhere, and nothing is strange about the fried egg that breaks and runs. But put wheels on the house-sized shoe and grind it like a heavy truck past your porch at breakfast and at the same instant find that the yolk of your fried egg has broken, and each comments on the other. The first question I want to ask this or any Edson poem is what brought these together? Was there an actual broken yolk on your breakfast plate? Had you been rereading your Mother Goose? Had a school bus full of children just ground up the hill past your house? Or were you sitting at your desk doing or thinking something else and the whole scene "flashed" on in your mind? Did it first come to you as a picture, a phrase, a sound?*

Yes, I like things. The more familiar the better, for it is only through the familiar that we can enter the unfamiliar. The poet doesn't want to know too much about the poem he is writing. If he has a good talent he's likely to get off a few good things and more in a lifetime without really having to understand the mechanism. Perhaps it is best to know very little about poetry; to start, as it were, from scratch. At a certain point, which comes rather early, there develops a kind of hunger. One checks the cupboard, albeit a figurative one. There a few fish tins of science, a cookie jar of admired paintings, a box of despair; all really rather bare. Yet it is possible to find a recipe from these few things. The brain is the big thing here. It is after all our elephant's trunk, our giraffe's neck.

What I've come to understand is that any knowledge will do for the writing of poems. But one must be careful to remain a novice. Otherwise one risks becoming a professional poet.

The proper study of poetry is anything but poetry. It is rather learning how to seem to be doing something with one hand, and doing quite another thing with the other. It is also learning how to think, this without burning the brain out. To write poetry is to learn how to enjoy one's own brain. This is why it is necessary to learn to do different things with each hand, to learn distraction.

In this sense it was one day that I wanted a large shoe, that is, I wanted to find it physically. All poems long to be physical entities. So little, in fact, nothing, is given of the nursery rhyme shoe, that it becomes a wonderful shoe, and possibly my shoe, if the brain will allow it. And that's the dodge. I think I'm going to be writing about the shoe, and consciously pursue its reality. And while I'm watching the shoe something else is happening, the poem is being written.

Earlier I had been thinking how rather like medieval shoes cured beef tongues look. More like shoes than organs of cud and moo. Perhaps an old woman could walk around in a poem wearing them? But unfortunately I left that poem in the supermarket, already written. This happens when the object of meditation is already too well described.

But still on this shoe thing; then came something that got written. It was a common old woman's shoe, and an old woman seeing it as her womb, albeit disembodied. I saw her approaching her old husband and asking him wouldn't he like to put some of his seeds in her *flowerpot* to grow them a child. But this wasn't the shoe; and the idea of a shoe was getting in the way of what I really wanted. Which was, of course, something I could not tell in the beginning. Because, when I can, I might just as well go to the supermarket and linger among the canned goods like a pair of ragged claws.

Actually, I was discovering that I was not all that much in a shoe mood. The brain was looking for something else. When I am in harmony with the unspoken mentality I realize that what we are after are psychological events that move with the cunning logic of a dream made into available language.

So the poem begins as a huge shoe out of fiction mounting up from the horizon. The rest of the poem develops as I watch with curious delight.

2. *The absurdity of the event is emphasized by the title. Surely we can't wound a breakfast—that inert stuff on a plate. We are safe from shame, so we can let ourselves*

be amused. But the absurdity has freed the reader's mind to make any connections it can, and the poem doesn't try to stop him. The woman and children in the poem are faceless, the familiar line "she had so many children she didn't know what to do" becomes, not a jingle, but a slow, squealing grind. Is this to suggest suffering, enduring, resolution? The egg bleeds like a person. Is it bleeding for envy? It will now bear no child. Sympathy? It can understand her toil. So the reader stops eating for a moment and, after chuckling, grows thoughtful. What thoughts did you want or expect him to have? What thoughts did you yourself have? Did you want or expect the reader to feel more somber than amused? To react differently to the poem each time he read it?

I do not ask the reader to do more than understand the poem physically, which was all I asked of the poem while it was being written. The event and the objects of the event are the language of the poem. But they are not just symbols, or conscious representations. As a writer I can only be interested in what is happening on the page. Not so much how the English was arranging itself, but how the story was finding itself. When the wounded egg arrived in the poem I was delighted. It was unpredicted, and yet so psychologically right, without my having to examine it further. Of course my brain knew what we were up to, and I didn't have to make a conscious analysis, until this writing.

In a general sense, and perhaps this is thin ice, I would suggest my method is opposite to the surrealists. As surrealists often are, I too am engaged with the absurd, but the work of my poetry is to rescue absurdity from chaos. I talk about letting the poem write itself, but this is not an open-ended process as might be suggested by terms like "automatic writing" or "stream of consciousness." What I seek in the poem is the discrete psychological entity, within which the arbitrary has been cast out; this, because the writing is true. Generally speaking, the job of poetry is to make available that which is otherwise unavailable. There is little use in writing about what is already known. At the same time the poem must earn its reality by being *true*.

3. *Would it make a difference to the poem if the reader saw the bleeding egg as one of those fertilized egg yolks with a red speck in it that one sometimes finds on one's plate?*

Naturally I would like the reader to see the physical fact of the yolk running out of its membrane as it is described. In this case it has more drama and immediacy, which is correct to the rest of the poem; this happens, then, that happens. I think the language describes exactly what is happening. Also, the reader ought to know that as I have it is more interesting and fitting than an inert red speck that, in fact, doesn't bleed or do anything except look annoyingly red on an otherwise appetizing breakfast.

4. *Is the shoe's progress from horizon to horizon and its "great shadow almost the size of the night" symbolic? Do you consciously imply that our posterity assures our mortality and that grinding toil is the diurnal sentence of the fallen?*

Obviously the poem describes a mental landscape. The man on the veranda with his breakfast might be seen as a man sitting in a theater box overlooking his own mentality. The huge shoe rises up out of the horizon as a thought rises to the surface of consciousness. And like a thought rides the surface for a portion, and then sinks back down into the brain.

And though the shoe is described more than anything else in the poem, it is still more ornamental than symbolic. It is mounted on wheels because it must have movement and the physical means. It grinds and squeals forward because it cannot be stopped from its course. And though it descends the opposite horizon, it will return.

Nursery rhymes, certain toys, century-long summers (so they seem when one is a child), all the collection of pre-adult memory become permanent objects of the mind.

Childhood is when we have not fully come awake. In human beings maturity is described less by the physical changes than the development of consciousness. I don't doubt that there may be a fuller wakefulness than our species knows. But by human standards of consciousness animals are sleepwalkers; children somewhat more than that, but still not fully awakened. This is why children do not write poetry in any real sense. It is only when the full consciousness touches the unconscious that poetry becomes possible, or even a *necessity*.

The shoe rises then, in a sense, out of childhood. The shadow it casts, *almost the size of the night*, describes the bigness of the shoe. But here the shadow is more important to the poem than the shoe. Almost the size of the night, but not fully the size of the night. Around it is daylight. Around it is adult consciousness that holds the shadow.

The man is having the early meal of the day, which places him in the morning, the childhood of the day. The poem recapitulates the journey into adult consciousness, consciousness touching the unconscious. The process is wounding, but not necessarily deeply wounding. After all, our greatest achievement is the development of consciousness. This is what has caused the rest of our brains to glow in the dark.

As in much of my other work this poem is an externalizing of mental process, where the shoe and the bleeding egg are almost incidental; a poem of witness and pattern. I do not write of experience, but rather the inscape formed by experience. The pattern and shape of thought. It is a language of images, where shape and movement are more significant than the meanings ascribed to the words that carry it. It is a language almost of hand signals, a language of gestures. It is given in the back-and-forthness, the mental swing of thought: a shoe mounts up, a man sits; morning, shadow almost the size of the night; the shoe sinking out of sight, the return of the man's attention to his own foreground. It is an attempt to describe the inner music that the brain sings to itself.

5. *Your most frequent poetic form is the short prose fable. Would you comment on why you chose it in this instance? What determined your choice of the long sentences, the various repetitions of word and sound, the ellipses at the ends of the paragraphs? What would this poem lose if it were written in Mother Goose rhythms or free verse with strategically placed line ends?*

I did not choose to write this poem in prose, it's just that the thought of doing it in verse never crossed my mind. If any formal structures in terms of language are found, they are strictly accidents of chance. I try to stay as far away from language as I can, even while writing it. The formal qualities that I seek for my work are psychological ones. Language, like a career in poetry, seem contradictions to poetry.

As I look again at "The Wounded Breakfast" there are long sentences. I hadn't noticed this before. This is probably the result of not having used enough periods. One never knows. It may just be the use of too many commas and semicolons. The repetitions are probably due to memory lapses and a poverty of vocabulary.

6. *Was the writing of this poem a single impulsive act or a series of revisions over a long period? What revisions over what period?*

Yes, the poem came all at once. It is too short and limited in content to have arrived any other way.

RUSSELL EDSON lives in Stamford, Connecticut, with his wife, Frances. He handset and printed his first pamphlets and is also a printmaker (woodcuts and etchings). Recently he won a Guggenheim Fellowship (1974–75) in "Creative Writing in Poetry."

His books include *The Very Thing That Happens* (1964), *What a Man Can See* (1969), *The Childhood of an Equestrian* (1973), *The Clam Theater* (1973), *The Falling Sickness, 4 Plays* (1975), *The Intuitive Journey and Other Works* (1976), *The Reason Why the Closet-Man is Never Sad* (1977), and *The Wounded Breakfast,* forthcoming from Wesleyan University Press.

ROBERT FRANCIS

*

Yes, What?

What would earth do without her blessed boobs
her blooming bumpkins garden variety
her oafs   her louts   her yodeling yokels
and all her Breughel characters
under the fat-faced moon?

Her nitwits   numbskulls   universal
nincompoops   jawohl   jawohl   with all
their yawps   burps   beers   guffaws
her goofs   her goons   her big galoots
under the red-faced moon?

1. *The title invites an answer, and the two stanzas ask the question again in a way that implies, "If we lost our 'blessed boobs,' we should lose one of our last vestiges of prelapsarian innocence. Watching boobs, even at times playing at being one, part of us becomes happy, even while the prune-faced part stands lonely, envious, and reproving." Is this the reaction you hoped for? One of several you hoped for? Or did you hope that the reaction would vary from reader to reader and reading to reading by the same reader?*

2. *The reference to Breughel recalls his painting "The Kermesh" and the rhythm of Auden's poem about it, yet one does not need to know Breughel or Auden to know that the boobs you enjoy are not the sad minibus-loads of retarded persons that we see on their way to special classes. Was this combination of hints a conscious courtesy toward several levels of readers?*

3. *Most of us who write in looser modes could not achieve your tight articulation of sound and rhythm with structure and sense (bumpkins implying the round, reddish, comical faces of pumpkins, your use of the affectionate terms for fool rather than the clinical or angry ones, the increasing looseness of the lines as the boobs grow more hilariously*

drunk, the blend of moon calf, man in the moon, *and* under the sun) *without years of patient revision and lots of luck. Just how did this poem get written?*

4. *What other questions would you have liked me to ask? (In answer to question four Robert Francis added: "Could the poem be, and perhaps has been here, misinterpreted?" His essay answers this last question directly and the others by implication.)*

"Yes, What?" is a celebration of words. I was, and am, fascinated with words themselves, their shapes and sounds, and in this poem, their down-to-earth "gut" character. They refer to certain types of men, but it is not the men but words about them that I am celebrating.

"Boobs," "blooming," and "bumpkins" wanted to go together, and "blessed" is a sort of contrasting oxymoron. In the first stanza the men are simply natural country fellows, hence "garden variety." In the second stanza we move to the brainless and dumb. For "yawps" I borrowed from Whitman's magnificent line: "I sound my barbaric yawp over the roofs of the world." No particular reason for borrowing the German "jawohl." For me (and I hope for others too) "her goofs her goons her big galoots" is especially delicious. When I say that line aloud I positively drool!

Why the "fat-faced" and "red-faced" moon? Somehow these earthly and earthy bumpkins seem most at home in moonlight. And the moon returns the compliment by becoming a bumpkin itself, fat, red-faced, and foolish.

How badly "Yes, What?" may be misinterpreted is demonstrated by the comment of a certain reviewer who said, "Robert Francis hates people: he calls them boobs and bumpkins." The poem itself seems evidence that I love them rather than hate them, for I call them "blessed" and ask "what would earth do without" them? But it is not, of course, the boobs and bumpkins that I love, but the words.

I could have started the poem without the initial question: "What would earth do" and so on. In any case, the question is not essential to the poem.

All poets love words, though not always in the same way or to the same degree. But so far as I am aware no other poet has done what I have done in "Yes, What?" and in similar poems. The point is explicit in my poem "Hogwash," which begins "Nobody ever called swill sweet, but isn't hogwash a daisy in a field of daisies?" No, I do not love hogwash, whether hog hogwash or political hogwash. What I do love is the name of it.

"Going to the Funeral" is also fundamentally a celebration of words and phrases. This is a gangster's funeral, a very important gangster. "High muck-a-mucks" is an expression my father used to use, and I borrowed it from him. Later I was pleasantly surprised to find it in the dictionary.

"Poppycock" is still another jamboree of words: "bilge bosh buncombe baloney."

As further evidence that in calling people boobs and bumpkins I do not hate them, I quote a poem not yet published though already included in poetry readings by myself and others:

Manifesto of the Simple

We are the dim-witted, the weak-witted, the half-wits
Your dunces and your dumbbells.
We don't know enough to do much harm.

The bright boys, the white-haired boys
Make the big bombs, the big bangs. We couldn't
Make even a little Molotov cocktail.

The bright boys, the white-haired boys
Make the sky dragons, the sky demons
And the bright boys run them.

We are the retarded who will never catch up
The mooncalves, moonrakers, the morons.
Progress is not our business.

Who said be simple? Jesus.
Who said it again? Saint Francis.
And the Shakers, the beautiful Shakers.

We are Mother Earth's simple ones.
We are Mother Earth's simpletons.
We are Mother Goose's Simple Simons.

     Peace.

Although this poem is full of word-love, it is not like the others we have been considering, for it has a message. The simple-minded and the simple in heart are not responsible for all the world's turmoil. With lifted hand the simple cry: Peace.

ROBERT FRANCIS was born in Pennsylvania in 1901, but it was not until 1926 that he reached Amherst, Massachusetts, his hometown ever since. On the way there he picked up two Harvard degrees. He is a writer of both poetry and prose. His first seven books of poems can be found in his *Collected Poems*. He has also been a teacher in various capacities. His rustic one-man home, Fort Juniper, was built in 1940. Though he is often said not to be well known, his "honors" are too numerous to be listed here.

STUART FRIEBERT

*

The Metal Fox

You sink the metal fox into the ground.
Years go by, you forget where it stands.
Don't dream it will cut his leg when he
goes into the brush to hide from you, it
was winter, who could miss it, branches
were bare. It was serious, shots needed.

And the florist decorated the room with
masses of scarlet yellow flowers, you're
the only ones on the corridor that night.
The room dim, the snow stopped. Someone
in a coma like that's your son, you want
baying hounds, hunting horns, anything
to make life huge, go right up to it.

No idea where to go, running off
like that, fleeing a father's anger,
drawing out of brush the metal fox
no one was looking for.

A Friebert poem moves by psychological leaps and syntactical ellipses, so that it gives the effect of dream and forces a waking reader to make emotional connections because he can't slide along the easier path of the usual logical ones, led by the usual grammatical clues. But underneath a poem like "The Metal Fox" is most often a consecutive narrative. This time it's an accident in which a father unintentionally injures his son, who cuts his leg on a rusty metal fox placed long ago by the father and forgotten. The next scene is in a hospital. The father and someone in a coma are "the only ones on the corridor that night." The father feels as if that other person were his injured son. The third stanza might apply to the son, to the father fleeing his own father, or to anyone who has fled a father. By this time the fox has become symbolic, with meanings raying out in all directions, depending on who reads the poem, how often, and in what context of his/her own life. The reader has to work very hard at this point because the poem does not explain. But the poet needs to talk about it, because unless readers are tilted toward this way of writing, they may sweat very hard indeed and still miss the excitement of what's going on.

I recall starting an early version in my usual rambling, notational way. A real experience was, as usual, involved: I broke my nose playing football and spent months in a hospital fighting off an ensuing strep infection (henceforth I have hated and feared hospitals). That was before there were wonder drugs, and I was in a coma part of the time. (By the way, another poem off this experience is entitled "Before There Were Wonder Drugs:" I frequently circle an experience for as many poems as I can get from it.) I soon picked up an unusual roommate: my father'd been planing wood, took a sliver up his arm which he ignored, and developed a wonderful case of blood poisoning. There we were in the same room, eating Thanksgiving Day dinner together. It was 1942, we were listening to the war news on the radio, and craning our necks out the window to follow the polo game being played on the grounds adjacent to the hospital, complete with shouts and Sousa-like music—where, no doubt, the "baying hounds, hunting horns" in the final version partly come from, by way of some minor transformation once I'd made the major move in the poem, changing what began as a metal flower into a fox (see below). At any rate, it was my usual odd mix, which has always challenged me: to see how many disparate elements I can juggle in a poem without anything falling.

I've always been fearful of being accused of writing the same poem over and over, which in effect I suppose I do! In a recurring dream, God says, "Sorry, mister, you've written just one poem all this while." Once I realize that's happening, that I'm writing the old father-&-me poem again, I try to swerve out of its way; relocating the story, changing the characters, anything to disguise that it's (mostly always) about a father and son whirling around each other, trying to connect. (Some recent poems have them taking care of each other, in a cabin in the woods, in a nursing home, a boat at sea.) Obviously, I haven't done anything drastic by changing "The Metal Fox" into a story about my own son and me, but it feels fresher, and that frees me to maintain some of the symbolic forces at work on my father and me, and all fathers and sons (see Alberta Turner's headnote), while I push in a slightly different direction. My main point is, it's important to keep tracking old themes, as well as seek fresh means in doing so to write yourself out of that proverbial corner.

Now more to the poem at hand: my son had been suffering a series of odd little accidents in his early years, and I'd rushed him to Emergency on occasion for shots and stitches. Once, I even caused the injury, threw him his first football much too hard. Its sharply pointed nose (the connection with my own broken nose story shouldn't be lost on anyone) cut his forehead and we were off to Emergency again. I was also a little angry, I realized in looking back, for his not having caught the ball, living up to my (impossible) expectations. That's an old, foolish pattern for some fathers and sons, I figure. (Currently, I'm exploring this theme on much more open ground, calling the poem, simply, "A Father's Anger"). Enter the next element: about the time of this little football incident, a student of mine gave me a wonderful metal flower he'd sculpted. We sank it into the ground in a grove of bushes and trees behind the house. I knew damn well it might be dangerous there, with its rough edges, but I couldn't put it away entirely either. It was summer, things grew, it disappeared. (Writing this now, I realize there's another dangerous object, an art object!, out back. Originally, it was a seven-foot figure called "The Bride," that we've since cut down to shoulders and head and leaned against a tree trunk where it can't topple over, if a child should hide there. So the 'final' cut by the metal flower on my son's leg has brought all this local danger stuff to an appropriate end).

As mentioned, the major move in the poem away from the real toward the symbolic (if that's what we need to call it), was my decision to convert the flower into a fox. That's consistent with the phase I've been in the past several years: writing all sorts of dislocated nursery tales. One whole series is about nursery rhyme characters seen in their old age, "Big Miss Muffet," "Big Jack Horner," "Very Old King Cole," "Sir William Winkie." Another group, to which this poem belongs, is an attempt to cast real experience in a nursery tale mode—an example that is similar to "The Metal Fox" is a poem called "Run Over Run Over," about running over a dog down the road a bit. To do so seems to me to shape the poem in a more lasting form, with phrases that lend themselves to turning over in the mind—"no one was looking for"; "the room dim, the snow stopped"; "who could miss it"—as well as allow poster-like images to float up—"baying hounds, hunting horns"; "masses of scarlet yellow flowers"—and the amalgam of the real and abstract, "to make life huge, go right up to it." In effect, I've tried to project the entire experience on the wall before the reader, make it seem to topple over on us. Finally, the whole poem, especially the last several lines, is an attempt to make the whole inevitable, and to catch us alone with our angers and fears, which can hurt us.

STUART FRIEBERT directs the writing program at Oberlin. His latest books of poetry include *Uncertain Health* (1979) and *Nicht Hinauslehnen* (1975). With David Young, he co-edited *The Longman Anthology of Contemporary American Poetry: 1950–1980*. He has also published many translations from many languages, and Wesleyan University Press has recently issued his and Vinio Rossi's translations of Giovanni Raboni's *The Coldest Year of Grace* (1984), from the Italian. In 1980, he held an N.E.A. fellowship in poetry.

JOHN HAINES

*

The Eye in the Rock

A high rock face above Flathead Lake,
turned east where the light
breaks at morning over the mountain.

An eye was painted here by men
before we came, part of an Indian face,
part of an earth
scratched and stained by our hands.

It is only rock, blue or green,
cloudy with lichen,
changing in the waterlight.

Yet blood moves in this rock,
seeping from the fissures;
the eye turned inward, gazing back
into the shadowy grain,
as if the rock gave life.

And out of the fired mineral
come these burned survivors,
sticks of the wasting dream:

thin red elk and rusty deer,
a few humped bison,
ciphers and circles without name.

Not ice that fractures rock,
nor sunlight, nor the wind
gritty with sand has erased them.
They feed in their tall meadow,
cropping the lichen a thousand years.

Over the lake water comes this light
that has not changed,
the air we have always known . . .

They who believed that stone,
water and wind might be quickened
with a spirit like their own,
painted this eye that the rock might see.

*I asked John Haines to what degree "The Eye in the Rock" is autobiography, whether the
speaker's point of view is his own, whether the poem's tone is reproof, regret, despair,
reverence, resolution or some combination of these or others. Then I asked him how the
poem grew and what technical decisions he made during the process. The following essay is
his meditation on those questions—and more.*

A high rock face above Flathead Lake,
turned east where the light
breaks at morning over the mountain.

It is an actual place on the west shore of Flathead Lake in western Montana, and
is known locally as Painted Rock Point. In company with five other people, I
went there one day in early summer a few years back. We had come, as I recall,
on a personal mission related to an environmental project for the Northern
Rockies, and were exploring some of the Indian past of the countryside.

We came by small boat from a landing two or three miles farther north on
the lake shore. The late morning was calm, the sun bright and warm. As we
approached from offshore, the rockface came into view, and what appeared
from a distance to be rusty splashes of lichen or patches of a reddish mineral
color in the rock, resolved into a scattered arrangement of small painted figures.

Roughly vertical, rising thirty to forty feet above the lake, and with numerous faults and planes, the rockface with its red-painted figures dispersed among
the gradations of rock color, is like a weathered mural, faded from its original

brilliance but, in full sun, still glowing and subtly dappled with light from the water below.

There is an irregular shelf of boulders below the face on which one can stand and view the paintings at close range. That morning we tied our boat to a length of driftwood lodged among the boulders at water level, and climbed up to the shelf. There we could move around and explore the face at our leisure.

From close up, the painted figures tend to blur into shadings in the rock surface and have not the definition and seeming coherence that they have when seen from the water. The figures are simply, even crudely, rendered in a bright rust or red brick pigment (ferrous oxide?); they are recognizable representations of bison, elk, and deer, and with many additional designs and markings, perhaps abstracted from something in nature, dispersed among them.

The figures are arranged in no immediately discernible pattern, mounting from somewhat below eye-level to a height out of reach of even the tallest man. The animal shapes are in profile, facing toward the left as one stands before them, and appear at times to be drifting across the face of the rock. Here and there a figure will be partly obscured by a break in the rockface; then, stepping a short distance to one side and shifting one's angle of view, another partly-erased figure will reveal itself.

The rock faces east, across more than a mile of water, into the rising sun. I am not certain now what kind of rock it is; pink quartzite is common in that part of Montana, but it is not that. The color of the rock ranges from tawny to a dusty blue or green, depending on the light and the time of day. According to one informed opinion, the figures are perhaps eight-hundred to nine-hundred years old, and may not in all cases be contemporary.

The most striking figure on the rock is an eye, an obviously human eye, many times life-size, painted at the far, or north, end of the face, and somewhat above average head height. The eye is painted as if looking back, into the eye-corner. Arranged around it are a number of vertical and diagonal slash marks. Neither the eye nor the markings around it appear to have any relation to anything else on the rock.

I had brought a camera with me, and in the course of the morning and early afternoon I took several photographs in color of the rock and its various sections, both from the water and from the shelf. Whatever conversation passed among us that day concerning the eye and the other figures, it is clear to me now that none of us had any real understanding of the significance of what we were seeing. It was not until later, when the film had been processed and the slides returned to me, and I had spent some time in studying them, that I realized that the eye which had so puzzled us was part of a face in the rock, that it had been placed in exact relation to a profile in one jutting edge of the rock, a profile that included a mouth, a nose, and a chin. It was clear also that the other markings around it—behind, above and below it—all contributed to form a face, a portrait perhaps of someone marked with ceremonial decoration. Once seen, the effect was so striking it was remarkable we had not noticed it at once.

They knew what they did, those who painted that eye, and there was surely nothing haphazard in the arrangement of the other figures on that rock.

I can't recover now all the stages that my poem went through. I recall it as being rather easy to write. With nothing more than memory to go on, I'm willing to say that the poem probably began with a few notes made on the spot, and was written out later that summer.

I have just written, "the poem probably began with . . ." And having said that and thought about it for a moment, I realize how tentative must be anything said about the origins of a poem. At one time, during the early nineteen-seventies, I made an intensive study of rock art in Central California. I combined a good deal of reading on the subject with several backpacking trips into the mountains of Santa Barbara and San Luis Obispo counties. With the help of a local authority on rock art, I was able to explore a number of remote and little-known sites. I camped alone in the hills at night, and by day I explored the rocks and caves, photographed, and made extensive notes on what I saw.

When I went to Painted Rock Point that day some years later, I had already an informed background from which to view it. And it might be as fair to say that as a consequence my poem had its beginning, not there on Flathead Lake, but some years before, on a sweltering forenoon in early summer when I first saw the sandstone redoubt of Pool Rock; and that somewhere in the underground of the poem there may be also some strange and still-unsorted emotion recalled from a night when I camped in a certain cave high in the Santa Ynez Mountains west of Bakersfield.

With that much said, I suspect that my sense of the poem's structure took shape early, and that the first lines, falling as they did into a three-line group, gave me a clue as to the overall form the poem would take. This three-line stanza is repeated at intervals, and its occurrence illustrates a convenient working principle: that by following what the poem suggests to us at any moment, we can shape it toward a possibly foreseen conclusion.

It may be, in this case, that the ending of the poem was formed early and I wrote the rest of it in order to get myself there. But what I *can* be sure of is that certain lines, images, and combinations thereof revealed themselves and served as keys. I am referring mainly to the third, fourth, and fifth stanzas and to lines like "not ice that fractures rock" and to the image of the painted animals "feeding in their tall meadow." Around these elements the poem grew. And "that the rock might see" was surely a perception worth writing towards.

The alternating long and short lines create a visual as well as an aural pattern. I notice, too, that the lines in most instances are long enough to contain the phrases and parts of sentences without breaking them. This is, let's say, a matter of choice at any given moment, but it cannot be arbitrary; every device employed, every part of "craft," must justify itself.

The very obvious rhyme that occurs toward the end of the poem was partly deliberate, though as nearly as I can now tell what was deliberate in this took its clue from the accidental. A certain amount of repetition of sounds seems to occur naturally to an ear attuned to language. I don't know how apparent this will be to a reader used to *seeing* a poem as print on the page, but if one reads the poem aloud and listens to it, the echo of syllables and consonants will soon be clear enough in the repeated sounds of "green," "grain," "men," "rock," "back," "lichen," "light," and so forth.

At one time I might have written a shorter, more compact poem out of the same circumstances. I will assume that all poems offer a kind of meditational process; but there is more than one way to meditation in a poem. There is that something brooded upon for a long time, possibly for years, and the result given expression in a brief and concentrated poem. For me, this sort would be represented by many poems in my first book, *Winter News*, and in many subsequent poems. And there is the poem in which meditation itself is in process and clearly given its full due, as rumination and extended commentary. Much traditional poetry is like this; or, to name a poet of our own time, many of the poems of Czeslaw Milosz. I would say, just for the occasion and assuming that such categories are useful at all, that "The Eye in the Rock" is a poem that falls somewhere between these two: that it is both immediate and discursive.

The foregoing discussion of some of the technical elements in the poem happens to be the least of my own interest in this poem and its circumstances, and for reasons which I hope will be clear.

My interest in rock art is that of an amateur, but it is of a piece with my passion for landforms, for earth history, and for all that belongs with and adorns these. I have sensed, and all too keenly at times, that in our time something may be dying: an ancient life-relation, and all its manifestations become the more valuable as they become rare, are cheapened or defaced, or disappear entirely from one cause or another.

A phrase in the fourth stanza of the poem, "blood moves," refers to the color of the pigment used in the rock paintings. Was the color red chosen because of its availability, or because of its closeness to the color of blood? Were there originally other colors on the rock that have since faded? I don't know. But my phrase also implies the feeling I had at the time that the rockface took on life from those painted figures, and that both the rock and the figures gathered a life-energy by virtue of the light and the moving water below.

What the eye may have meant to the people who placed it there is, so far as I know, impossible to say exactly. That is, I cannot know with any certainty what the "Indian's belief" was. And since I can know very little of the original thought and purpose behind the eye in the rock, nearly everything in the poem is a projection of mine. But to the extent that I can recover in myself something of the mind that looked on nature in a way very different from our habitual attitude of "use"—a nature that was alive in every detail and filled with meaning, with *spirit*—it may be that my projection verifies a felt truth.

It could be said that the eye and all that surrounds it, the rock of which it is part, constitute a fossil language, decipherable now only to a limited degree. The figures and the markings, the rockface itself, are evidence of a communication with the visible and invisible world. We have lost the key to that language, but if we had it we could read the rockface as a book. Or, to put it another way, and to answer one of the questions posed about the poem: if we were able really to see with the *eye of the rock* we might read the entire history of the earth—past and future, mineral, seed, and flesh.

I would say, then, that the tone of the poem is that of reverence mixed with a keen sense of loss. A remark by Ortega y Gasset seems to make an appropriate connection here:

> There are people who believe in good faith that we have no obligations toward the rocks. (Jose Ortega y Gasset, *Meditations on Hunting*, p. 103)

This observation makes an intellectual event out of what was once an immediate kinship with the elements. In our time we must think our way back through many centuries in order to regain a kind of understanding in place of what was once intuitive.

It is "only" rock, to be sure; but then this is "only" earth, and we are "only" flesh, and finally, perhaps, nothing but dust. And yet it's true, even from a plain geological viewpoint, that the rock *does* give life—gives it back continually in the work of centuries of consolidation and soil-building. There is also, alas, a point of view from which we can all nowadays be seen as "sticks of the wasting dream."

It is I who speak the poem, as representative man muttering to himself some interior thing, but assuming at the same time that he will be overheard. Perhaps because I saw the rock in company with other people I was led to speak in terms of *we* rather than of *I*. But I notice that among the poems of which "The Eye in the Rock" forms a group, from my book *In A Dusty Light*, how consistently I have used the pronoun *we*. This is something I had not thought much about until now. Here, at any rate, I seem to have written as if *we* were the natural self.

There is a sense in which I could speak of this poem as having been "found." Maybe all worthwhile poems (and things and persons, for that matter) are found. They are found by us in the act of living, of walking and looking, and often in the act of thinking. Now, I know that it is possible, with a little skill and practice, to write poems about almost anything, and by taking any clue in the world around us as a starting point. But let me be clear about this: I do not believe in using the world as a source of egotistical aggrandisement—in going through the world looking for things and events to set a poem in motion. This is a trick that can be learned, but to me it is the literary equivalent of that material exploitation that in one way or another is wasting so much of the life of this planet.

I believe in the poem as a gift. I believe in that fortunate meeting of attention and object which results in an essential and necessary recognition: of the thing felt, understood in a way that precludes any choice or equivocation. I believe also in silence, in keeping still when one has nothing to say.

Rereading my poem now, rather like a distant friend of the occasion, I find in it things that please me. After the preparatory ground of the opening lines, I note a certain gathering of energy, a breaking forth in the third stanza, and again with intensity in the fifth. And from there on it seems to me that the poem sustains itself pretty well to the end. Assuming I'm right about this, none of it, naturally, was plotted out beforehand. Only an inborn sense of balance, of *rightness*, allows these things to happen in the right order and with the right weight of emphasis. (But who is to say that we aren't all originally gifted to some degree with this sense)? The effect is similar, I suspect, to the way a good piece of music reveals itself with alternations of tone and pitch. And somewhere here, *craft* turns into vision, though as I say those words I know how trivial they can be made to sound.

As an aesthetic object the poem satisfies me. If it were worthwhile to try and reduce the poem to its message, it seems to me it could be expressed in this way: "Here is something you have not thought about, fellow citizens. You think that rock is dead matter, and that these red daubings are the play of children now gone. But you are wrong. This rock and these figures are alive, and they are telling you something: that the past is not past, and that despite your certainties and amusements life has not changed much in these thousand years. What *has* changed is your perception of values. But keep looking, for if this rock and this poem say nothing to you now, some day they might."

Reviewing what I have written about this poem, I feel that the explanations I have offered are substantially true, that things occurred as I have said and with their approximate meaning. At the same time, the reader should beware of taking at face value anything said in this way about something as mysterious as a poem. I know that the poem itself says more fully and deeply what it means and is. Any attempt to say more about the eye, the rock, and their combined significance would require another approach than this brief essay—an approach more nearly poetic, though not necessarily another poem in verse.

JOHN HAINES, born in 1924, has taught at the Universities of Washington, Alaska, and Montana. He did not study creative writing, but spent a number of years homesteading in Alaska. His books include, among others, *Winter News,* 1966, revised and reissued, Wesleyan, 1983; *Living Off the Country: Essays on Poetry and Place,* Michigan University Press, 1981; *Of Traps and Snares,* essays, Dragon Press, 1981; *News From the Glacier,* Selected Poems, 1960–80, Wesleyan University Press, 1982; and *Other Days,* essays, Graywolf Press, 1982. He received the Governor's Award for Excellence in the Literary Arts in Alaska, 1982, and an Honorary Doctor of Letters degree from the University of Alaska, Fairbanks, 1983.

DONALD HALL

*

Names of Horses

All winter your brute shoulders strained against collars, padding
and steerhide over the ash hames, to haul
sledges of cordwood for drying through spring and summer,
for the Glenwood stove next winter, and for the simmering range.

In April you pulled cartloads of manure to spread on the fields,
dark manure of Holsteins, and knobs of your own clustered with oats.
All summer you mowed the grass in meadow and hayfield, the mowing machine
clacketing beside you, while the sun walked high in the morning;

and after noon's heat, you pulled a clawed rake through the same acres,
gathering stacks, and dragged the wagon from stack to stack,
and the built hayrack back, up hill to the chaffy barn,
three loads of hay a day from standing grass in the morning.

Sundays you trotted the two miles to church with the light load
of a leather quartertop buggy, and grazed in the sound of hymns.
Generation on generation, your neck rubbed the windowsill
of the stall, smoothing the wood as the sea smooths glass.

When you were old and lame, when your shoulders hurt bending to graze,
one October the man who fed you and kept you, and harnessed you every
    morning,
led you through corn stubble to sandy ground above Eagle Pond,
and dug a hole beside you where you stood shuddering in your skin,

and lay the shotgun's muzzle in the boneless hollow behind your ear,
and fired the slug into your brain, and felled you into the grave,
shoveling sand to cover you, setting goldenrod upright above you,
where by next summer a dent in the ground made your monument.

For a hundred and fifty years, in the pasture of dead horses,
roots of pine trees pushed through the pale curves of your ribs,
yellow blossoms flourished above you in autumn, and in winter
frost heaved your bones in the ground—old toilers, soil makers:

O Roger, Mackerel, Riley, Ned, Nellie, Chester, Lady Ghost.

1. *Perhaps because my first memories are of two large, empty box stalls with the smell of
   dried manure and the names Billy and Marjorie Daw, and of our 1922 Apersen car
   caught coming home from the station behind a slow team, and of a mildewed buggy
   harness in the cellar, every muscle tensed with recognition when I read this poem. But
   when the poem was first published, in* The New Yorker *in 1977, how many readers
   could it have "happened" to in that way? What sort of experience can readers have
   when the experience has become a historical curiosity associated with calendar towels
   and department store windows at Christmas?*

Exactly. I share the worries that the question entertains, and not only in
connection with *this* poem. Everybody knows about horses—from a Budweiser
ad on television: great manicured Clydesdales pull beer wagons through landscape reduced to scenery, pretty as a picture. I worry that in my rural poems I
may fabricate calendar art, make postcards of covered bridges, or Norman
Rockwell magazine covers. Putting manure into a poem like this may help to
avoid Norman Rockwell, but I suppose there is such a thing as Norman Rockwell manure.

Obviously if I print the poem I hope that it survives the danger you speak of.
How? Well, if any poem succeeds, its subject matter is only ostensible (which is
why thematic anthologies never work). I question your premise that the poem is
about horses.

Of course it's about horses, but on the other hand two elements in the poem
seem to me to point somewhere away from these ostensible dobbins. Half of the
poem is about *work*—about muscles, labor, making land, and about the difficulty or harshness of that life. Maybe the other half is a universal *ubi sunt*, an
elegy not merely for horses but for people who hayed and cut ice and went to
Church and spread manure and shot horses, by extension for all the country of
the dead. Think of Villon's list of the dead beauties: is his poem about mythology? Is it even about beautiful women? When I had worked on "Names of
Horses" for a long time, I came to hope that it was no more about horses than,
oh, Keats's ode is about an object among the archeological plunder in the British
Museum.

2. *How did you determine the nature and sequence of the names of the horses? Are they
   the names of actual horses you have known, names associated with a single farm, or a
   composite? Did you invent any of them for their sound or connotation, Lady Ghost,
   for instance?*

I wrote the poem over two years or so. As I first worked on it, I did not list the horses' names at the end of the poem. After each stanza I repeated a refrain in which I rhymed the names. Many of the names are remembered. Riley was the first horse of my childhood; then I remember a Ned, a Roger, a Nellie; I remember hearing about a great Chester who ran things before I was born. I made up "Lady Ghost"—you suspected!—not for the sound itself but for a rhyme. The refrain ended with "but Riley the most." "Lady Ghost" was born to rhyme with "most." When I abandoned the refrain idea and went to the one-line list at the end, I kept her around.

3. *How much of the rest of the poem is autobiography? I note that Eagle Pond Farm, for instance, is your present address. Is it the farm where you grew up? Was the stove a Glenwood? Did you have a Holstein herd? Did you yourself help bring in "three loads of hay a day from standing grass in the morning"?*

This is the farm where I spent my childhood summers. My great-grand-father bought it in 1865 when he was almost forty. He was a sheep farmer, and had worked a hill farm for many years; I suspect that he made money, during the Civil War, selling wool for uniforms. Originally, people farmed up the hill because the frost came later, but when the railroad came through, late in the 1840s, the flatter farms in the valley became more valuable. You could raise corn and hay to feed milk cattle, then ship milk by railroad to Manchester and Boston.

My grandmother was born here, and my mother. My mother when she married went to Connecticut, and I lived in a suburb of New Haven during the schooltime of the year. Summers I spent here haying with my grandfather— what a contrast it was! It set the suburbs of identical families in identical houses against the farm country where nothing was like anything else. The suburbs never had a chance.

And I moved into the past, because my grandfather farmed as people had farmed for a century or so. Farms were poor then—the agricultural depression started early in the '20s—and he farmed with one horse. I worked here sum-mers, milked a Holstein on occasion, hayed every day with Riley.

We still have the Glenwood stove; the range is also a Glenwood.

But then you ask: "Did you yourself help bring in 'Three loads of hay a day from standing grass in the morning'?" A sore point. Once or twice a year, we did that. For the most part, you do *not* load in the afternoon the hay that you cut in the morning: it is too green; it might burn your barn down. You leave it to dry for a few days, then bring it in. This line is an exaggeration that I must change. It was early this year at a poetry reading when I finally understood that I *must* revise this line. (If we do many readings, we keep examining our old work; we keep finding things to change. I tinker with old poems continually.) In January when I read my poems in Buffalo, I saw Wendell Berry sitting in the third row; he was reading elsewhere in town the same day. When I read this poem aloud, I stopped after "Three loads of hay a day" and left the line short. I couldn't look Wendell in the eye and say the rest of the line.

4. *What determined your choice of the unusually long lines, the line breaks, the stanza groupings?*

I didn't choose the long line; it chose me. On several occasions during the last thirty years, the sound of my poems has altered; it has become exciting to make a new noise. After years of working with short-lined percussive, enjambed free verse, in the fall of 1974 I found this long line coming . . . When I began this poem—in 1975, I think—it arrived in a line that made the new music. Over the many drafts, over years of working, gradually these stanzas found their present shape.

As I have said before: I intend a thing *after* it happens. It happens first because one day I write it that way. If I do not change it, then I have intended it. I am careful indeed. But I am not careful ahead of time; I do not say to myself: "Let me see, I am writing about horses. I guess a long line would be good because horses are so *big*." I don't write the way Poe said he did, when he told about writing "The Raven." (I'm not sure Poe did either.) I cannot predict what I will end up doing. But one thing I *can* do is to take a long time; I can make sure that by the time I print something, I intend most of what is there.

5. *The poem shows signs of a very careful ear, a matching of the sounds to the action, as in the alliteration and the final spondees of the line, "of the stall, smoothing the wood as the sea smooths glass." Could you comment on the strategies and accidents in matching the poem's sounds and rhythms to its sense?*

I don't believe in spondees; spondees are like the Easter bunny. Another time. . . .

As with the gross matters of line-length and stanza-form, so with the more intimate matters of alliteration and assonance. I don't know ahead of time what I am going to do. When I see what I am doing, I search for ways to do it better. Although I try to understand what I'm up to, *before* I print a poem, it is common for me to keep on noticing things about my poem later, after I have published it and read it aloud many times. Here I have come to notice, for instance, that there are two moments when the sound becomes especially prominent—two separate moments, with quieter patches in between. If you try all the time to make sound that draws attention to itself, you will draw attention to nothing but sound. Wild sound must coincide with a high moment. It will always *make* a high moment anyway, and if it makes a high moment out of low matter there will be disparity.

For me ecstacy signals itself by assonance. In the work-part of this poem, with all its attention to short *as* and to *ks*, there is a *revelry* in the day of haying. This is the first high moment. The second is lamentation and elegy, especially the sentence that ends with the poem's penultimate line. Here I am wholly conscious of *song*. Here I want to belt it out. If I can't make this happen, let the poem collapse in the trash of its phonemes.

I make writing sound like a performance. All right. It is a performance arrived at slowly, in solitude, morning after morning.

There is one other phrase I may change but which I am loathe to revise because I like the sound. Late in the poem I speak of how "Frost heaves their bones in the ground . . ." Once after a poetry reading somebody asked me if their bones were really so close to the surface. Damn! I doubt it. One buries the bodies deep, or a dog will dig them up. I am afraid that these bones reside below the frost line, despite my poem. Maybe in an *exceptional* winter the frost would sink deep enough?

6. *The genre of the elegy has been used for animals since its beginnings. Did you make any conscious use of or variation from that tradition in writing this poem?*

I was reading a lot of Thomas Hardy; I think some Hardy comes into the poem. I remember Edwin Muir's wonderful horse-poem, about the strange horses returning after nuclear war. But I was not aware of using animal-elegies as a source, nor was I really conscious of the genre.

7. *What started this poem? What changes did it go through? How long did it take to complete? If you have saved the worksheets, could I see a copy?*

The poem started when I returned to live here, after years of towns and suburbs. Forty years ago my grandfather met me at the depot with Riley drawing a carriage; he never owned a tractor, much less an automobile. (My wife and I are the first people to live at this place with a car.) I thought about the horse-labor that had gone into this place, to keep it going over the many years; to control and maintain the land.

I do not own the worksheets. They are down at the University of New Hampshire with my other papers. I suppose that I took seventy or eighty drafts, and worked at the poem over a couple of years.

I always show poems to my friends—after I have worked on them alone for a year or so. I remember W. D. Snodgrass helping me with this poem, as he has done with many. This time Louis Simpson helped me more than anyone else. He's always so good on narrative—a master. It was he who persuaded me out of the refrain, asking me who did I think I was, Thomas Hardy? (The answer was doubtless yes.) And it was he who suggested that I might save the names of the horses for the end of the poem. I am grateful.

8. *What other questions would you have liked me to ask?*

"Has anyone set this poem to music?" Some years back the composer William Bolcom set three of my poems. When I knew he wanted to do something with "Names of Horses," I tinkered with it toward the notion of a setting. I piece-cut old stanzas and restored the refrain . . . When he set it (he has performed it with his wife Joan Morris) I called it "Horse Song" to distinguish it from the poem. This is the poem he set:

Horse Song

All winter your brute shoulders strained against collars,
padding and steerhide over the ash hames, to haul
sledges of cordwood for drying through spring and summer.
In April you pulled cartloads of manure to spread on the fields,
dark manure of Holsteins, and knobs of your own clustered with oats. . .

> *O Ned the Elder, Ned the Less,*
> *Riley, Chester, and Sister Bess,*
> *O Sally-Maggie, Billy Blue,*
> *Nebuchadnezzar and Roger too,*
> *O Babe and William, Lady Ghost,*
> *Jesse, Ted—but Riley the most.*

All summer you mowed the grass in hayfields, mowing machine
clacketing beside you, while the sun walked high in the morning;
and after noon's heat, you pulled a clawed rake through the same acres,
gathering stacks, and dragged the wagon from stack to stack
and the built hayrack back, up hill to the chaffy barn. . .

> *O Ned the Elder, Ned the Less,*
> *Riley, Chester, and Sister Bess,*
> *O Sally-Maggie, Billy Blue,*
> *Nebuchadnezzar and Roger too,*
> *O Babe and William, Lady Ghost,*
> *Jesse, Ted—but Riley the most.*

When you were old and lame, one October the man who kept you
dug a hole beside you in sandy ground above Eagle Pond
and lay the shotgun's muzzle in the boneless hollow behind your ear,
and shoveled sand to cover you, setting goldenrod upright above you,
where by next summer a dent in the ground made your monument. . .

> *O Ned the Elder, Ned the Less,*
> *Riley, Chester, and Sister Bess,*
> *O Sally-Maggie, Billy Blue,*
> *Nebuchadnezzar and Roger too,*
> *O Babe and William, Lady Ghost,*
> *Jesse, Ted—but Riley the most.*

I like "Names of Horses" better as a poem—whatever that means. But with Bolcom's setting and the voice of Joan Morris, the song is gorgeous.

DONALD HALL was born in 1928, and has published eight books of poetry and fifty-some other books—textbooks, juveniles, biography, essays, memoirs, and one encyclopedia. He taught for many years at the University of Michigan; in 1975 he quit teaching in order to live in New Hampshire as a free-lance writer.

MICHAEL S. HARPER

*

Landfill

Loads of trash and we light the match;
what can be in a cardboard box
can be in the bed of the pickup
and you jostle the containers onto the side road.
A match for this little road,
and a match for your son riding next to you firing,
and a match for the hole in the land filled with trees.
I will not mention concrete because theirs is the meshed
wire of concrete near the docks, and the concrete
of burned trees cut in cords of change-sawing,
and we will light a match to this too.

Work in anger for the final hour of adjustment
to the surveyors, and to the lawyers speaking of squatting,
and the land burning to no one.
This building of scrap metal, high as the storm that will
break it totally in the tornado dust,
and to the animals that have lived in the wheathay of their bedding
will beg for the cutting edge, or the ax,
or the electrified fencing that warms them in summer rain.

My son coughs on the tarred scrubble of cut trees,
and is cursed by the firelight, and beckoned to me to the pickup,
and washed of the soot of his sootskinned face,
and the dirt at the corners of my daughter's mouth will be trenchmouth;
and the worn moccasin of my woman will tear into the bulbed big toe,
and the blood will be black as the compost pile burning,
and the milk from her dugs will be the balm for the trenchmouth,
as she wipes her mouth from the smoke of the landfill filled with fire,
and these loads of trash will be the ashes for her to take:
and will be taken to the landfill, and filled, and filled.

77

1. By the time the poem is finished, the title, "Landfill," has come to mean not only a euphemism for dump, but the stuff that our land, including our society, is filled with and on which we must build its future—trash, fire, ash, charred lives. In stanza 1, the match that lights the conflagration and destroys the trash seems to be a tool of reform held in an aware and righteous human being's hand, yet he and his are stained and infected by the fire they willed, and the pit will never be filled with such ashes. This is an angry poem, something between a dirge, a curse, and a threat. It leaves this reader ashamed and swinging between resolution and despair. Is this how you wish me to feel, or do I react too strongly? Do the words "Work in anger" epitomize the poem's theme and tone?

2. In places I have difficulty with the syntax: Is ashes or landfill the subject of "and filled and filled" in the last line? To whom does theirs refer in line 8? Is to implied between and and the in line 3 of stanza 2? The series "to the surveyors," "to the lawyers" seems to be continued in "to the animals" in line 6 of stanza 2. Is "This building of scrap metal" the subject of "will beg" in line 7 of stanza 2, or is the subject "the animals" in line 6?

3. Is scrubble your own combination of scrub and stubble? Change-sawing of change and chainsaw? Were these deliberate neologisms or happy accidents?

4. Why did you select trenchmouth for the disease endemic to our condition?

5. Is the son's sootskinned face and the black blood of the woman's toe an ethnic reference or a reference to the way the landfill society has blackened all its citizens? Or both?

6. The long sentences and sustained series of the poem suggest the rhythms of the Old Testament Prophets. The fires and smoke of the hole suggest medieval representations of Hell Mouth. Are these the contexts in which you wish the poem to be heard and seen?

7. What started the poem? How long did it take to complete? What revisions did it go through?

The poem is intended as an angry poem, but the anger is meant to project an internal state as well as describe the landscape of the poem. "Work in Anger" is the tone and theme of the poem.

The syntax is meant to be categorical; to some this means confusing. The poem is about violation, and about the consciousness which cannot embrace a true telling of what has happened, in time, in history; so much of the telling of the landscape is cosmetic, superficial, and therefore insisted upon. Scrubble and Change-sawing are neologisms and quite deliberate; trenchmouth is "combat disease," what soldiers contracted by deprivation in the name of some honor-able cause ("gingivitus": foul odor, pain, gray film over diseased area). It is the spoken utterance of survival and, therefore, duplicity—it is both true, in the sense of what is lived, and false as a prism on what is true; it is "personal." On the question of 'sootskinned' face, it is both racial, which includes the Indian (Chippewa, Sioux) and black, and the citizenry as a whole. The poem is meant to suggest prophecy and could be seen in the mode of the Old Testament, and the dark ages, from which we continue to struggle to rise.

The poem started when an actual fire broke out near our home in central Minnesota; the fire was set as a deliberate rite of maintenance, to control weeds, but escalated into something more, including the jeopardy of the house and children. A volunteer force from town came to the rescue, after several hours of family effort; the area is often dry, site of a gravel pit, with buildings that have been used for storage of throwaway items too large to burn or bury: old cars, refrigerators, ranges, bald tires, broken water heaters, magazines, bedding, salvation army clothes.

What might also be relevant is something not included in the poem but is in the consciousness of this poet. The site is near a highway, going east and west; not far is an historical marker which offers commentary on a local incident. A farmer "officiates" between two Indians, one Chippewa, the other Sioux, who are in dispute; the farmer settles the argument with the aid of a broom. The Chippewa (Ojibway) migrated from Ontario, forest dwellers, makers of canoes, and excellent fisherman; the Sioux, with the aid of the horse, were called Plains Indians. The question is one of domain, or territory, and the act of naming; the county is Kandiyohi, which can't be translated, though there is a large brass statue in the county seat: an Indian carrying several pike, dressed up in "hunt-ing and gathering" garb, including braids and a headband. Who owns the land is he or she who names, a sacred function larger than dominion; the act is spiritual, makes utterance to higher law.

W. C. Williams is a master of idiom. And so is Wallace Stevens. The syntax is meant to recall the innovations of speech and reference, to leaps that seem illogical; the landfill can't be filled by any ashes, there is no *to* implied between *and* and *the* in line 3, stanza 2. *Animals* is the subject. Freud made much of one's capacity to *work* and to *love* as civilizing modes of conduct in confronting the landscape, ourselves as caretakers.

MICHAEL S. HARPER was born in 1938 in Brooklyn, New York, spent his teens in Los Angeles, California, and studied at CSU, Los Angeles, and the

University of Iowa. He has published eight collections of poetry, including *Dear John, Dear Coltrane* and *Images of Kin*, New and Selected Poems. He teaches at Brown University and was recently named I. J. Kapstein Professor of English. He is married and has three children.

STRATIS HAVIARAS

*

The Gypsy and the Man in the Black Hat

What is the gypsy searching for in the rain?
And this man in the black hat,
what does he want in the snow?
His face
at my window
tormented by the sun
doesn't melt.
Look
he hurls out a plastic thread
pulls down the sun
now you see it, he shouts
now you don't
and stuffs it inside his hollow rib cage.
Then changes, turns into a priest
turns into a hawker of everything
an antique dealer
displaying holy relics
Byzantine sorrows
flags of Saint Lavra
with holes artfully scorched
as though from enemy bullets—
and the gypsy envies him

the gypsy who is really a king
searching in the rain for his monkey.

Translated by Ruth Whitman

To be attracted to a poem until you are almost mesmerized by it and not to be able to
explain what it is about is embarrassing. Yet Stratis Haviaras's "The Gypsy and the Man

81

in the Black Hat" has me by the throat, though I do not know whether the gypsy or the man are figures in traditional Greek folk tale or surrealistic figures of the poet's imagination or perhaps fictional cloaks for political persons or points of view that discretion would disguise. I don't know why the gypsy should search in the rain and the man in the snow, whether the man's pulling down the sun and putting it in his rib cage and his subsequent metamorphoses make him stand for all crafty survivors, or why the gypsy should envy him—unless the gypsy stands for idealists, who can search only for what they cannot find. But though I cannot identify the gypsy or the king or the monkey, I sense the hopelessness of his loss and his envy for the artful man in the black hat, who can invent what he doesn't have quickly enough to fool his masters and survive.

These Gothic figures and their bizarre acts create a tension that keeps a reader watching even if he is not sure who's doing what to whom. Would you enlarge or redirect my participation by telling me what initiated this poem, what audience you were particularly speaking to, what reaction (s) you hoped they would have, what reaction (s) they did have, and how often and to what extent you revised the poem before it reached its present form. Also, would you comment on how many times the poem has been translated and how it has changed in translation.

And please feel free to answer any questions that I should have asked, but did not think to ask.

"The Gypsy and the Man in the Black Hat" was originally published in Greece during the reign of the military dictatorship, and its cryptic nature and surrealist devices helped it pass through that regime's censorship. In fact, the man in the black hat represents the Regime itself in the poem: the crafty, spying, arbitrary, tyrannical joker that such governments become. Let's say then that the man in the black hat is the personification of political tyranny. Its face, unaltered even by the Greek sun, prevails against the snow, the political winter. The gypsy, on the other hand, is the opposite extreme: the helpless, displaced, confused Greek people—the paying-dearly-for-his-freedom gypsy (as elsewhere in Greek poetry, as also in a major long poem by the national poet, Kostis Palamas: *The Twelve Words of the Gypsy*).

The man in the black hat tears down the sun, hiding it for his exclusive use. He then transforms himself from one expedient form to another: a priest (the dictator's slogan was, "a Greece of Christian Greeks!"); an antique dealer (peddling the "glory that was Greece!"); a hawker of everything (an opportunist, exploiting national sentiments and symbols, such as the grandure of Byzantium and the banner of the revolution of independence from the Turks, kept in the monastery of St. Lavra.)

The gypsy throughout the Balkans often earns his bread by training a monkey or a bear to dance and to imitate people. "The gypsy who is really a king/ searching in the rain for his monkey," brings briefly to mind the unfortunate king Alexander of the modern era, who was bitten by a pet monkey and died in 1920. But make no mistake: the gypsy here is the people, searching for what was rightly theirs: their identity, however disputed, their bread, and above all their freedom.

Note on the translation

Was it Robert Frost, who said, "Poetry is what translation leaves out"? If by poetry he meant imagery, sound and rhythm, and a wide variety of lesser devices to be found in the original poem, then this statement is not far from the truth. Let me skip the problem of reconstituting images and reinventing the lesser devices, as lesser in importance yet greedy in attention, and let me concentrate on sound and rhythm, which seem to be extremely important to me.

Once, I attempted to translate my own Greek poems into English, and I caught myself changing the words, and sacrificing their meaning, in order to accommodate each poem's musical content and general mood. It then occurred to me that this is precisely what happens with many popular songs when they become international hits: when "Never on Sunday" became a success in this country (following its introduction by Melina Mercouri in the movie of the same title), the Greek-speaking Americans realized that the producers of the disc had retained the music but altered the words. But poetry, which is less profitable in the marketplace than popular songs, is far more serious business to those who create it. The poet is by nature a perfectionist, and the compromises involved in the craft of translation depress him, discourage him. In addition to those drawbacks, I am also impatient, so my career as a translator was indeed short: I supervised and edited an anthology of post-war Greek poets (in English), and translated some of the poems in it myself, but not my own poems. That I left to the competence and patience of my friend Ruth Whitman, the poet from Brookline. What Ruth salvaged and reconstructed in "The Gypsy and the Man in the Black Hat" is considerable: if it is not compared to the original it does not sound like a translation; and yet other features, names, and devices betray it as such. But then many experts say that a translation ought to sound like a translation. These are usually academics, who would not and cannot remake a poem so skillfully as to seem an original, and are content to bring to their readers some flavor and some aura from all those distant, exotic poetries.

"The Gypsy and the Man in the Black Hat" did not cause the suppression of the entire book, in which it appeared in Athens, in 1972. The price is that it continues to be a difficult poem even after the fall of the military junta there. That book's title was *Apparent Death*. Two years later, Greece re-emerged as a democratic society. Two more years later, this author began his second life as a poet and novelist writing directly in English. After all he is, as the U.S. Immigration Service classifies him, "a naturalized American."

STRATIS HAVIARAS was born in Greece in 1935, and came to the United States in 1967. He edited *Arion's Dolphin,* a quarterly of poetry (1971–1976), and *The Poet's Voice,* a collection on tape of major American poets reading from their works. His own work in English includes *Crossing the River Twice,* a book of poems published by Cleveland State University Poetry Center, and *When the Tree Sings* and *The Heroic Age,* novels, both published by Simon & Schuster. Haviaras, who works as a librarian at Harvard, is also the author of four books of poetry in Greek.

MIROSLAV HOLUB

*

Collision

I could have been dead by now,
he said to himself, ashamed, as if
it was the heart's malediction, lifting a bundle of
    bones
to a man's height, as if it was
a sudden restriction from even touching the
    words—
Danger / High Voltage.
Anyway, he was afraid to find
his own body pressed in that metal. Painful—
down to the capillaries.

The streetcar stood jammed over him
like an icebreaker's bow; what was left
of the car was a funny pretzel
bitten by the dentures of a mad angel.
Something dark was dripping onto the rails,
and a surprisingly pale wind
leafed through the pages of a book
that was still warm.

People formed in a ring and with deaf-mute
sympathy waited for the play's
catharsis, like black mites
creeping from under the wings
of a freshly-beheaded hen.
A distant siren's wail moved closer,
turning solid in the hexed air-conditioning
of that day and that minute.
Dewdrops fell on the back of the neck,
like remnants of atmospheric dignity.
Painful, down to the capillaries.

No thanks, he said, I'll wait;
because a silent film had begun to run,
without subtitles, without colors,
without answers.

And what about magnetic monopoles
fleeing seconds after the Big Bang,
protons violating the principle
of time reversal variance.

The giant molecular cloud complexes
delivering embryonic stars.

The loneliness of the first genes
accumulating amino acids
in shallow primeval puddles,
on the collateral of entropic loan sharks.

Dried starfish
like hawk's talons, grasping the bottoms
of vanishing seas.

Mortal migrations of birds
obeying the sun's inclination
and the roar of sexual hormones.

The caged, half-crazed
orangutan who vomits to pass the time.

Mice that learned to sing
and frogs, balancing on one foot like the thigh
of a Mesopotamian beauty queen.

Poetry, an occupation
so messy it makes the slide-rule bend,
and supervisors increasingly cross-eyed.

What about the girl in the leukemia
            ward
on the toilet, wanting to show

what a mustache the good doctor has—
when she gestures with her skinny sticks of hands
she starts to slide through the seat, grabs it,
gestures, grabs, again and again.

And what about the lousy egghead,
the associate professor who almost
understood the approximate universe
and forgot about the traffic rules?

No thanks, he said to some uniform,
I don't need anything. I have my license
in my pocket, but I can't reach it.
And he tried to smile a little
about this painfully embarrassing,
finished creation.
It's all my fault, he said,
thank you.

And then he died.

*Science and history show contemporary man that he is an incomplete animal in an
uncompleted universe. Yet some individual thrust or instinct or will lets him assert his
uniqueness before he dissolves. Your poem "Collision" demonstrates how single entities,
from the first violating proton to the associate professor who dies telling the officer, "No
thanks . . . I don't need anything," all assert themsleves effectively for a moment against
mere flux.*

1. *The tone of the poem seems to be shock and grief suffused with wonder, pride, and
affection. Do I read it correctly?*

I don't expect the reader to share my tone. By intention I leave the tone
ambivalent. You may describe the poem as cynical just as well as very affectionate. My own tone was something like consternation, but I don't like to expose
my tones and feelings. At many occasions I have described poetry as some sort
of infection: the virus may be the author's virus; the reaction, i.e., the disease,
depends on the reader.

2. *Is any part of the experience autobiographical?*

The incident is real, it happened some time in 1967, and the dying man was
my professor of physiology. I knew him for fifteen years; I have published his
article about bird migration and bird orientation in space in my magazine. To
me he was one of the kindest men I have ever known. What is in a sense
autobiographical is the "silent film" which I experienced once aboard a plane
which caught fire and dropped about two thousand feet down to a lower flight
level and then returned safely to the Kennedy airport. I don't know whether the

film was about molecular clouds, protons and orangutans, but I know it was about something very impersonal.

My personal association with the incident was the shock on hearing the story of the collision and, in the first place, the fact that the death may have been caused by the refusal of the streetcar operator to back up his vehicle until the police would come, investigate and establish the guilt of the dying man. In Prague I wrote an article in my magazine "About the Death of Professor H.," where I exposed this fact. In the poem, which was written in Oberlin fifteen years later, almost simultaneously in a Czech and in a rough and primitive English version; I did not mention this fact. I did not find the way how to explain it to the American reader. It has a lot of meanings for the Czech reader, which can't be shared. The basic motive of the poem was an attempt to render the monstrosity of the incident by other means.

3. *The expected sentiment of grief is undercut by anger ("lousy egghead"), ugly details ("black mites . . . freshly beheaded hen," "orangutan who vomits," girl on the toilet), humor ("funny pretzel," "dentures of a mad angel"), understatement ("painful— / down to the capillaries," "What about . . . ," "It's all my fault . . . ," "And then he died."), distancing of the characters ("some uniform," the characters unnamed, the speaker not speaking in the first person). Is this flattened way of telling the story a conscious strategy to represent the first shock of grief more realistically than the traditional method of hyperbole and self-consolation?*

It is a routine strategy which I have to use almost every time. When I am too close, I mess things up. And I want order by all means. In poetry I realize that I am at distance whether I want it or not. Besides, I don't believe in noises, assuming that silence may be louder. That coolness may be hotter. That hints may say more.

This is not a choice of strategy. This is necessity. This is a style established by the pressure of natural selection. If you wish, by conditions in which hyperboles and emotions may be luxury or an impossible burden.

4. *"Collision" is the first poem in a group of poems called "A Theory of the Theater," and in the poem you say, "People formed in a ring and with deaf-mute/ sympathy waited for the play's catharsis." In what sense is the accident a play? Are you using catharsis in the same sense as Aristotle used it?*

The poem was conceived for the book *Interferon or On Theater* (I try not to write poems, but books of poetry); the first section is entitled "Biological Poems" and the second "Towards a Theory of the Theater." I realized that the traffic accident is some sort of elementary theater and some sort of biological drama. At the theater, I am much more concerned with the drama than with the performance. I never believe that *Hamlet* or *Oedipus Rex* will end this evening the same way. I always hope. . . . This hope is my sort of catharsis.

The spectators at the traffic accident hope—in spite of the blood, in spite of the black mites, in spite of the weird reactions of streetcar operators.

Another purifying effect of the theater was in my mind in the whole volume *Interferon* and in the title poem: simply, that onstage and in the play you are *elsewhere*.

5. *What do "protons violating the principle/of time reversal variance," "molecular cloud complexes," "genes/ accumulating amino acids," "dried starfish," "bird migration," a sick orangutan, singing mice, balancing frogs, poetry, a leukemia patient, and an associate professor who "forgot the traffic rules" have in common?*

With some hesitation I would admit that all these items have something in common. They mean a victory of the "lousy egghead" over the streetcars. The professor who forgot the traffic rules must be taken in this context strictly as the one saying to some uniform, "No thanks, I don't need anything."

In this sense, this poem and most poems mean a victory in the situation described by Rilke as "Wer spricht vom Siegen, überstehen ist Alles."

6. *Unlike many poets who keep up with the latest advances in science, you make metaphor from scientific facts as often as from urban, rural, domestic, and political sources. Do you do this just because you have both sources of metaphor conveniently at hand or because you are fulfilling a more specific theory of poetics?*

I can imagine a poem about the bad luck of multipotent stem cells turning into precommitted progenitor cells through this alarming effect of endotoxin, but hardly anybody would understand it. I don't feel I can detach myself from the common points of reference. I don't like "scientific poems"; what I try to do is poetry with a hard-centered approach. I try to look for metaphors in every aspect of my personal and professional life, but I am continually made aware of the need for more or less general interest and comprehensibility. Again, because of conditions, I find myself always facing the reality that endotoxins have a much broader sense in sociology than in biology, or no sense at all.

7. *How did the poem start? How many revisions did it go through? In what order, over what period? If you have saved the worksheets, could I see a copy?*

The poem starts for me always as a coincidence of an idea, of the basic or general metaphor or leap in Bly's sense, with the feeling that it can be technically done and that it may work. I make a mind-picture of the whole structure days or weeks ahead. When I start writing—i.e., exposing the preconceived structure to the free oscillation of wording—I do it at once and almost never do revisions, knowing that they would not help when the first attempt failed.

In this concrete instance, "Collision" was started as one in a series of poems based on shocking events far back in my memory. I felt at that time that shocking situations and associations are communicative, unambiguous, objective and help to get safely through the thicket of words.

As in most cases, I had only one worksheet and threw it away immediately; this is another catharsis. I don't remember doing any revisions; I only checked in *The Scientific American* and *Discover* about the molecular clouds and magnetic monopoles and made some corrections in the respective stanzas. The whole thing may have been written within one or two hours one weekend afternoon.

8. In what ways has the poem been affected by translation into English?

As mentioned, immediately upon completion of the Czech original, I did a very rough English translation and in a couple of afternoons did a more polished English translation with one of my students, Beki Bloyd. To protect the translator from being pressed by the limits of a single English interpretation of single sentences, we used several possible wordings at many places and judged them from both the author's and the English reader's point of view. We had a hard time with the Danger/High Voltage line (in Czech it is a better metaphor, "Don't touch the words even fallen to earth" based on a sign on every electricity pole "Don't touch the wires even fallen to earth") and with the *lousy egghead*, which feels slightly different in the Czech context. The silent film from the magnetic monopoles to the leukemic girl went very smoothly compared to the street realities. This translation was then forwarded to David Young with a few comments, and he did his version which went exactly in the direction I wanted and could not find at some places myself. In my feeling, the final version is in every respect as close to the original as I can imagine.

9. What other questions would you have liked me to ask?

None. Have you ever seen a patient on the table handing scalpels to his surgeon? Anyway, I must admit it was a pleasant surgery and the patient has learned something. Thanks.

MIROSLAV HOLUB, born in 1923 in Plzeň, Czechoslovakia, earned his M.D. in 1953 from Charles University, Prague, and his Ph.D. in 1958 from the Czechoslovak Academy of Sciences. He has worked as a medical researcher in cellular immunology for the Czechoslovak Academy of Science, the Public Health Research Institute of New York City, and The Institute for Clinical and Experimental Medicine in Prague. He has written 110 scientific papers and two monographs. He has been publishing poetry since 1958, 12 volumes in Czech, and 11 volumes of translations—in English, German, Polish, Greek, Dutch, and Gujarati. He has also published 4 books of essays. In 1979 and 1982 he spent two semesters teaching creative writing at Oberlin College in Oberlin, Ohio.

TED HUGHES

*

Crow on the Beach

Hearing shingle explode, seeing it skip,
Crow sucked his tongue.
Seeing sea-grey mash a mountain of itself
Crow tightened his goose-pimples.
Feeling spray from the sea's root nothinged on his crest
Crow's toes gripped the wet pebbles.
When the smell of the whale's den, the gulfing of the crab's
                                            last prayer,

Gimletted in his nostril
He grasped he was on earth.

                                    He knew he grasped
Something fleeting
Of the sea's ogreish outcry and convulsion.
He knew he was the wrong listener unwanted
To understand or help—

His utmost gaping of brain in his tiny skull
Was just enough to wonder, about the sea,

What could be hurting so much?

I asked Ted Hughes chiefly about Crow's personality (Reynard the Fox? Bugs Bunny?), about his own attitude toward Crow (Sympathy? Admiration? Superiority?), and about Crow's voice (the Anglo-Saxon quality of his language, sounds, and rhythms). Mr. Hughes answered that he welcomed "the chance to put on record in the U.S. my own notion of Crow's cultural context, and of my own motivation in composing it."

Any reader who is unfamiliar with the Trickster Tales of early and primitive literatures, or who doesn't think those "folk" productions have any place in the canon of serious literary forms, will probably try to relate Crow to something more familiar within the Western modern tradition. What usually comes up is Black Comedy of the sort that became fashionable for a while in postwar western Europe. But to make this relationship can be misleading.

Black Comedy (as I understand it) and Trickster literature have superficial apparent resemblances, to be sure. But they are fundamentally so opposite that those seeming resemblances are in fact absolute opposites, as negative and positive are opposites.

Black Comedy is the end of a cultural process, Trickster literature is the beginning. Black Comedy draws its effects from the animal despair and suicidal nihilism that afflict a society or an individual when the supportive metaphysical beliefs disintegrate. Trickster literature draws its effects from the unkillable, biological optimism that supports a society or individual whose world is not yet fully created, and whose metaphysical beliefs are only just struggling out of the dream stage.

In Black Comedy the despair and nihilism are fundamental, and the attempts to live are provisional, clownish, meaningless, "absurd." In Trickster literature the optimism and creative joy are fundamental, and the attempts to live, and to enlarge and intensify life, however mismanaged, fill up at every point with self-sufficient meaning.

It is easy to confuse the two with each other, because historically they sometimes coexist, and psychologically they often do so—or at least they do so up to the point where the negative mood finally crushes out all possibility of hope, as often demonstrated in our own day, so that the biological processes of renewal and reproduction simply give up and cease. Black Comedy expresses the misery and disintegration of that, which is a reality, and so has its place in our attempts to diagnose what is happening to us. But Trickster literature expresses the vital factor compressed beneath the affliction at such times—the renewing, sacred spirit, searching its depths for new resources and directives, exploring towards new emergence and growth. And this is how the worst moment comes closest to the best opportunity. "When the load of bricks is doubled, Moses comes," etc. From the point of view of someone trying to cope with external circumstances just as they are, Black Comedy can seem too narrow and cynical, in its selection of evidence, almost like the statement of a paranoia, but Trickster literature can seem irresponsible, in its refusal to be daunted by the opposition.

That is only a proverb of course. If the load of bricks is quadrupled, Moses might be squashed flat. Trickster's appearances guarantee nothing. In fact, they might be ominous—coming disaster can be aphrodisiac.

Trickster and sexuality are connected by a hot line. In an individual's life, Black Comedy is like a metaphor of inescapable age and illness, as if it were founded on the chemical disillusionment and breakdown of the cells. But Trickster literature corresponds to the infantile, irresponsible naivety of sexual love, as if it were founded on the immortal enterprise of the sperm.

It needs a sharp eye to separate the two. In Black Comedy, the lost, hopeful world of Trickster is mirrored coldly, with a negative accent. In Trickster literature, the doomed world of Black Comedy is mirrored hotly, with a positive accent. It is like the difference between two laughters: one bitter and destructive, the other defiant and creative, attending what seems to be the same calamity.

Maybe at bottom that is what Trickster is: the optimism of the sperm still battling zestfully along after 150 million years.

Cultures blossom round his head and fall to bits under his feet. Indifferent to the discouragements of time, learning a little, but not much, from every rebuff, in the evolutionary way, turning everything to his advantage, or trying to, he is nothing really but an all-out commitment to salvaging life against the odds. All the other qualities spin round that nucleus, on long ellipses, but his confidence and trajectory are constant. The sperm is looking for the egg—to combine with every human thing that is not itself, and to create a new self, with multiplied genetic potential, in a renewed world.

In the literature, the playful-savage burlesque of Trickster's inadequacies and setbacks, which is a distinguishing feature of the mode, is an integral part of the intrinsic humane realism. And it is this folk-note of playfulness, really of affection and fellow-feeling, which does not date, no matter how peculiar and extravagant the adventures.

The recurrent quest of Trickster, as the spirit of the sperm, is like a master plan, a deep biological imprint, and one of our most useful pieces of kit. We use it all the time, spontaneously, like a tool, at every stage of psychological recovery or growth. It supplies a path to the God-seeker, whose spiritual ecstasy, or the ecstasy he works for, hasn't altogether lost the sexual *samadhi* of the sperm. A little lower, like the hand of his Fate, it guides the Hero through his Hero-Tale, embroils him, since he's mortal, in tragedy, but sustains him with tragic joy. Beneath the Hero-Tale, like the satyr behind the Tragedy, is the Trickster Saga, a series of Tragicomedies. It is a series, and never properly tragic, because Trickster, demon of phallic energy, bearing the spirit of the sperm, is repetitive and indestructible. No matter what fatal mistakes he makes, and what tragic flaws he indulges, he refuses to let sufferings or death detain him, but always circumvents them, and never despairs. Too full of opportunistic ideas for sexual *samadhi*, too unevolved for spiritual ecstasy, too deathless for tragic joy, he rattles along on biological glee.

Each of these figures casts the shadows of the others. The Trickster, the Hero, and the Saint on the Path meet in the Holy Fool. None of them operates within a closed society, but on the epic stage, in the drafty arena of "everything possible". And each of them, true to that little sperm, serpent at the center of the whole Russian Doll complex, works to redeem us, to heal us, and even, in a sense, to resurrect us, in our bad times.

This particular view of the Trickster Saga was my guiding metaphor when I set out to make what I could of Crow.

In "Crow on the Beach" Crow confronts what he thinks is the sea. Yes, it is the sea. Simultaneously, at this moment, his eye is overshadowed by a sub-conscious vision of the womb. The womb that he has forgotten, the one that bore him, and the womb of his Beloved—which he will find when he overcomes his own perversity, and learns what he is looking for (and what is looking for him).

The hopeful sign is that he recognizes pain—or rather "travail." He does not recognize it, so much as become conscious of it by projecting it, because he too is in pain, though he doesn't know it. Everything in himself that he refuses to acknowledge is in pain. And pain calls to pain. Mystified, he detects this. He experiences the whole exchange, yet observes it as a non-participant. In other words, he is still infantile—he evades the reality in himself. Or, for some reason or other, cannot yet recognize it, so does not take responsibility for it, and so remains infantile.

The language of this piece—as of most of the CROW pieces—is really determined by the fact that it is a song-legend. It is not an argument, or a natural description, or a realistic narrative, or a discursive meditation. As a legend the archaic perspective requires simplicity of a particular kind. The whole problem of composing a song-legend, in the thick of contemporary literatures, is the business of reaching the right kind of simplicity—and then hanging on to it. So it seems to me. And one has to have a taste for simplicity.

Complexity, as a fact of our consciousness, is highly attractive, and tends to commandeer all the available blood, in any constructive mental effort. There is a simplicity on the near side of it, which is a matter of selecting and generalizing the teeming external effects. There is another simplicity on the far side of it, which is a matter of handling the nuclei. As styles of language, they provide opportunities for different kinds of penetration, but successful legend employs the latter.

Considering "Crow On the Beach" as a song among songs, the dominance of melody (the kind of melody that will carry a legend), in the voice of it, tends again to select for itself an elemental vocabulary—one that has, like music itself, kinaesthetic or at least physical roots. That seems to have happened, sure enough, but I only offer it as an observation. I suppose a close analysis of the vocabulary might come up with some account of the melody as a variant of a certain species, pinpoint its psychosomatic characteristics, etc. Whatever that may be, the melody controlled the selection of words—as a physical act summons just the right hormones. The special function of the melody is the only law to the language of Crow.

Perhaps it should be said that *Crow* grew out of an invitation by Leonard Baskin to make a book with him simply about crows. He wanted an occasion to add more crows to all the crows that flock through his sculptures, drawings, and engravings in their various transformations. As the protagonist of a book, a crow would become symbolic in any author's hands. And a symbolic crow lives a legendary life. That is how *Crow* took off.

TED HUGHES was born in 1930 in Yorkshire, England; was graduated B.A. and M.A. from Cambridge University; and is a full-time writer. In addition to children's books, plays, and anthologies, he has published over twenty volumes of poetry. *The Collected Poems* appeared in 1981. Well known on both sides of the Atlantic, he has been awarded, among others, the Queen's Medal for Poetry, the City of Florence International Poetry Prize, a Guggenheim Fellowship, and the Order of the British Empire.

LAURA JENSEN

*

The Candles Draw Well After All

The candles draw well after all.
By night they might have been
flickering.
Tallow; wax and tallow;
the story is a circle and a band.
The unseen circles of air
make a silent story. So tells
the ring and the rowboat round the isle,
the zero and the handles of scissors.
So tells the circle swinging from the cord,
the noose of the windowshade.

The sun is passing
from the Atlantic to your day.
The sun has passed the eddies of rain
and is coming fast as a runner.
It is coming from a bath of rain
to its absence.

Sister braid, the skull
is not along today. Elemental word!
She is never ready for morning.
Reel up the little masquerade.
The summer will not be dreadful.

*I did not ask Laura Jensen specific questions about "The Candles Draw Well After All."
Instead of aiming answers, she has drifted back through the experience of making the
poem—its light, weather, place—its relation to her other poems—the ways that structure
and sound became incantation. In this memory she has presented both intuitively and
analytically the poetic process by which she harvests her "underwater mysteries."*

The days have lengthened and the first week of hot weather is here. Memorable things have begun to happen . . . not in the news, although that is memorable enough—the first woman is scheduled to take a space flight—but memorable things in daily life. The real memorable events are in the gardens. One particular rhododendron hangs like blooms of moist pink tissue, these flowers everywhere are at their best, along with azaleas and other flowers blooming in abundant gardens—lilac, hawthorn, lavender, forget-me-not, indian paintbrush. The air is scented with mown grass.

But a fear everyone felt or sensed during the winter remains. There is a recollection of cold or hunger, of endless gray sky and no snow (see C. S. Lewis), dripping gutters and short dull days.

An originality of scope should allow an artist to project a spring coming. But she is filled with location and the location works on her senses in such a way that she must interpret through her story, her poem, her drawing, not her sense of future. Suppose we did "all live in a yellow submarine," as the Beatles sang, (and we do in springtime). That puts us under the influence of imaginary and real terrors and delights. These mysteries in this sense would be underwater and enter sensually at all times. But there is an intellect within us that necessarily scopes up into the air, intellectually, and interprets and scopes ahead and around. In the case of the artist, the scope is not used for self-protection but for the creation of her work.

When you walk or ride, a person at times forgets where she is and continues on automatic pilot. An artist continues in the person of automatic artist, and should view or work or interpret until there is not other. Surely this is like rising from the position of four-points-to-the-ground and finding oneself able to walk on two feet. How does the artist scope in this way for individual survival when she is accustomed to interpretation of what she sees, standing or walking, into a poem, a story, a picture?

How do you scope for viewing of a future? Seven years ago this month, in May 1976, according to a workbook I was using at that time, I was writing poems that would be included in the last part of *Bad Boats*. "The Candles Draw Well After All" was not a part of that book, but in composition it follows "Amigo Acres" and precedes "Faces Passing Your Garden." In the same workbook I was also planning stories and noting down letters answered or received. I had recently received a copy of Tom Lux's *The Glassblower's Breath*. I remember my delight over that book. My feelings at that time over my own life seem much the same to me now as they are written in these poems—they are poems about a half-imagined neighbor boy, a poem (this poem) about day coming, a poem about viewing other people's gardens.

Isolating "The Candles Draw Well After All" separates the night from the daytime and limits the poet to her own rooms. So I will isolate the poem now and mention nothing further here about the neighborhood in which I live, and concentrate on "The Candles. . . ."

I see that I have used internal rhyme and consonance and kept this within each line, although similar sounds are repeated in recurring lines. The first

three lines follow from a's and l's to i's to a third line of a single word—
"flickering." The single word stresses the opportunity to concentrate on the
sound and appearance of the candle. In the fourth line is a return to the a and l:
"Tallow, wax and tallow"; then there are the three terms *story, circle, band.*

It is necessary to use the magic three to state that day is coming, because
this is an incantatory poem. First day "Is passing" then it "has passed" then it
"is coming."

And the third stanza is the lighter, more cheerful arrival. The hair is the
sister of the skull, which should refer to the mind or the psyche affectionately or
offhandedly, "skull" or a bone, because she cannot gain hold of the day quickly.
We return to the windowshade from the last line of the first stanza—"Reel up
the little masquerade"—the day, the shade presenting the day, the people who
go about their work, and the last line is a charm.

Seven years before last May, in 1969, I was a student at the University of
Washington in Seattle, which is about forty miles north of Tacoma by freeway. I
was drawing at all times then. A drawing I did then, or later in the spring or
summer, decorates the facing page of *Tapwater,* the chapbook "The Candles
. . ." did appear in. The drawing faces "The Candles . . ." and pictures a dresser
with square top drawers, a glass jar of ten tulips, a water glass half-full, a thick
candle on an elaborate candle-stand, some cigarettes, a hairbrush, a bottle of
some cosmetic, a box of tissues, and behind it, a square paper taped to the wall.

The same household items occupy my mind and life now, and they still find
their way into poems. But other matters occupy my thoughts as well. How to
deal with my economic level, how the food bank in town is doing, the state of
being of good friends. . . .

LAURA JENSEN was born in 1948 in Tacoma, Washington, and attended the
University of Washington and the University of Iowa. She has lived and written
in Tacoma since 1974 and has taught a poetry workshop at a community college
there. She has published in many magazines and a half-dozen anthologies, and
traveled in the United States to work and to read. Her book and chapbooks
include: *After I Have Voted* (Gemini Press, 1972), *Anxiety and Ashes* (Penumbra
Press, 1976), *Bad Boats* (Ecco Press, 1977), *Tapwater* (Graywolf Press, 1978),
The Story Makes Them Whole (Porch Publications, 1979), and *Memory* (Dragon
Gate, 1982). She has received awards and grants from the Washington State
Arts Commission, the National Endowment for the Arts, and the Ingram-
Merrill Foundation.

DONALD JUSTICE

*

Bus Stop

Lights are burning
In quiet rooms
Where lives go on
Resembling ours.

The quiet lives
That follow us—
These lives we lead
But do not own—

Stand in the rain
So quietly
When we are gone,
So quietly . . .

And the last bus
Comes letting dark
Umbrellas out—
Black flowers, black flowers.

And lives go on.
And lives go on
Like sudden lights
At street corners

Or like the lights
In quiet rooms
Left on for hours,
Burning, burning.

1. "Bus Stop" seems to be a poem spoken in a very soft voice between clenched teeth.
The "quiet lives" lived in "quiet rooms," standing "so quietly" in the rain, the lives that
are led and "follow us," can either flash on "Like sudden lights/At street corners" or be
"Left on for hours,/ burning, burning." Do you hear the last line as a praise of incandes-
cence? A threat of conflagration?

2. Do the line "When we are gone," the umbrellas as dark flowers, and the reference to the
last bus imply that the leader of the quiet life dies (goes) before he dies, that perhaps the life
each of us leads is his own incineration?

3. The poem's structure seems both circular and horizontal, like the face and pendulum of
a large clock. Burning in both the first and last lines, the same rhyme or slant-rhyme
sounds recurring from beginning to end of the poem (ours, flowers, hours; lives, quietly,
lights; rooms, own, rain, on) create a circular effect. The duple meter and the doublings
of so quietly, and lives go on, and in quiet rooms suggest a pendulum's swing. Did you
choose this structure and rhythm to create a sense of pressure on the quiet lives?

4. In other words, how did the poem start? By what strategies and accidents did it grow?

That fall and winter we were living in a rented house on Potrero Hill. From
the back porch on the second story, where the living quarters were, you could
look down into the neglected garden below or off across hills to the bay and the
lights of Oakland. It was an exemplary view, but in a dark mood it could leave
you feeling remote and isolated. We seemed to be perched insecurely on the top
of an unfamiliar new world, teetering on the continent's very edge. Every evening I would walk our dog, Hugo, up and down the steep sidewalks, past the
rows of narrow two-storied San Francisco houses, as the sun faded across their
pale pastel fronts. High wooden fences surrounded some of them, and through
the palings you could see strange plants in tubs and the deep-hued blooms of
exotic flowers.

Our nearest corner, the intersection of Kansas and 20th Streets, was a
municipal bus stop. It seemed that often, just as we were setting out on our
walk, a bus would be stopped there, discharging passengers. At that hour they
would be city workers coming home from their day in shop or office. There
must have been an unusually long period of rain that year, two or three weeks of
it, and I remember the passengers one after the other opening their great black
umbrellas as they stepped down from the bus, which waited purring and
quivering in the mist and drizzle of early evening. I sensed something symbolic
in this, as if centuries hence it might be recalled as part of an ancient urban
ritual whose meaning had been forgotten. And vividly there rose up before me a
picture of the raised umbrellas which had represented the dead in the last scene
of Our Town, called back now from the pages, years before, of Life magazine.

Sometimes, as we walked, the streetlights would wink on all at once, perfectly timed. Gradually more and more lights would be visible in the upper
windows of the houses. From the playground you could see headlights moving

along the Bayshore Highway just at the foot of the hill; or, from another bluff, the distant shunting in the Southern Pacific yards; all around, masked at times by fog, hung the various glows of the fanned-out districts of the city. It was beautiful. But the Potrero Hill of those days was like a lost village high in the Caucasus, with old Russian women peering doubtfully out from windows and doorways at passing strangers. All that fall and winter I felt like an exile, no part of the life around me. I knew none of the bus passengers alighting, no one in the lighted rooms above, certainly none of the wrinkled old women in their babushkas, who would yell and gesticulate sometimes at the quiet and well-mannered Hugo.

Such was the background from which "Bus Stop" gradually emerged. Other poems from that time share the same moods: "Poem To Be Read at 3 A.M." (with its own image of a burning light), "Memory of a Porch," "In the Green-room," and "At a Rehearsal of *Uncle Vanya*." (I was with a theater company that year, The Actor's Workshop.) The somewhat visionary "To the Hawks" came just after.

Connections between the life a writer lives and the work that comes out of that life seem much more important now than I once thought them, and in fact I would insist on their importance. Even so, in my work I have preferred to deal with connections of this kind indirectly, which is, as I believe, the way of art. Thus it is not the mere undergoing of a terrible or a beautiful experience, neither suffering nor exaltation, which leads to poetry, at least not for me. Only when the experience itself, or more likely no more than some singular aspect or broken small tangent of it, comes somehow to be deflected or translated into something else, into some mysteriously larger other thing—which in another day might have been called the universal or archetypal—does any poem of mine begin to come into focus. I think of it as a merging of the personal with the impersonal; the singular commences to disappear into the plural.

But the exact relations between art and life are not legislated. We know that Dorothy had seen the ten thousand daffodils, too, but in the poem only William is left wandering "lonely as a cloud." So also did poor Hugo vanish from the Potrero Hill evenings of "Bus Stop," though he had been my faithful companion through many glooms. If he does survive now, it is only as a generalized ghost, one of

> The quiet lives
> That follow us—
> These lives we lead
> But do not own.

I did sometimes picture him, as the poem goes on to suggest, standing there, if I should die, puzzled but infinitely patient. That whole time in San Francisco, as a matter of fact, I went about, for reasons that scarcely enter the poem, in the grip of a fear of death. No doubt I did "own" Hugo, if it came to that, but I did

not feel at all in possession of my own life. There were times when my life felt
ghostly to me, and, as in some special effect contrived for film, I could picture
the husk of my body left behind on a street corner waiting faithfully for the real
self to return. But in writing the poem I was not tempted to spell out or to make
very much out of so slight and evanescent a feeling, scarcely strong enough to
register on the most sensitive emotional scale. As I concentrate now in an effort
to bring back the time and the place, I see all at once and for the first time that
the buses stopped at the corner were like a modern equivalent of Charon's ferry,
and rain-wet 20th Street a paved-over Styx. The gathering gloom—mist, drizzle, twilight, fog—would have filled out the infernal impression. It seems obvious, now that I think of it, but even if so literal a transcription of what the
scene suggested had then occurred to me—and it did not, not consciously—I
would have kept it out of the poem. It would have been false, too explicit, too
histrionic.

The first actual lines—I am sure of it, though I have lost or mislaid the
worksheets—began with mention of the lights burning upstairs in unknown
rooms. An image with overtones of Weldon Kees, no doubt, and of the very city
from which, not quite a decade before, he had disappeared; only a block or two
along Kansas Street his best friend still lived. I worked at lines meant to evoke
the lives of the strangers in those rooms, a motif perhaps retrieved from "Anthony St. Blues," a much earlier poem of mine:

> Withindoors many now enact,
> Behind drawn shades, their shadow lives.

But I was too much absorbed in my own broodings to want to brood long in
others; besides, they were very much like us, surely, which was a good part of
the poignancy. I had my sense of exile and loneliness, my neurotic fear, my
divided self all to find words and figures for, and there, in the very circumstances of daily life, in that extraordinary neighborhood, were facts and details
vivid with symbolic presence, only waiting to be mentioned in right relation
with one another in order to glow with meaning.

Finding the structure was no problem, as I recall. I had been trying to teach
myself to write short free-verse lines; also short syllabics lines. I theorized that
there was more control in the short line. A curious problem in syllabics had
always interested me and nobody else, apparently, among all the poets—many
more then—attracted to that metric. It was the possibility of keeping the
number of accents and the number of syllables the same from line to line, but
without letting them fall together into the regular foot-patterns, iambs and the
like, too often and too familiarly. It's a very technical matter, not awfully
important, but it did interest me. Lines in syllabics had usually seemed to go
better in odd numbers—sevens, nines, elevens—since the odd number was a
help in avoiding iambics. But now I wanted to try *evens* and, to make it harder
on myself, shorter lines than I had attempted or will probably attempt again in
syllabics. My sense of syllabics is that as the count gets shorter the line gets

harder to compose, but, as though in compensation, more "musical," as people like to put it. In "Bus Stop" each line, it will be noticed, has only four syllables. (*Flowers* traditionally may be counted as either one or two syllables; in the line, "Black flowers, black flowers," it counts as one.) Some lines gave me trouble, however easy they may now look, but on the whole they did turn out to be more "musical" than average. The majority are autonomous, more or less end-stopped; they can be heard as lines, which is rare in syllabics. Readers who hear them as accentuals are not wrong to do so, for each line does have two accents. But if these were pure accentual lines no one could expect 24 lines in a row to fall by chance into the same syllable count. Because I was keeping this double count, the lines come very close, after all, to being iambic dimeter; yet to those who understand such intricacies, it must be clear that a few lines refuse to submit to the usual iambic conditions (lines 1, 20, and 24).

As for other sound-effects, mostly rhyme or something like it, the thought of calling the poem a song did enter my head, or even of subtitling it "An Urban Song," but a subtitle seemed pretentious. Even so, this was unmistakably a lyric poem, which by its nature could stand quite a lot of *sound*, and I was willing to seek out a fair amount of it, though not very vigorously. I wanted anything which had to do with the sound or "music" to come in very simply and in a completely natural way, almost as though by chance, and chance did, as always in such matters, throw up some coincidences of sound. My intentions in this, being largely impulse and instinct, I was able to carry out more successfully than with the meters. If rhymes showed up—and they did—they were to remain casual, not part of a deliberate scheme, not predictable. Repetition—a type of rhyme itself—turned out to play a larger role in the sound of the poem than the usual rhyming. The rule I set for myself in this was simple and indulgent. I would repeat whatever I wanted to, anything from a single word to a whole line, and at any time. The effect came to resemble what you get in a poem with multiple refrains, or, more fancifully, when several bells are set swinging at different timings. In the old ballads or in comic songs, not to mention in the master Yeats himself, the meaning of a refrain will seem to shift sometimes with its new context, and I made an effort to imitate that effect. The most obvious case involves repeating "And lives go on." First it is a complete sentence, signifying only that lives continue, persist, endure. But, chiming back in at once, it starts now a longer sentence which before it is done will turn the original meaning into something very different. The lives no longer plod along but are suddenly bright and giving light—beacons. A hopeful note, it seems now, looking back. Yet I was prouder of the more hidden repetition, for those who would notice it, between lines 4 and 23, *hours* echoing *ours*. One of the buried motifs of the poem—that of the displaced self—is here suggested, I would like to think, in the pun on *hours*, but quietly, secretly, perhaps escaping all notice. Read the lines again and see if it is there at all. Perhaps I have imagined it; or has everyone always seen it at once? It only remains to say that whatever the reader is willing to find in *burning* was probably intended, from the simplest turning on of lights to the ardent yearning of the self baffled in loneliness. But perhaps not. Only this instant has it occurred to me that at the end St. Augustine may have blundered into yet another Carthage, *burning, burning.*

Certainly the world seemed that year on the point of conflagration. Goldwater bullies had roamed Nob Hill, our navy was attacked by phantoms in the Tonkin gulf, Kruschev fell, China exploded a nuclear device, the first defiant Berkeley students were dragged roughly down marble staircases, and at Thanksgiving General Taylor took off on his futile fact-finding mission to Vietnam. By late February the official bombing of North Vietnam had begun. The theater company was breaking up, and I fled the city. It sounds dramatic now, but it did feel that way at the time. Not long afterwards, across the continent in Miami, I came upon most of the lines of "Bus Stop" jumbled together on a few pages of the old chemistry notebook I'd found in the Potrero Hill house and, unscrambling them now with ease, finished the poem in an hour or two.

DONALD JUSTICE was born in Miami, Florida, in 1925 and graduated from the University of Miami. He teaches now at the University of Florida. He has edited the poems of Weldon Kees and coedited an anthology of contemporary French poetry. His first book of poems was *The Summer Anniversaries* (Wesleyan, 1960) and his most recent, *Selected Poems* (Atheneum, 1979), for which he received the Pulitzer Prize.

SHIRLEY KAUFMAN

*

The Mountain

1

In the morning I am alone in the icy room
everyone has gone to climb the mountain
the only sound is the noise in my head
machine of my anger or my fear
that won't shut off
the wind keeps cranking it.

My daughter has fled to the mountain
a piece of her dress in my hand
it is green
and I hold it next to my ear
to stop the wind.

What she took out of me
was not what I meant to give.
She hears strange voices.
I dream she's the child I grew up with
kneeling beside her hamsters
soft things she cared for
cradling them in her hands.

I want to make my words into a hamster
and nest them in her palms
to be sorry again
when she falls out of the tree
and breaks her arm.

She runs to an empty house
with her own prophets
they sit shoulder to shoulder
waiting for the sky to open
they can already see through a tiny crack
where the path begins.

2

Yesterday we saw how roots of mangroves
suck the warm sea at the desert's edge
and keep the salt
the leaves are white
and flaky as dead skin.
My ankles swell.
I must be drowning in my own brine.

A Bedouin woman stands veiled
in the ruined courtyard
there's a well
a hole in the ground
where she leads the camel by a rope
I watch her fill the bucket
and the camel drinks
lifting its small shrewd head
rinsing its teeth with a swollen tongue.

The woman is covered in black
her body her head her whole face black
except for the skin around her eyes.

My daughter watches me watch her
with the same eyes.

She picks up a handful of rocks
and hits the camel
shrieking she strikes it
over and over to make it move.

I am alone in the icy room
everyone has gone to climb the mountain
the only sound is the woman
chasing the camel with the rocks.

I look out at the dry river bed.
I let her go.

Unlike many personal poems this one is complex and ambivalent without being obscure,
intense without being hysterical. The subject is the mother-daughter relationship. In Part 1
the mother is angry and/or afraid. The daughter has "fled to the mountain," rejecting the

mother's gift of nurture. The daughter has heard "strange voices," sits "shoulder to shoulder" with "her own prophets," sees a crack in the sky where "the path begins." We know without being told that the path leads only outward. In Part 2 the scene becomes middle-eastern, biblical. The mother watches a Bedouin woman, swathed in black except her eyes, water a camel, then pelt it with stones to drive it away, while the daughter watches the mother watch. Here the pronouns point in different directions: Who is watching whom with the Bedouin's eyes? Who is casting the stones? Then we realize that the mother has seen herself as the woman stoning the camel, and the daughter has probably seen it too, and/or she may have seen herself as the woman stoning the camel too. In anger, fear, tenderness, regret, and inevitably some guilt, the mother has driven the young from the nest, and the daughter has wrenched herself away, both of them because they had to. Though told from the mother's point of view, there is no reproach in the tone of this poem, just a grave acceptance.

1. Was the poem written after you had resolved the theme in your mind, or did the different scenes come together in a more accidental way?

2. Is the trip to the mountain an actual trip to an actual mountain, or was the mountain always a metaphor, a reference to Pisgah or Nebo as a place from which to view the Promised Land?

3. Was the incident of the woman stoning the camel autobiographical? Am I overreading to infer that the mother and the daughter both see themselves in the Bedouin woman?

4. Is the reference to the daughter's sitting shoulder to shoulder with her own prophets autobiographical or metaphorical?

5. Is the reference in Part I to the child you played with a reference to your daughter as a child or to a childhood friend of your own? If the former, do you consider the relationship of mother and child equivalent in some ways to two children growing up together?

6. You have written other poems which deal with the mother-daughter relationship. Are these a sequence that should be read together, in a certain order? Are there more of them to be written?

7. Why is the poem written in two parts? What determined your stanza breaks and line breaks? Your rhythms and sound repetitions?

8. What triggered the poem? What form did it first take? How many revisions did it undergo, what kinds, in what order, over what period? If you have saved the work-sheets, may I see a copy?

9. What other questions would you have liked me to ask?

1 and 2. As an answer to what triggered the poem, let me begin with a journal entry:

January 4, 1976

Bedouin woman—veiled—her black dress covering her skin—the veil around her head, her face covered—only the eyes in one bare strip of skin exposed—black and brilliant—fire—then she bends down, picks up a rock on the dusty ground to throw at the camel

In the ruined courtyard—a well—she lowers her bucket—draws the water out to feed the camel—the camel drinks, raises his head and rolls the water around in his mouth—he runs his tongue over his great stained teeth to rinse them

a new Dodge pick-up truck by every shack—the children dressed in rags—their teeth are brown, pitted with decay—they smile and smile, hands out for anything

the great wadis strewn with rocks—sense of violence—all the stones tumbling off the mountains—swept by torrents of water through the whole river bed to bleach in the sun—granite

mangroves growing at the water's edge on the Red Sea (on the way to Sharm el Sheik) they drink the salt and it evaporates through the leaves—the smooth, shining, pointed leaves covered with salt

> smooth leaves of mangroves crusted with white
> they drink the water at the desert's edge
> and the salt stays on their leaves

The poem was written several weeks after a trip to the Sinai peninsula from Jerusalem, where I live. The Sinai desert is well known for its recent battles, but most famous as the scene of the wanderings of the tribes of Israel after their escape from slavery in Egypt on the way to the Promised Land. In the Bible it is written that here, before the Exodus, God spoke to Moses for the first time out of the Burning Bush. And here, at the top of Mt. Sinai, Moses received the tablets of the Ten Commandments which became the foundation of the Jewish religion.

On our two-day trip, the highlight was a visit to St. Catherine's Monastery, built by the Byzantine Emperor Justinian in the sixth century. According to Greek Orthodox tradition, the church of the monastery is located on the site of the Burning Bush at the foot of the actual Mt. Sinai. Historians, geographers, and archaeologists have determined that this could not have been the "holy" mountain, but belief in myth is stronger than belief in facts. People come daily (crossing the Egyptian border now), tourists from all over the world and those who live in the area, to visit the monastery and to climb the mountain at dawn.

When the surrounding peaks are lit by the rising sun, the effect is overwhelming. Locally the mountain is known as Jebal Mussa, the Arab name for it, meaning Mount of Moses.

The line between fact and metaphor disappears in this part of the world where most places mentioned in the Bible and in our literary tradition have actually been located by modern archaeology, and where impossible events assume mysterious credibility. One can indeed see the wilderness bordering the Promised Land from the top of a mountain in Sinai, a great and awesome emptiness. Response to that could be another poem. But the nature of the wilderness, the dry river beds (raging with water after a rare rainfall), the enormous limestone and granite rocks, narrow canyons, and steep mountain where the Law might have been received—became for me the emotional landscape of a mother's ongoing struggle to accept and release her daughter, another exodus, another uncharted trek. And since the emotional landscape was what finally generated the poem, I did not name the mountain.

As I reread my journal notes some time later in the quiet of the small room where I write, and recalled each visual detail of Sinai together with its history, the memories became so huge and unmanageable that I thought of the first lines of the *Duino Elegies*— . . . *for beauty is nothing but the beginning of terror.* And if Sinai dramatizes one's loneliness and failure in a universe too vast and magnificent to offer any comfort (*who, if I cried out, would hear me . . . ?*), on a much smaller scale, some human encounters enforce a similar loneliness and sense of failure.

The image of the children in the journal entry, their smiles, "hands out for anything," did not get into the poem. But they seem to have opened a conduit in my mind to some aspect of my own daughter. And there is more about Sinai which may have led me to the resolution of the poem. If one stays long enough, confronting the silence and depth of the sky at night, the unrelieved splendor, the towering cliffs and ravines with their ever-changing colors, it becomes so impersonal, nonjudgmental, and persistent, that one gives in to it. Reliving the ancient Exodus in fantasy, but in the very place, one finally can do nothing but let go ("let her go"). This is the point where *making the poem* took over. My daughter had not been with us on that trip to the mountain. But I had to put her there. My total experience of Sinai became the metaphor for our relationship. The mountain, the icy room, the mangroves, the Bedouin woman, and the camel are all part of the actual journey. And I recalled the actual hamsters and broken arm of my daughter. The rest was invented.

3. As you can note from the journal entry, I saw the woman stoning the camel. When the poem turned out to be about my relationship with my daughter rather than about my encounter with Sinai, the single figure in black, feminine and intense, seemed to mirror mother and daughter at the same time, until they reflected each other.

4. The empty house with the prophets is metaphorical. It was a way of projecting our alienation and suggesting how the daughter's first assertion of

independence, her new relationships, her own way of seeing the world, were leading her away from the mother.

5. Jung wrote, "Every mother contains her daughter in herself and every daughter her mother. Every woman extends backwards into her mother and forward into her daughter."

Jung was speaking of feminine immortality. I was breaking the linear concept of time, wanting to say something about growth as a repetitive process, not simply moving from one stage to another. At any given moment, we not only live in the present. We may be acting out some past experience (our own and even the history of the race), and even anticipating events that have not yet happened. So it's not that mother and child are like two children growing up together. Rather, that an adult mother can repeat the growth process sometimes with her own children.

That's a lot of meaning to compress into "I dream she's the child I grew up with." But I'd like to think some of this gets through!

6. I have been writing mother-daughter poems for more than fifteen years now, and I suppose there are more to be written. I believe the subject is very central to my work, defining myself as a woman in relation to my own mother and my daughters, in order to arrive at some understanding of my relationship to others and to events, to the time and the place in which I live.

Often, at poetry readings, I group some of these poems together, and then I am always struck by the endings—some of them quite final (as in "The Mountain"), as if the struggle were successfully concluded. But there's always a new poem on the same subject, so, of course, there is no conclusion. A more recent mother-daughter poem, "Perfection," is less certain, and ends "There is a smell of goat cheese/ ripening." Well, *ripeness is all!*

7 and 8. The separation into two parts is something I can't explain too well. I think there was a shift in perspective with the introduction of the Bedouin woman, and I needed to pause. In the first section, the movement is inward in space and backward in time. The second section marks a movement outward in space and forward in time. I remain in the icy room, but the vision of the mangroves and the Bedouin woman moves the poem out of the room into the courtyard and forward to its final resolution.

I remember first writing the poem in two parts to correspond with the two days of our trip. And I began it as a narrative, though the daughter was there from the start. Later, the sequence of events was not important. (I actually saw the Bedouin woman and the mangroves on the first day.) And I knew I wanted to end with the same image of being alone, but also with the resolution I felt at the time.

I have not saved my worksheets, but it might be interesting to compare the three lines of poetry about the mangroves at the end of the journal entry with the description in the first stanza of section 2 of the finished poem. There's something to be said for revision.

Stanza breaks often work like paragraphs for me. In this poem, I dropped all commas, trying for greater urgency, breathlessness—wanting to be in touch with something more primitive, before punctuation and syntax. Except for periods, mostly at the end of stanzas, the line breaks became the only stops, frequently serving as punctuation.

Sound repetition: I use sounds sometimes not even consciously, for musical effect or to enhance a mood. In the first stanza, there are many combinations of *o* with *n*, which draw out the sound, and slow the words down: al*one*, every*one*, g*one*, m*oun*tain, *only*, s*ound*, w*on*'t. "Anger" was meant to work with "cranking." And in the beginning of the second section, "swell" was deliberately rhymed with "well," "fill," and "smell," leading to "swollen." (Identification with the camel as well as the woman.)

The rhythm in this poem is very uneven: flat statements, some almost lyrical passages as in the second and third stanzas, and very staccato lines. I may have intended the lack of unity to increase the tension and anxiety. Or the tension and anxiety, that took over as I was writing the poem, produced the lack of a unified rhythm. That's probably a more accurate way of putting it.

9. I think you have asked as much as I can answer! You must be aware that while we can write all this after the fact, poems develop usually in a purely intuitive way. If I had worked on this analysis before, I don't believe I could have written the poem. Now I'd like to return to Sinai and rewrite the poem!

SHIRLEY KAUFMAN, born in Seattle, Washington, in 1923, graduated from UCLA and received her M.A. from San Francisco State University. She won the 1969 United States Award of the International Poetry Forum for her first book, *The Floor Keeps Turning,* and an N.E.A. fellowship in 1979. Other books are *Gold Country* (1973); *From One Life to Another* (1979); *Claims* (1984); and two volumes of translations from Hebrew: *A Canopy in the Desert,* Selected poems of Abba Kovner (1973) and *The Light of Lost Suns,* Selected poems of Amir Gilboa (1979). Since 1973 she has lived in Jerusalem, where she has taught at the Hebrew University.

ABBA KOVNER

*

Potato Pie

1
The father wore an overcoat with a narrow velvet collar.

2
Once in a while there was a striped suit underneath and a shirt
always neatly pressed.

3
Sorrow already lay on his clothes
like an eternal crease.

4
There was no radio at home. And there was no end to his curiosity,
his thoughts awake at night walking
everywhere.

5
In his time he figured correctly
the results of the Russo-Japanese War, a bit late.

6
He liked potato pie with salt herring.

7
When he couldn't have herring he made do
with the brine.

8
Suddenly the first World War
was over. A year later
Poland's liberation began. In 1919
he inherited a stone building

9
in the capital. On the bank of the river, with
condemned apartments. When he was already
a landlord, with tenants

10
and creditors

11
he still loved potato pie his wife
made in all seasons.

12
They loved the sea
because another country came close
reflected in its waters.

13
He dreamed he'd go back

14
. . . .

15
So he went back. On the day he imagined
his father returned
he lost his voice. And more.

16
He stood on the threshold.

17
There was no witness to see
the father
still standing on the threshold

18
and not remembering the time. How long
his mouth was wide open

19
                  and silent.
Until he moved his lips. Until his tongue
began to work, until his voice was back
and the echo
            the father

20
behind the muslin curtain and the boy,
a buzzing in his head.

21
From that time on he feels a buzzing
in his head. Like pieces of a heart scraping his temples
and not only when

22
                    there's an uninvited guest,
present without coming. Or
when he plays with his grandson: all the colors of the rainbow
in a soap bubble ready to burst
on the window screen.
                    Then
it's there—this buzzing in his head!

23
The pain passes as it comes.
Often
there's nothing in its place.

Translated by Shirley Kaufman

Although the New Criticism, which formed the reading habits of most Americans between the world wars, insists that any poem can be apprehended fully by a close reading of its unaided text, I suspect that this principle applies only to poems written by members of the same culture who have had the same linguistic and historical experiences. The Odyssey read by Pope is not the same poem as that heard by Heroic Age listeners; Paradise Lost read in an American university classroom is not the same experience it was to Milton's "fit audience though few"; and "Potato Pie," unaided, is likely to be read by Americans, who have no firsthand experience of military occupation or starvation or genocide, as a poem which begins as affectionate nostalgia but turns unaccountably terrifying. To them the loss of home usually means that when one drives back through the town where one grew up, one is saddened by the fact that the elm tree in front of the house has died or the empty field next door is now a parking lot. Their reaction is a sweetish or at most a bittersweet nostalgia. They cannot quite conceive a memory so terrible that the mind blanks it out or translates it to physical pain. Therefore, as one such reader, I can ask only questions that reveal my lack of full awareness and my need for all the help you can give me with the poem's context.

1. *What specific occasion prompted you to write the poem? When?*

2. *The father in the poem appears to be poor (he has no radio, sometimes he couldn't have herring with his potato pie, he inherits condemned apartments); yet his shirt is always pressed, he is politically aware, enterprising. Why does sorrow lie "on his clothes like an eternal crease"? Are you suggesting what will happen to him?*

3. *Why is #14 blank? What happens between the time the poet dreams of going back (to his father's home?) and does go back? Is it too painful to write about?*

4. *Why does he (the poet?) lose his voice when he imagines his father returns (#15)? What did he lose besides his voice ("and more")?*

5. *Did you write the first half of the poem to prepare us for the son's loss and pain? What is the significance of potato pie? Is it a staple of the Jewish diet?*

6. *Is the buzzing in the head of the boy the sound of his memory? Why is it so persistent?*

7. *Is the poem autobiographical?*

8. *What determined your verse form: line and stanza breaks, use of numbers for each stanza, putting the parts of the same sentences into several different stanzas?*

9. *How many revisions did the poem undergo, over what time?*

10. *What, if anything, has translation changed in the poem?*

11. *How does this translation, in your opinion, differ from other translations of the same poem?*

Imagine, only imagine, that America disappeared. As a result of a sudden shocking and unexpected catastrophe, the United States was erased from the earth. That is to say, the people, not the continent. The nation and the entire American civilization simply faded away, went up in smoke.

Tommy is a young boy from Cincinnati who survived somehow. He arrived at a safe harbor in Kasrilevka.* Where is Kasrilevka? It doesn't matter—it is in another world. And Tommy clung to the new place that gave him friendly shelter. While he was trying to get over his anxiety and loneliness, he made an admirable effort to adjust to the customs of the place and to rebuild his life.

And Tommy, the boy, became a man. He married, had children, built a new home. His name was no longer Tommy, but Tomiel. In the local language it meant the "innocence of God." He learned to speak the language of the

---

*A small Jewish town—*shtetl*—frequently the setting in stories by Shalom Aleichem.

Kasrilevkers, to dress like them, and even to enjoy their exotic food. Actually, that was one of his more difficult experiences. More even than reading the local newspapers of Kasrilevka. But all that passed. And Tommy, Tomiel, is now quite a happy man, loves his new homeland. He is satisfied.

One day (it's a pity we didn't mark the exact date though we still remember the exact place where it happened), in the middle of the street, on the stairs in front of G's restaurant, suddenly he smells the long forgotten smell of . . . . hamburger. God! What is a hamburger doing in Kasrilevka? Tomiel rubs his eyes, rubs his nose, excited and confused. What is real here? The hamburger or Kasrilevka? At that moment . . .

The undersigned, Abba ben Israel Kovner—whose forefathers were expelled from Lithuania, who was born on the shore of the Black Sea in the Crimea in Russia, grew up in Vilna, and since the end of World War II has lived in Kibbutz Ein Hahoresh in Israel—at that moment he was visiting in Tel Aviv. The distance between Kibbutz Ein Hahoresh and Tel Aviv is fifty minutes by car. But in other ways, the distance between the two is much greater, when it comes to possible surprises.

The windows in Tel Aviv during most of the year are not closed tight. Only covered by screens against mosquitoes. Maybe the mosquitoes can't get through, but all the voices and noise of the big city do. When I woke up at the home of my friends, it was daylight. But what woke me from my sleep was a voice singing from under the window, "Alte zachen. Alte zach . . . ennnn!" It took more than a few seconds for me to realize that the room I was in was actually in north Tel Aviv, in the nineteen eighties. And not in Vilna, in another generation. And when my senses functioned again, I got out of bed and went barefoot to the window to look out and to make sure that I was not mistaken.

Every month, on Monday, in the first week of the month exactly, he came to our courtyard. The man did not have a loudspeaker, no electric amplifier or anything else. He didn't come with a bell, like the kerosene man. Nor with a trumpet announcing himself like the travelling musicians (those beggar artists ashamed to simply beg), but only with his voice: "Alte zachennnnn. Alte zach . . . ennnn!"

Windows opened on every floor. Women would come to him with sacks. And we children would get there first, joyously surrounding the peddler's cart. Actually Reb Zalman was not a peddler in our eyes. A peddler sells. And Reb Zalman sold nothing. He only bought. He bought and he paid. Not much. Only pennies. But he paid. Always. And what didn't he buy! Everything. From an old piano to copper buttons from the Czar's army. My mother was too busy to find time for Reb Zalman, and I would beg her to let me sell him some old pitcher or anything. It seemed to me that as long as you had something to sell to Reb Zalman, you existed. And after all, we were landlords. So, of course, we had to exist!

Once I told my mother that someone with nothing to sell might as well be dead. My mother looked at me shocked: is it written in the Bible? Yes, I said without blinking. And with one word, I committed two sins—I lied and I didn't honor my mother. Because right then, Zalman was more important to me. And so I ran, following Reb Zalman until he disappeared around a corner and only his voice remained in the air: "Alte zachennnnn. Alte zach . . . ennnn!"

For the little ones who helped him to tie all his chattels to his cart, he always had candies to give as a reward. They were broken, but sweet. And I always wondered how Reb Zalman managed to extract the candy from the cellars of the ten pockets of his shabby coat. Another thing I didn't understand, which is still a mystery to me, is what did this man do with all the junk that he bought?

In Vilna, in those days, they did not know about flea markets. Youngsters did not dress in their grandmothers' clothes, and people did not furnish their living rooms with antiques that you buy today at garage sales. What did Reb Zalman do with all those leftovers of life? I was too young to know what to ask. And when I knew what to ask, Reb Zalman was already in a limepit in Ponar.[†]

The poem "Potato Pie" is titled in the Hebrew original "Alte Zachen," spelled as it is in Yiddish, not Hebrew. I remember that I wrote that title on the page before I began to write the poem. And I didn't know then what I was going to write. And although *alte zachen* is not mentioned at all in the poem, I left the title as it came to me from the beginning.

A friend, a well-known Israeli poet, reacted with amazement—that I could call a poem about my father "Alte Zachen" (worn-out clothes, rags, junk). But I was not thinking of the meaning. Rather, the sound, the melody—the same melody that woke me up in Tel Aviv (and by the way, there it was a Yemenite who did not understand Yiddish, and who pronounced the words alte zachen with a Yemenite accent—but with the same melody). And this brought the image of my father back to me after many years of distance and forgetting. Why father and not mother? I don't know. Maybe because mother was waiting for another time. With this title I wanted to preserve the first glimmer in the process of remembering and its transformation into a poem.

How did "Alte Zachen" become "Potato Pie?" That is one of the mysteries of translation. When my translator told me she had a problem translating the title, that to readers of poetry in English, it would seem strange and without the original connotations, I accepted her suggestion to title the poem "Potato Pie," because that image does appear in the poem, and because a title is, after all, only the hat and not the whole head.

I'm not used to interpreting my poems—not to someone else, and not to myself. Therefore, forgive me if I skip some of your questions. I shall just make some comments on question number 2: The father in the poem appears to be poor (no radio, etc.).

If my parents were alive, I assume they would have a radio, and also TV today. I'm not sure if they would have preferred color or black and white. But what I am sure of is that my mother and father would not have hurried to put an antenna on the roof before they had running water and a toilet in their

---

†Or Ponary, the infamous place near Vilna where Nazis murdered thousands of Jews and dumped them into a pit covered with lime.

apartment. During the thirties we didn't have either. But we did have, in that small apartment in Vilna, three cupboards of books. One that my grandfather bequeathed to us, a second that father acquired, and a third, my own proud selection.

When I wrote in the poem "no radio," I did not mean that as a suggestion of social status, but rather of time and place. The era before the mass media entered our lives.

Was the father a poor man? In whose eyes? From the point of view of income tax—he was very heavily taxed because he owned property. At least twice a year the tax collector would come and confiscate our furniture because of late payments. The twenty-two tenants in the building were late with their rent, and most of them didn't pay at all. The wheels of justice grind slower than our teeth. In our home we experienced some days close to starvation.

Once I walked with my father on the main street of my city when, suddenly, the sole of his shoe fell off. Embarrassed, my father bent down and began to fix his torn shoe. And then I discovered, to my dismay, that the shoe was already fastened together with wire. One can inherit a house with twenty-two apartments that will not support the owner. Self-dignity is something you must struggle for day after day.

In answer to question number 8, "What determined your verse form . . . etc.," I think the process of the return of memory. The content of the poem came to me like Morse code, or something like that. Short, cut, condensed. Like an outline with a much larger experience hidden behind it. That's it.

And what about potato pie? Well. Grate 8 to 10 potatoes on a thick grater. Add 2 teaspoons of salt. One tsp. of black pepper. Two eggs. Two tablespoons of white flour. Fried onion. One tsp. of melted butter. Mix everything. And put it in a very hot frying pan with oil. After a few seconds, turn the gas to a small flame. Fry 20 minutes on each side. You can eat it hot or cold. And if it's successful, it is very tasty. (Copyright © 1985 by Abba Kovner.) Like a poem.

In different places it was called different names: *tagchetz*, *kartofel-bobke*, *kartoshniak*, etc. But always based on potatoes. Because the fundamental ingredient of every poor kitchen—Jewish, Chinese—is whatever is cheap and available.

Here is a simple Jewish folk song that every Jew used to know by heart:

On Sunday potatoes
On Monday potatoes
On Tuesday potatoes
On Wednesday potato soup
On Thursday potato pie
On Friday potato stuffing
On Saturday potato *tcholent* (stew)
and on Sunday again—potatoes . . . .

Translated by Shirley Kaufman and Nurit Orchan

ABBA KOVNER was born at Sebastopol in the Crimea in 1918 and grew up in Vilna. After the Nazi invasion of Poland, he joined the Jewish underground partisan organization, and in 1943 took command of the United Partisans Organization of the Vilna ghetto. Shortly before the extermination of the Vilna ghetto, he led the Jewish Partisans' Battalion in the neighboring forests. In 1968 he won the Brener Literary prize for *My Little Sister*, a book-length poem about the Holocaust. In 1970 Abba Kovner won Israel's highest literary award, the Israel Prize in Literature. In 1971 he received the International Remembrance Award for excellence and distinction in literature relating to the Holocaust. In the spring of 1973, the University of Pittsburgh Press published three of his book-length poems and selections of shorter lyrics in a volume titled *A Canopy in the Desert: Selected Poems of Abba Kovner*. In 1977 he won the Bialik Prize for his new book, *Observations*. Abba Kovner is the spiritual creator of Bet Hatefutsoth—Museum of the Jewish Diaspora at the Tel-Aviv University. He has published 12 volumes of poetry, a novel, *Face to Face*, and a volume of essays, *On The Narrow Bridge*. He has received an honorary doctorate from Tel-Aviv University, and has served as chairman of the Israel Writer's Association.

PHILIP LEVINE

*

Angel Butcher

At sun up I am up
hosing down the outdoor abattoir
getting ready. The water
steams and hisses on the white stones
and the air pales to a
thin blue.
        Today it is
Christophe. I don't see him
come up the long climb or
know he's here until I hear
my breathing double
and he's beside me smiling
like a young girl.
        He asks
me the names of all
the tools and all
their functions, he lifts
and weighs and
balances, and runs a long
forefinger down the tongue
of each blade.
        He asks
me how I came to this place and
this work, and I tell him how
I began with animals, and
he tells me how
he began with animals. We
talk about growing up and losing
the strange things we never
understood and settling.
        I help
him with his robes; he
has a kind of modesty and sits

on the stone table with
the ends of the gown crossed
in his lap.
                    He wants to die
like a rabbit, and he wants me
to help him. I hold
his wrist; it's small, like
the throat of a young hen, but
cool and dry. He holds
mine and I can feel the
blood thudding in the ring
his fingers make.
                    He helps me, he
guides my hand at first. I can
feel my shoulders settle and
the bones take the weight, I can
feel my lungs flower as the
swing begins. He smiles again
with only one side of his mouth
and looks down to the
dark valley where the cities
burn. When I hit
him he comes apart like a
perfect puzzle or an
old flower.
                    And my legs
dance and twitch for hours.

Butchering's a craft like any other: you begin with animals and work up to angels. Such questions as why you're doing it and what it's worth as a profession and whether you could have made a better choice have been settled long ago. When you reach the top the question is, how sharp are the tools, are you in good form? In a new place with a new audience you're always a little nervous. But once you have started the performance, your professional control and confidence take over. You "can feel [your] shoulders settle and/ the bones take the weight, [you] can/ feel [your] lungs flower as the/swing begins." Agreed, for a golf pro, trapeze artist, concert pianist, surgeon, or even a poet. But "Angel Butcher" puts this comfortable truism in a new context—a professional butcher promoted out of this life and demonstrating his skill to, for, and on an angel. The situation is impossible enough to make a reader laugh, at least at first. Angels can't bleed or die. At most they can come apart. But this one looks, talks, and acts like an amiable man. He has a name, a wrist, and a pulse. He admires the tools and shows perfect faith in the butcher's skill. The demonstration goes splendidly, but the angel never learns what it's like to die like a man (he just comes apart), and the butcher never learns what it feels like to be an angel (his legs dance and twitch for hours, in the reflex of a newly killed lower animal).

1. The poem has made no statement of idea, yet it has shocked the readers into looking very hard at something most of them take for granted: the nature of being alive and the worth of what they practice, save for, deny themselves for, and take pride in. What did you hope the readers would do in response to this shock? Laugh? Feel shame? Reevaluate their own professional goals? A mixture of these? None of these?

2. What is the significance of the angel's name, Christophe? Does the title apply to both the butcher and the angel he kills? Does "he began with animals" mean that the angel began in some other way with animals and then, like the butcher, began "growing up and losing/ the strange things we never understand/and settling"?

3. Why does the angel want to die? Is it curiosity to know what it's like to be a man? Why does he want to die like a rabbit?

4. Why did you have the butcher tell the story?

5. The visual effect of starting each new stanza at or after the middle of a line gives those indented lines great emphasis. One is tempted to read them vertically, and they can be read vertically with almost the effect of a chorus. Did you wish them to be read that way?

6. What determined your stanza breaks and line breaks?

7. What strategies or accidents determined your rhythms and sound repetitions?

8. What started the poem?

Your questions certainly seem relevant, and if I were able to answer them more fully I believe I could contribute to a reader's understanding of the poem. The poem was written in the spring of 1968, fifteen years ago, and many of my choices and intentions are now a mystery to me. At that time I was "hot," writing poems I was very excited by. I was full of trust in my own talent and my inspirations; I rarely questioned what I was doing. To question now is a bit difficult.

A few opening remarks that might help a reader. In the late 1960's the inner populations of some of our cities were burning parts of those cities, not for the usual reason—to collect the insurance—but to express their outrage with an America that was forcing them to accept less than full citizenship and equality. I grew up in one of those cities, Detroit, indeed in the very neighborhood most damaged. Another key fact: I am an identical twin. It was first pointed out to me by a shrewd reader that many of my poems contain a dialogue or confrontation between two adult male figures who embody very different visions of the world. In all of these poems the figures come together in some sort of physical or spiritual embrace before the poem concludes. It's very likely that I believe in the Platonic notion that each human soul strives for a lifetime to recover that half of the self lost at birth.

Now the questions. What did I hope the reader would do in response to the shock of the poem? I did not, as you suggest, hope that he or she would reevaluate his professional goals. I don't believe the poem has anything to do with professional goals although it is concerned with the tools and techniques of a trade. I believe a good poem is about what it's about, and this poem is about butchering. Certainly both the poem and I are interested in the way the human body works and the magic of its movements even when those movements lead to slaughter; the common magic of that body in motion is the splendor of the poem, more amazing even than the presence of the angel. I'm sure I hoped my reader would be horrified that one being could do this to another being, and I hoped to intensify that horror by creating two lovely creatures who until the end display great tenderness for each other. They are very close, they speak of common experiences, they touch each other, they help each other, and they share this act almost as though they were two parts of the same being. One part kills the other part, and the killing part goes on living in the world. Perhaps I am suggesting that to be human we must murder a certain portion of the self, and thus, mutilated, we survive.

The name Christophe. I knew a boy with that name who was so delicate he seemed insubstantial and almost totally spirit. I wondered if he could survive as an adult in this world. His name was Christopher, but his father called him Christophe as though in recognition of this intense delicacy, for without the final "r" the name seems more open and vulnerable.

The title does try to suggest that both angel and butcher are closely related, but I do not conceive of Christophe as a butcher, although the butcher may also be the angel of butchers as well as the butcher of angels. The two creatures say they began with animals, but by this they don't mean the same thing, and I leave the reader to discover that. The butcher began his career as butcher with animals, which is to be expected. The angel began his career as an angel with animals. As to the strange things they lost, that is childhood, the same for both, an existence in which they accepted both their spiritual and animal natures. Now they have matured and settled: one is a butcher, one is an angel.

The angel wants to die because he cannot abide the world or love it any longer as an angel. He must die as a creature bound by time, an animal, and so he comes to a butcher of animals for help. The angel chooses a rabbit, a creature threatening to no one. This choice is in keeping with his character in the poem and very convenient for me, for a rabbit may be killed with one good sock, and in my poem I didn't want all the blood and gore of the slaughter-house.

I chose the butcher to tell the story because I wanted to get as close to the event as possible, and I wanted to avoid the problem of the volume of description and explication third person would have required. Imagine the poem in third person, and you'll see what I mean. I wanted also to suggest something ordinary about the occasion—for the reader it may seem sensational but to the butcher it's another day—and that was easily done by establishing a certain offhand tone by the speaker. I couldn't use the angel as narrator; for one thing I want him to die in the poem, and I wasn't prepared to deal with the state of dying, and for another I doubt I could ever capture convincingly the inner life of the angel. I felt capable of capturing a butcher's version of even so remarkable an event.

Why the indented beginnings of the stanzas? I'm not sure. I'd used the technique before. I didn't want the reader to rest on a rounded, full line. I wanted something more upsetting, stark, aggressive. I think I felt that the breaks, the staging of the lines, would lead the reader, force the reader deeper into the poem. I didn't want a single full rest until the end of the poem.

I can still recall the two events which back then seemed to sponser the poem's rise into my conscious awareness. I went home to Detroit some months after the riots or, as they are called there, The Great Rebellion of 1967, and I discovered walking through the neighborhoods of my youth that I was an utter stranger and an intruder. I felt that our history, America's, had taken my home from me and turned those who were formerly my neighbors and friends into my enemies. Furthermore these people had a right to their hatred of me because as white, middle aged, and middle class I was dressed in the uniform of their keepers. The other event was only a moment. I was in the library skimming through the Swiss magazine of graphic arts, GRAPHIS, when my eye fell upon a reproduction which depicted a conveyor belt upon which rode the amazing organs of some unworldly creatures, angels, I supposed.

PHILIP LEVINE was born in Detroit in 1928, where he attended the public schools and Wayne University. After several lousy jobs there, he left to make his fortune in poetry, settling finally in Fresno, California. He has three sons, all grown now and employed. He has taught at a number of schools, most recently at Tufts. His books have won the American Book Award, the National Book Critics Award, the Lenore Marshall Award, and other prizes. In the spring of 1984 Atheneum published his selected poems.

THOMAS LUX

*

Farmers

Force-feeding swans—let me tell
you—was hard. And up
every morning 4:30 counting

the lambs out to pasture,
each one tapped on the forehead with a stick
to be sure it's there.

Uncle Reaper half the time so drunk
he'd pull his milkstool
under the horse: more work

explaining the difference. Gramma
and Cousin Shroud putting up
8000 jars of beets, Auntie Bones

rapping her wooden spoon
against my ear: "More bushels, bumbler!"

I'll tell you—I understand
how come the dancing bear tore off his skirt

and headed back to the Yukon,
how come all of a sudden jewels in avalanche
down the spine of my sleep. . . .

But still, still when it rains
I remember all of us: farmers, simple sweat mongers
of the dirt whose turnips depend on it,

I remember how we called it down, how down
we desired it to fall: the rain.

1. *The poem "Farmers" seems to be a comic spoof of the rural life, a sort of anti-back-to-nature poem: the farm chores are made grotesque (force-feeding swans instead of geese, tapping lambs on the head to see if they are really there, trying to milk a horse, canning 8000 jars of beets); and the names are grotesque (Uncle Reaper, Auntie Bones, Cousin Shroud). But toward the end of the poem the speaker has taken their point of view, as he remembers how it felt to pray for rain. At this point the tone becomes at least half serious, even though the mockery persists in the exaggerated self-deprecation ("simple sweat mongers of the dirt"), the selection of turnips as the important crop, and the garbled parody of a much-anthologized medieval lyric, in the last two lines. Did you intend this ambivalence of tone? Was the humor all along a defensive gesture?*

"Farmers" *is* a kind of comic spoof, a satire, really, not on rural life but on people who romanticize rural life. It was meant—although I did not know this until the poem was in progress—to be a comment on many members of my generation, particularly those who talked (they seldom acted, successfully anyway) dreamily about "getting back to the land" etc. There's nothing wrong, of course, with getting back to the land, but farming is *not* for dreamers. It is a hard, relentless, and very risky way of life. So, the tone *is* deliberately ambivalent—the point is to praise real farmers and to poke fun at naive dreamers. I don't know if the humor is a defensive gesture. The best I can hope for is that the humor is humorous.

2. *Are you farm bred? Were your forebears farmers?*

I spent the first several years of my childhood on a working dairy farm in Western Massachusetts. It was owned by my grandmother and worked by my uncle. My father was the milkman. We all helped with various aspects of the work. It was a small operation: about thirty milk cows at any given time. We also had chickens, an occasional hog, or beef cattle for our own consumption. When I was eight or nine my uncle took the cows and moved to Vermont, where he thought the farming would be better. From that point on we used the barns and pastures to board horses and we rented the rest of the surrounding land to local truck farmers in return for hay for the horses.

3. *Your diction and sentence structure are casual, elliptical, even slangy in a colloquially offhand manner. Is this a conscious strategy?*

The diction and sentence structure of the poem are carefully constructed to sound casual. I wanted to create the sense of someone actually *speaking*. Since many of the things the speaker is saying are absurd, it was important to make him sound offhanded, matter of fact.

4. *The form of the poem punctuates three-line stanzas with two-line stanzas. What determined this pattern and its variation?*

Since the poem was written over five years ago (spring 1978) and I don't have any of the notebooks or drafts of the poem on hand right now, I can't remember how I came upon the stanzaic structure for this poem. Sometimes I use very regular stanzas, but this time I apparently tried different stanzas until I found the ones that I thought worked for the movement of the poem I had in mind.

5. *What determined your line breaks?*

The line breaks are determined for all the usual reasons: emphasis, music, surprise, pacing, breath, etc.

6. *The poem has relatively little sound repetition, except for humorous emphasis ("More bushels, bumbler!"; "simple sweat mongers," "dirt whose turnips depend"). How much did your ear rely on accident, how much on plan?*

Nothing after the first draft or two of a poem happens by accident. Usually I have a lot more sound-play (including preconceived meter and rhyme schemes) in a poem, but this one apparently didn't call for more at the time. I must have been satisfied with its sound as believable speech.

7. *What proportion of your readers do you think will recognize the second line of the fifteenth-century anonymous "Western Wind" ("The small rain down can rain") in your "how down/ we desired it to fall: the rain?" What will they make of your inversion if they don't recognize the source?*

I have no idea what proportion of readers will hear the "Western Wind" echo. Anyone who has read that poem *should* recognize it. The last lines of the poem are meant to be serious, to stop, abruptly, any laughter that the earlier part of the poem might provoke in a reader. I use the inversion to wrench the readers' syntactical expectations a little and also because we use inversion in speech a good deal. If they don't recognize the source, they should still be able to understand the sentence. "Western Wind" is a love poem, a lyric. "Farmers" is more of a monologue that has elements of longing, of love, in it. I should mention, by the way, that I would gladly trade *every* line I have ever written, or hope to write, for "Western Wind," which is one of the most beautiful lyrics ever written. Anonymous was one of the greatest poets in our, or any, language.

8. *How did the poem start? What revisions did it undergo?*

As I've said, I don't have access to any of the notebooks or early drafts of "Farmers" right now, but it started like most of my poems: with a few lines, a rhythm, an image or two that I had written in notebooks and that somehow announced that they belonged together and wanted to try to be a poem. From then it was all process, conscious process and work. Certainly the poem went through at least twenty drafts and probably more to get to the point it is at now. I worked on it over a period of three or four months, which is about average for me with shorter poems.

THOMAS LUX was born in 1946 in Massachusetts. He has published four full-length books and six chapbooks. He has taught writing and literature at several colleges and universities. Since 1975 he has been a member of the Writing Faculty at Sarah Lawrence College.

HEATHER McHUGH

*

Breath

What I want from God, feared to be
unlovable, is none of the body's
business, nasty lunches
of blood and host, and none

of the yes-man networks,
neural, capillary or electric.
No little histories recited
in the temple, in the neck and wrist.

I want the heavy air,
unhymned, uncyclical,
the deep kiss—absence's.
I want to be rid of men,

who seem friendly but die,
and rid of my studies
wired for sound. I want
the space in which all names

for worship sink away,
and earth recedes to silver
vanishing, the point
at which we can forget

our history of longing
and become
his great blue breath,
his ghost and only song.

1. *The history of western religion has been the story of wagging or snarling obedience to "stand," "sit," or "sic-em," the personification of a master in our own image and a freedom like one of the gentler slaveries. In your poem "Breath" you reject all the conventions of incarnation, including obedience and worship, and ask to become something wholly non-human. Yet you retain the personal pronoun: "his great breath, / his ghost and only song." Is this a deliberate irony? An "accommodation" to a limited human understanding? A need to re-see and re-state the conventional God of the Bible from a more accurate perspective? A merging with the God, not of love but indifference? A disgust with self and a desire to destroy it?*

2. *The tone is impatient, like the impatience in throwing off a heavy coat or brushing a lock of hair out of the eyes. Is this a brief, once-only impulse or a recurrent and lasting one?*

3. *What determined your choice of the four-line, short-line stanza form? What determined your line and stanza breaks? Several of the stanza breaks require a quick double-take. For example, the last line of stanza 3 seems to say "I want to be rid of men" (angry, perhaps as opposed to women), but the first line of stanza 4 suggests the generic meaning of the term men and a feeling of loss rather than anger. Do you mean both? To what extent was this a conscious strategy, to what extent a happy accident?*

4. *What determined the poem's rhythm? Repetitions of sound?*

5. *How did the poem start? How did it change?*

Back when I wrote this poem, what I wanted from God was not a history of men, not a chronology of inheritance, not a line. I was forswearing patriarchies—religious ones among others—but the poem's vehemence was personal: I wanted to be rid of the suffering at the root of passion. My passion is man.

This meant to be rid of the body love took place in: the pointedly masculine possessive. I didn't want another father, didn't ask for another son.

The person or character of holiness left for those of us with crosses instead of arrows coming off our o's seemed to be, in Christian terms, the third: tertium quid, rara avis, least carnal, personless. Of the three of them, I guess I always loved the ghost.

Wordsworth called poetry "the breath and finer spirit of all knowledge." I knew what a woman afflicted in faith and love might know: I sang the song I felt then, something of an anti-hymn. Only in body is god unlovable; only in brown studies, wired words, is he untrue.

I was trying, I suppose, to dispel a little loss with a lot of letting go; to fight the pain of being partial by pretending to take no part at all, invoking a peace of utter impartiality. If men hurt us, species and genus, by their very nature, always dying, don't we wish sometimes to be some kind of cloud-trace, breath of a breeze, freed from the bloody ribcage? The poem was, in its moment, my dream of invulnerability—not through physical empowering, but through physical relinquishing. It was the dream of leaving earth, with all its beds and boxes and carpenters, with all its priests; turning (silvered and cerulean) to images made of space, imagination of flight. The afterlife and ship of ghosts is a blue song. I wanted God to give me spirit.

Inspiration is held to be (funny how said is said to be held, understanding held to be grasp—as if the truth were still life)—inspiration is *taken* to be—the medium, the atmosphere, of poetry. The poem *"Breath"* wants expiration for its muse. The air is of death. In the poem's prevailing verb "want," wishing and missing are one. I no longer remember much about the act of composition—the poem's years old at this writing—but I know I wrote in seizures of feeling, bursts of desire. The music of poems seemed to me a running rhythm—a current, as of water or air or electrons—from which thoughts take shape. I studied the stills falls made, the ribs bays made, x-rays of the anima. I could watch rivulets down a steep dirt street for hours.

The poem's music is expressed, in part, in approximate aabb rhymes until, at the end of stanza four, the physical is dreamt to fall away; but not for long; longing, in the last stanza, leads to song. The preponderance of 3-stress lines is a sign, I suspect, of my trinitarian concerns. Generally I revise until the flow raises repeating visual patterns on the page, until I hear the shape in the shell. When the poem's running right, it's usually thinking right. In the end, the invocation is of breath *with* tone: spirit is discernible; air has weight; and water sound. Feeling takes a body to fill, feeling uncontainable, and human hearts are where spirit is loved, though spirit is so much lighter. The poem is what I did, in throes, in love, instead of renting a skywriter.

HEATHER McHUGH was born on the West Coast, raised on the East. She is the Milliman Writer-in-Residence at the University of Washington in Seattle six months a year, and at home in downeast Maine the rest of the year. She is also a faculty member in the nonresidential M.F.A. Writing program at Warren Wilson College in Swannanoa, North Carolina. Her books include *Dangers* (1977), *A World of Difference* (Houghton Mifflin, 1981) and *D'Après Tout: Poems by Jean Follain* (Princeton University Press, 1981), a translation. She is sensible of Enesco's cautionary epigram: "Autocriticism does honor to the poet, dishonor to the critic.

SANDRA McPHERSON

*

Collapsars

The problem with
black holes is

She would see
if I had a problem.
She read my birth
and I grew cold.
The chart held a "dark time"
for a "near" woman
in the snow stars of Christmas.
No, I said,
tragedies like that—

> *there is no way*
> *to see them*
> *or hear them.*

As one hears
even in sleep
a man shouting Fire!
in the street.

> *They are stars*
> *that have collapsed,*
> *suffered what*

even hard winter
doesn't bring:
snow fallen between houses
like a body
between bed and door.
Inhaling then choking

> *is called an implosion.*

Without realizing
what happens,
you reach intensity . . .

> *The matter*
> *in such stars*
> *has been squashed together*

like a victim
of a fire
carried down in a bag,
half size,
but then again and again,
fire after fire,

> *into forms*
> *unknown on earth,*

because our knowledge
has made us rare
and cold. How
can I look at it,

> *matter so dense*
> *its gravitational field*
> *prevents any kind*
> *of radiation*
> *from escaping.*

I have kept my body heat
in heavy sweaters
and weatherstripping,
while earth's night grows colder
and what was burned
freezes.
        From that body
could a soul be escaping?

> *You couldn't see one*
> *if it was right*
> *next to you;*

Miss Nugent was like that.
She must have walked
right by our house
twice a day. I never

saw her, never saw
her take the steps
one by one up to her apartment
after work and switch
on the light.

> *if you shone*
> *a light on it*

today, in the noon
after the fire broke out
like the sun's own rooster
rising from her window,
way too early
in the dark holiday morning,
licking up story after story,

> *the light would*
> *simply disappear*

like a Christmas present
we missed
and sifted the ashes for,
thrown away with its wrapping,

> *into the black hole.*

And what spark doesn't
desire all? And what
kind of star
visited a woman that night,
thirty-five,
of a secretary's passions,
ninety-eight point six?

When I asked Sandra McPherson about "Collapsars," I was probing a cauldron with a knitting needle, a mystery almost too hot and too dense to separate into its parts. She answered with the poem's full biography, which reveals her poetics and her working habits, yet preserves the mystery.

It was a little over fourteen years ago that I began to attempt to write what became "Collapsars." A woman two doors from our house had died in a fire that broke out in her apartment in the early morning hours two nights before Christmas, 1968. I stood on the porch and looked at the flames. My husband went up the street to see if he could do anything. The firemen said, "We've got a crispy here." Her name, in the paper the next day, was Jene Nugent, age 35 or 36. I wrote down notes on what I'd seen because I didn't want to forget any details. Both of us felt hopeless and dark. I felt that no poem was possible because there was nothing beautiful or redeeming in Ms. Nugent's fate, and a poem has to bring pleasure even when it deals with thoroughly dismal subjects.

However, I kept trying. The results were not alive. I didn't want "art" to be some kind of lacquer shining up a list of depressing facts about the fire, but that was all I seemed to be getting. Then one day about two years later I was reading *Natural History* magazine (April 1971, p. 63) and ran across a description of a collapsar, a black hole. As I read, it recalled the way the burned-out apartment looked the next day—a black hole in the midst of clean, white, untouched apartment units. This was the entrance into the mystery.

I attempted to write "my" parts in prose too; that relaxed me and words came more freely. I found that my sentences could be integrated with *Natural History*'s phrases much more easily than I expected. I only had to cut two *that*s from the magazine's passage; their wording still reads to me like poetry.

When my daughter Phoebe was born, an astrologer warned of a terrible thing happening to some woman close to her in Phoebe's 46th or 47th week of her second year: "Neptune goes retrograde and may mark a major event either in Phoebe's life or the life of her parents, as when children are that young the pattern reacts on the parents . . . At the same time . . . progressed moon will pass over Uranus, signifies separation or illness of a woman and in her case it could also be a close or distant relative." As the time approached, we wondered if anything would happen, and if it would be to me or to one of her grand-parents. This fire was that event, or that coincidence. It changed my life pro-foundly; I remember thinking that those who choose suicide would think twice if fire were the form it had to come in. "If you want suicide you must want death any way it comes," I find on an early draft. For the poem's sake I changed the astrological prediction to refer to myself, not to my daughter.

The way the metaphor of the collapsar worked was, I believe, to give me something distant and unemotional against which the close and chaotic could be viewed.

The pre-*Natural History* drafts are too embarrassing to make public in their entirety. In June 1970 I tried to join Nugent's story with the fire at the local Grandma's Cookies factory: "There was no way to bring joy to such light/ Or the despair to art that we smelled still in our hair." On another draft I asked, "What is the rhyme for *corpse?*" and instructed myself with "There must be certain degrees of seriousness, called playing with matches, I can play with fire— verbally—" I have found thirty-six pages of drafts. I had forgotten that I incor-porated an idea from Bachelard: "to be aware that one is burning is to grow cold; to feel an intensity is to diminish it; it is necessary to be an intensity without realizing it" (*Psychoanalysis of Fire*, p. 112). I eliminated a pathetic detail—people had heard her cat screaming in the fire. Very early I find an egoistical reference to "a woman who died for me." In the first typed draft, November 1969, I had the essence of the current ending; now that surprises me, for it seems less to grow out of that early draft than of its current setting. (The star was Bethlehem's as well as the astrologer's.) A draft a month later contained these lines:

> Many ashes strewn by the water down the street
> stuck under cars and stayed in piles
> as, in fall, leaves rise against stones.
> Why don't they sweep the cinders and put them
> in a bag—
>
> night grows colder and what was burned will freeze.
> Why don't they carry the street off
> and give us a new street.
> The macadam is so black and it seems to need
> new surfacing. It leads
>
> into the night where we cannot sleep
> for the fire. Why don't they give us a new night?

The original prose description goes like this:

> Christmas was not the same this year because the morning of
> Christmas Eve day, early morning, about 2:15 or 2:30 we woke up
> hearing a man shout from the street—I thought it was just some
> beery happy student cooling off outside from a party but
> Henry heard better: the man was yelling, "Fire, fire, get
> out of a burning house," and Henry put his clothes on
> running down the stairs, ran outside and said it was just
> up the block. I looked out the window at the fronts of the
> houses across the street—the red barn one and the gray
> clapboard one were lit up from the glow, a reddish, warm
> yellow light as if from a large iridescent lightbulb and
> I thought not so much of fire as Christmas until I looked
> up our side of the street to an apartment house next door
> across a yard to the house beside us and saw a great fire
> the bulge-shape of a turkey's breast blowing up from one
> unit to the apartment above it with a great rush—I do not
> remember at all with what sound; my ears must have censored
> it.—I began to feel as if I might vomit. It occurs to
> me now I did not watch the fire for more than a few seconds
> perhaps. I saw it; then I came in and watched the crowd and
> the firemen; then later I stepped out and saw that it was
> under control and the smoke was swelling out.

All the next day, as the engines came back to inspect and
to sift the ashes, Henry and I kept seeing the fire—it
would flash on us every thirty seconds or so like labor
pain. We found out from someone who had heard the news in
the morning that a woman had died in that fire—they found
her wedged between the wall and the bed—suffocated first.
She had burned and the firemen carried her out in a rubber
sack. The man yelling "Fire" was from the upper apartment
(she was in the lower)—when he saw the fire in his room
he had leaped two stories to the ground and been seriously
burned in that action—2nd degree burns. When Henry saw him
walking with a fireman last night the man, who Henry said
looked American Indian, was shaking badly and had gone into
shock.

Henry had taken pictures—there was a lit Christmas tree
in the window of the apartment (untouched) next to the blazing
one—he asked a newsman that came the morning after and the
newsman said his station might like to buy it. That was
before he knew a woman had died; he told the newsman then
he didn't want to make money off somebody else's misfortune.

When we listened to a newscast in the afternoon nothing was
reported about the fire but there was news of a double murder
on Sauvies Island—a decapitated woman about 20 wrapped in
six sheets and a blanket and down the beach a 4 yr old girl
with a ponytail who showed signs of having been beaten around
the head.

And when you came home and went to bed your hair smelled of
smoke and for some reason my hands did too, from standing out
on the porch maybe and it was very hard for both of us to
sleep—my dream at least was no different from what I saw
in reality a few minutes ago—the flame like a belch, you
reporting back to me news, the man yelling for people to
wake up. The smoke in your hair, since it was not the good
smell of a camp fire in the mountains, of gathered wood,
reminded me of burning bodies—it did not occur to me at
the time that I had never smelled such a thing. And the
day after as I was eating meat I felt that I was eating
flesh.

The poem has interested some readers for the way it integrates science with
poetry. Yes, it does, I guess. But now I think too it integrates poetry with poetry,
mystery with mystery.

SANDRA McPHERSON was born in San Jose, California, in 1943 and was educated at Westmont College, Santa Barbara, San Jose State, and University of Washington. She has worked as a technical writer for Honeywell, Inc., and has taught at the University of Iowa, University of California, Berkeley, Portland State University, and the Oregon Writers' Workshop at Pacific Northwest College of Art. Ecco Press has published the following collections of her poems: *Elegies for the Hot Season* (1970 and 1982), *Radiation* (1973), *The Year of Our Birth* (1978), and *Patron Happiness* (1983). Meadow Press published *Sensing* (San Francisco, 1980). She lives in Portland, Oregon.

JOHN MOLE

*

Less Than Sixpence

Now let us educate you, let us, let us . . .
Cracking the crust, this rare politico's
A brave one, a home-baked
Brilliant blackbird, beaked
And gaping far beyond his pastry—
Listen to the facts, now, listen to me . . .
God save the Queen in her parlour,
God save the Counting House forever
And the silver spoon, the gold plate
And all those words which are good enough to eat.
Nobody loves Peace more than he does,
Of course, but he'd peck off any nose
To spite her face, poor maid
Alone in the garden with nowhere to hide
When the world ends. It's the *balance*
She doesn't understand, the courtly dance
Of money and power. *Oh listen, listen . . .*
If only she'd hang out reason
With the clothes. Things are not simple;
They are history's manifold example.
You can't just wash them and hope.
Oh keep faith with the faith we keep.
If not for you, for the sake of your children.
Of course we hope it will never happen.
That little white shirt on the line
Which waves at the future, take it in, take it in.
It signals surrender. The skull and bones
Could not be more fatal. So *we come into your homes*
Tonight and tomorrow and tomorrow and tomorrow
Telling you why and when and how
Until you understand. We have baked the pie
And now you'll eat it. Your destiny
Must be to go on listening to reason, its song
Of so much less than sixpence . . .

But no, this is wrong, wrong.
Switch off, walk out in the garden, there's time yet
To hang out a whole wardrobe. Why not?
And remember, a pocket-full of rye is something.
Plant each grain of it, then let the blackbirds sing.

After asking John Mole the usual questions about how his poem started and how it grew, I asked him somewhat ruefully about his idea of the nature and function of political poetry in England today. Relatively little of American poetry of the sixties and seventies seems to me to have been written on political themes, and it often seems to bring out the rant in us rather than the wit. John Mole does not answer the question directly, but his implication is clear: "To tell someone that he or she 'doesn't count' is to challenge that someone to stand up and be counted" and "I have . . . taken that opportunity to be playful about matters that concern me deeply."

Talking about "Less Than Sixpence," a recent poem, will not be any the less difficult because it is recent. It surprised me at the time, and is still curiously unfamiliar, as if willed on me by its occasion. I agree with Randall Jarrell that a poem is a way of making you forget how you wrote it. Going back, you are amazed, grateful, puzzled, detached, proud, and embarrassed by turns and in equal measure. Did I commit this? In whose name? Why? What next? Will too close a look at water under the bridge jeopardize the direction of the current? I suspect that questions of this kind occur to many poets when they are asked to comment in detail on what they have written. So, beset with superstition and misgivings, I shall proceed in this case cautiously and at random, uncertain—even then—about the extent to which I may be inventing a portrait of myself as the working poet for the sake of convenience. In short, the more coherent you find this essay the more you should mistrust it, whereas the poem itself can only be granted authenticity by a coherence which is beyond paraphrase.

What I do remember clearly is the immediate occasion. There's a popular program on British television which has run, now, for several series. It goes out quite late at night, is adult after a fashion, and is called *Question Time*. Chaired abrasively by Sir Robin Day, a thoroughly established political commentator and TV personality, it assembles four men or women (the latter often introduced with coy gallantry) around a polished, purposeful panelists' table. Questions are then taken from a judiciously invited audience, and it is pot-luck whether they are answered or merely serve as fodder for contention and polemic. Sometimes the questioners are brought into the debate, but they are subsidiary and often patronized or manipulated by the professionals' expertise. It's the kind of program I find addictive and profoundly disconcerting; a media vision of democracy—prerecorded by a few hours, so that, politically, it is almost immediate but at the same time entirely safe.

I wrote "Less Than Sixpence" in a white heat of laughter and outrage, as a way, perhaps, of sorting out by mimicry, comment and an intense playfulness, my response to a particular edition of this program. One of the panelists was a representative of the Conservative government, committed to preserving the balance of nuclear power. He was urbane, unflustered, rational and smiling. *That one may smile and smile and be a villain*, says Hamlet—but, of course, it would be simplistic, even sentimental, to cast him as the villain. My hackles rose at everything he said and at the way he said it, but the sentiments were unexceptional. "Nobody loves peace more than I do." There's no arguing with that, and he certainly wasn't going to allow any argument. The case for unilateral disarmament was put by another panelist, a woman, who did not have a seat in parliament and was immediately reminded of this fact by Mr. Balance-of-Power, who told her that, although he could not question her sincerity, she "did not count." After smiling and nodding his way through her humane and strikingly intelligent analysis of our present dangers, he informed her that she couldn't possibly appreciate the intricacies of high-level political decision. "Now let me educate you . . . " he began, at which point—as they'd no doubt have said in Hollywood in the heyday of Ronald Reagan—"Less Than Sixpence" was born. I'd completed it within twenty-four hours of watching the program.

The painter Goya wrote that "the sleep of Reason begets impossible monsters." I think that my poem is, in part, suggesting that Reason itself becomes an impossible monster when it is sure of itself to the point where it patronizes those who would put the case against it. The well-intentioned, innocent ogre in a smart suit, committed by temperament to the *status quo*, is perhaps the most terrifying ogre of them all.

And speaking of ogres, I suppose, leads on to the particular shape in which I cast the poem. Ogres make a nursery of the world because that is where they belong; in the child's imagination, as a monolithic aspect of all that the child doesn't understand and which it finds terrifying. The rhyme on which "Less Than Sixpence" is built, as a kind of ironic superstructure, is the familiar nursery-rhyme "Sing a Song of Sixpence." Like so many of its kind it is, on the surface, whimsically delightful, but with a strong undercurrent of puzzling violence. It has been appropriated, since it first gained currency in the early Eighteenth Century, by many political allegorists, and a fascinating summary of its history can be found in *The Oxford Dictionary of Nursery Rhymes*, edited by Iona and Peter Opie (Oxford University Press, 1951). I discovered this, however, after I had written the poem, and was rather gratified to learn that I had been elected to a club without ever realizing that I had been put up for membership. At the time of writing, it was just the *words* that were running through my head, and they were these:

Sing a song of sixpence,
  A pocket full of rye;
Four and twenty blackbirds,
  Baked in a pie.

When the pie was opened,
  The birds began to sing;
Wasn't that a dainty dish
  To set before the king?

The king was in his counting-house,
  Counting out his money;
The queen was in the parlour,
  Eating bread and honey.

The maid was in the garden,
  Hanging out the clothes,
When down came a blackbird
  And pecked off her nose.

A later version, softened for children who it was felt couldn't take the rhyme neat, appends a couple of lines in which little Jenny Wren puts the nose back on again. But I hardly need point out that such an ending has no place in my poem. If there is to be a happy outcome, *we* must work for it. It's no use hoping that the wrens of this world (or the doves) will prevail simply because they are nice. The blackbirds (or the hawks) are adept manipulators of mere niceness. They make it look not only ineffectual but also irresponsible. And, in my book, they're not entirely wrong. They are an inevitable part of the historical process. To tell someone that he or she "doesn't count" is to challenge that someone to stand up and be counted.

Yeats observed that we make rhetoric from our quarrel with the world, and poetry from the quarrel with ourselves. He also wrote, in "The Second Coming," that "the best lack all conviction while the worst are full of passionate intensity." The two voices in my poem, indicated by the italic and roman type faces, for the most part act out this "quarrel" between reason and imagination, confidence and anxiety, destruction and growth, and, yes, the prospect of global annihilation and the will to survive. "Less Than Sixpence" is a kind of debate, I suppose. It is not polemical but, rather, shifts about, exploring, within the pattern of the rhyme it has adopted. I should like to feel that it might be taken as wholly serious and yet properly witty. As a character from Henry James says, "the increasing seriousness of things is the great opportunity of jokes." I have, I suspect, taken that opportunity to be playful about matters that concern me deeply.

Finally, even if I could do so I should resist making precise symbolic identification of the Queen, the Counting House, the Maid etc. They are a vital pat of the argument and as such they must remain alive in the imagination of each reader. However, having been asked by the editor of this anthology to say whether the last two lines of the poem are serious, I won't end with an evasion. Yes they are. Utterly.

JOHN MOLE was born in 1941, grew up in the West Country of England, where he attended various schools, and studied English Literature at Magdalene College, Cambridge. He is coeditor of The Mandeville Press, a teacher, and regular poetry critic for *Encounter*. He has published five collections, and a sixth, *In and Out of the Apple,* appeared from Secker and Warburg in the summer of 1984. With Anthony Thwaite he has edited *Poetry, 1945–1980* (Longman, 1983) and has collaborated with his wife, the artist Mary Norman, on a book of riddles for children, *Once There Were Dragons* (Andre Deutsch, 1979). He broadcasts for the BBC as a compiler of feature programs and anthologies, and is, in his spare time, a jazz clarinettist.

CAROL MUSKE

*

Biglietto D'Ingresso

I rented a house
in the old Roman wall
in Barbarino Val d'Elsa.
It was like a treehouse

overlooking the wine-blue valley
and faraway, the towers of San Gimignano.
Three stories down, beneath the stones
of the street, slept a few
of the town's Etruscans, city fathers,
happily buried below year
after year of the famous chianti.

The day I arrived
I sat in a red chair
and looked out the windows
at the olive trees
and thought of August.

How the house, like a month
in a year, kept its privacy,
its calendar address,
guarded its doors, front
and back, as if each day

made a family of watchers,
then a family of revellers,
as the presses in the winery
made liquor from the hobbled vines.

Out of that crude, useful mouth,
as from the hand of the lord
came the bounty of Harvest:
the single light by which
the books of reckoning are read.

There was a familiar
still life I'd composed around
my solitude, laying my knife
across the plate like a hunter
discarding his weapon in the sun
next to a stream, watching it
become the brightest object

in the landscape. I watched
the scirocco leave the trees
trembling, one by one,
brushing them with studied casualness,
like people stroking the hair of orphans—

as if loss, in its beauty,
was an accusation, growing
stronger with each act of careless attention.

I stalked what the wind said,
tree by tree, I stalked grief—
but grief didn't want me—

like the homeless child in the street,
her face a little mirror held up
against each solicitous expression:

Grief didn't need me, it never did.
Grief had other subjects.
Grief had doors carved in the great churches.
Grief had its family.

So what was I thinking of
that morning I left the Uffizi early,

the ticket of admission forgotten
in my hand? I was going

to meet you. It wasn't yet noon,
but we were already in the day
kept private by every night
we did not know each other.

As I walked, I saw
the kitchen of my crooked house
in the trees. On the sideboard,
a pair of scales that tipped,

off-balance, letting a handful
of fava beans outweigh a loaded coin,
a lead counter-weight, and hang,
trembling like each space

the wind vacates. When we shook
hands, the stamped ticket fluttered
away and I was happy to see

all around us, paintings
of the local miracles: the saint
who cheated no one, but believed
in making things even
occasionally, in this world of inequity.

The light was perfect that day.
I can see us clearly, weighing
each other below the mild eyes
of the saint, the orphans and the ill,
transformed by Giotto into angels.

All along the street, and at
the doors of the embassy
were those same children who
belong to no one, not even grief,

and I see now
how the angel of justice
spins in the painter's eye,
tips the ancient scale

in favor of the left hand, the fistful
of fava, the lop-sided smile, the dirty
curls, the stunted lamb, the crooked door
of love, opening where we stand
that second before recovering,
at our feet, held still in the wind,
the *biglietto d'ingresso.*

*The poem is ostensibly a leisurely narrative about two lovers meeting in a strange city—
Florence—but the cool, detached tone and the long passages on the house, the wind, the
kitchen scales, the pictures of the saints, and the children of the city make the narrative less
important than the meditation on still life versus life, balance versus imbalance.*

1. *The repetition of the title in the last line suggests that the "ticket of entrance"
represents the theme. Are you using* ticket *in the sense of* right to, price of, *as in
"Incompleteness is the price of completeness"?*

2. *Is the poem based on an actual incident in which a dropped ticket was picked up? Are
other details in the poem, such as the scales with the fava beans, the paintings of the
local miracles, the house over (or by) the winery autobiographical?*

3. *The images which build the contrast between still (or inert, alienated) life and animate
life are carefully threaded throughout the poem: the active personification of house,
wine presses, wind, even of grief versus the stasis of the discarded knife, the still life;
and then the interaction of the two: the tilted kitchen scale, the ticket fluttering but held
momentarily still by the wind. Was this deployment of images part of a plan made
before starting the poem, the result of one or two happy accidents extended in revision,
or neither? In other words, how did the poem start and grow?*

"Biglietto d'Ingresso," or "Ticket of Entry," is the theme of this poem, as
well as the title. The ticket implies the cost of admission, as well as the right to
enter. What is being entered is a place unavailable to the narrator of the poem
before this moment. The poem's accumulated images are meant to suggest a
change in consciousness that *allows* entry into a new place.

If the poem works at all, it works as a mechanism, like a scale. Something is taken away, or added (cost of, right to), but there is a restoration of balance implicit in the place entered: a church, an art museum, the charged aura of a saint's presence, the miracle of love (and I use the term *miracle* quite intentionally). We used to say, when I was a child (before Communion) in the Catholic Church, "Lord, I am not worthy that thou should enter under my roof, say but the word and my soul will be healed."

In the poem, balance, or entry, is only possible through imbalance, unbalancing the scales, and this is done in favor of the unlikeliest of heroes and heroines: the orphaned, the imperfect, the doubters, the stunted. This is, I guess, a familiar theme of Christian renewal. The "justice" of Christ's miracles was this: that those who appeared lost or cursed, or undeserving—who had, in fact, accepted this view of themselves—were raised suddenly to that plateau of light, that miraculous dimension where their true selves are revealed and acknowledged. What is taught is humility, the necessity of acknowledging one's "unworthiness" before one can be healed.

I don't mean to sound like an evangelist. The poem is actually based on an experience I had the summer I spent in Italy on a Guggenheim fellowship. I did live in a roomy, airy house across the street from a winery in a little town between Florence and Siena—and its kitchen did possess a pair of skewed scales. I did go regularly into Florence, to see museums and churchs. I noted the floating hippie population and the "real" orphans of the city, cared for by nuns. And I did meet the man I'm now married to in Florence; we had mutual friends we were going to visit in Perugia, and we went together, at their suggestion. I had just come from the Uffizi when I met David at his hotel and carried the ticket of admission somewhere on my person. The ticket never dropped, only in my imagination.

None of the "facts" add up to the "moment" of the poem, anyway. That moment came to me, a year later, in August of 1982, when I was looking at some photos from the previous summer and the long-forgotten ticket came fluttering out of a pile of pictures. At that moment, the ticket seemed to stand out in relief and then, in the odd manner of a poem's inception, became an integrating symbol, thus a catalyst, for bringing together all the pieces of the experience. In endowing the experience with significance beyond the ordinary, I found the representational to be key: the ticket with its ornate margins, the works of art remembered, the churches and the Church, which I had left so many years before, then rediscovered in Italy in all its liturgical metaphor. I did not sustain a religious conversion there, nothing so blatant as that, but I did recall how transformation works, in a domestic sense. Water into wine. In all the frescoes of Cimabue and Giotto the faces were the faces of the people in the streets: St. Francis and Christ looked like Tuscan waiters, and all of those faces and attitudes brought back my childhood, a place and time when one freely crossed between the countries of the real and the miraculous. I suspect that in my own life I had been waiting for this to happen again.

I came to Italy in the wake of an unhappy, lengthy, love affair. I wanted nothing more, and expected nothing more from my life, than to be alone with my work. I found the seclusion in my house to write. When I had time for introspection I realized, appalled, the force of my own will, the way I had always *insisted* that things happen. I felt that I had coerced my life into being. Now, in Italy, I simply allowed things to happen to me. The "hunter laying down his knife by the stream" passage is a description of this abandonment of the will. When the knife is touched by light, there is wonder. One has to be as willful and cynical as I am to know the immense relief and feeling of gratitude in watching that knife turn to light. I could say I had nothing to do with it, but it loved something unconscious I did, the light. That for me is a miracle. When this unconsciousness becomes innocence (in other words, when it is raised to a superior dimension by faith in the light), it becomes art, it becomes justice; the blind see, the impossible is painted.

We all talk about the sense of loss inherent in poetry, the falling away from a world of light. Art's ability to restore that light will always be associated for me with righteousness—not in the sense of a vengeful diety, but in the sense of "seeing things right," re-setting a rightful balance. To include the creatures of exclusion, to bless and transform them, to reveal their virtue freed from cruel disguise.

I was one of those creatures of exclusion—imagining the poet as orphan, the orphan as some exceptional detour in human ancestry. Like a cripple or a dwarf, I felt absolutely enclosed within my difference, my consciousness of my self derived from my distinction, my flaw. (I was not in any way exclusive. However, I *made* myself so, by my own will, which is as good as being orphaned for real.) I should have known that the mind makes too many false distinctions. I should have known that a greater will than my own was in operation ("Grief didn't want me . . ."), that fate is so often provider of the "inspired accident." In August of 1981 I had an inspired accident, and it changed my life. I met my husband, David, was put in touch with another world, a different art. I had to re-order my perspectives. We traveled to Arrezzo and Assisi and saw the frescos. David's son traveled with us, and I saw how easy it was (if one worked hard at it) to include a child in one's life.

It was August. The significance of the month, of course, has to do with the obvious metaphor of harvest and fruition. But also of stasis, like the scales, the held-breath of near equity. In the poem, when balance occurs, the wind stops, it *holds* the moment.

When I first sat in my rented house in Tuscany I felt the energy of August at the foundations of the house. The grapes were being gathered and crushed, the olives picked and pressed, hay mown, figs, peaches, apricots and tomatoes stacked in the stalls of the fruit sellers. I had such a sense of things coming to a conclusion, a point. Because my life seemed to lack this orderly progression, I suppose, I felt August as a reminder (but gentle) of what James Wright says in a little poem "Piccolini": "But I care now for the poetry of the present moment." I wanted to be a Sufferer, but I was chosen to be happy. The present moment in the poem is the past and future coming together, the way it happens in harvest, in August.

The worksheets don't vary much from this overview; my greatest sense of confusion came at the ending, which I could "hear" in my mind, like a rising crescendo, like the cumulative effect of Latin, say the Credo in the Mass, the rhythm of the words, without actually having the words. Until I got the words ". . . fistful of fava, lopsided smile, the dirty curls, the stunted lamb, the crooked door of love, opening where we stand. . . ." etc., I had, as Frost says, the "clothesline," with nothing on it. I could *feel* the rhythm, but I kept trying to impose an idea. When I just said the words, they came like a trance language, with the authority of common expression, simple speech.

I don't know if the poem works as it should, ultimately, but it is a poem I found necessary to write, to clarify who I was and am. Someone stunted, a doubter, a cynic, who despite all this was blessed. Allowed to "enter" the world again. It seems significant to say that this August, 1983, I will give birth to my first child, my daughter, exactly two years, almost to the day, from meeting David, from holding the ticket, from seeing the way to enter the harvest.

CAROL MUSKE was born in December, 1945, grew up in Minnesota, and received her M.A. in Creative Writing from the State University of San Francisco in 1970. After traveling in Europe and Eastern Europe, she spent eleven years in New York City, where she was an editor at *Antaeus* magazine, founded and directed a writing program for prison inmates called Art Without Walls, and began a teaching career. She has now taught in several writing programs throughout the country, including Columbia University's MFA Writing Program, the University of Iowa's Writers' Workshop, the University of Virginia, and most recently, the University of California at Irvine. Her books include *Camouflage*, from the University of Pittsburgh Press, 1975, and *Skylight*, from Doubleday, 1981. She has recently completed a third book called *Wyndmere*. In 1981 she was the recipient of a John Simon Guggenheim Fellowship. She notes her most important achievement as the birth of her daughter, Anne Cameron Muske Dukes, on August 19, 1983.

HOWARD NEMEROV

*

On Being Asked for a Peace Poem

Here is Joe Blow the poet
Sitting before the console of the giant instrument
That mediates his spirit to the world.
He flexes his fingers nervously,
He ripples off a few scale passages
(Shall I compare thee to a summer's day?)
And resolutely readies himself to begin
His poem about the War in Vietnam.

This poem, he figures, is
A sacred obligation: all by himself,
Applying the immense leverage of art,
He is about to stop this senseless war.
So Homer stopped that dreadful thing at Troy
By giving the troops the Iliad to read instead;
So Wordsworth stopped the Revolution when
He felt that Robespierre had gone too far;
So Yevtushenko was invited in the *Times*
To keep the Arabs out of Israel
By smiting once again his mighty lyre.[1]
Joe smiles. He sees the Nobel Prize
Already, and the reading of his poem
Before the General Assembly, followed by
His lecture to the Security Council
About the Creative Process; probably
Some bright producer would put it on TV.
Poetry might suddenly be the in thing.

Only trouble was, he didn't have
A good first line, though he thought that for so great

---

[1] "An Open Letter to Yevgeny Yevtushenko, Poet Extraordinary of Humanity," advt., Charles Rubinstein, *New York Times*, November 3, 1966.

A theme it would be right to start with O,
Something he would not normally have done,

O

And follow on by making some demands
Of a strenuous sort upon the Muse
Polyhymnia of Sacred Song, that Lady
With the fierce gaze and implacable small smile.

1. *Occasional verse is not as common as it once was. Epitaphs tend to be just names and dates. Great men are more often honored by TV interviews, and victories by televised speeches. If the president of the United States visited Ashtabula, he'd be unlikely to be greeted by poems tacked to the walls of the buildings he passed, as Queen Elizabeth I was on her progresses about England. But the urge is still there. Books are being written on the poems that were written against the Vietnam War. And your poem gently but firmly lays bare the motive behind the whole history of occasional verse—the desire to sieze the occasion to glorify the poets. After all, a poem is a project, not an impulsive gesture. It was always a calculated risk, an invitation to fame. The fact that Joe is both the author and his readers softens Joe's blow, so that the resulting tone is both mocking and affectionate. Could you talk to us about your own idea of the poet's function, especially as it relates to the moving and shaking of events? Does this poem imply that you assign to poets a more lace-like function? Do you value Catullus above Martial, Herrick over Milton, Stevens over Whitman? Or are you trying to let just a little air out of the vatic balloon, to achieve a classical proportion?*

    You do ask difficult questions, don't you? But I shall try to answer by the numbers.

    Surely, as you seem to allow once you get past the first few sentences, occasions are of many sorts; our great men are perhaps best honored by TV interviews, as they are too visible to bear the scrutiny of poems. Marvell's Horatian Ode on the Lord Protector's Returning from Ireland would be hard to write for our statesmen (always returning from somewhere or other), who require praise praise praise, if only to balance up against their daily excoriation in the news.

    When Goethe was asked his opinion of an anthology of verses by Young Germany, he said mildly that they were pretty nice poesies, only they lacked any occasion whatever for being; in his sense, any poem is an occasional poem if it's worth having at all.

    It'd not be appropriate for me to say if the present instance had an occasion sufficient to make it worth having at all; but the occasion was thus: I was in Washington, D.C. in '70–'71 during the Troubles, visiting with friends. Indeed, the pilot of our aircraft, coming in past the White House and the protesters' fires on the Mall, exclaimed a touch righteously against them folk down there polluting the atmosphere, this while emitting, as was his and our god-given right to do, a heavy kerosene smoke that many campfires could not have equalled. O Smiling Jack, I thought, why don't you just fly the airplane and . . . and what?

Our firstborn was in town that night, not as a partisan but as part of a paramedical team come down in an ambulance from Hobart College to be some use; as I remember, the ambulance was overturned and set on fire during the evening, but he escaped harm.

The other part of the occasion was my friends' keeping us up, not sober, while they explained to me how it was my duty to write a poem against the war in Vietnam. Their seriousness may be measured by our not getting to bed till two in the morning. I probably kept saying "Poetry makes nothing happen," though it'd be more like the truth that poetry makes many things happen but never what the poet expects or intends; consider *Hamlet.*

This was during the era of "read-ins" (still with us, the latest variant of protest against nukes being called "die-ins"), and while some of the poets participating in such performances were no doubt expressing a sincerely indignant helplessness, I thought that reading one's little verses in public was an odd means of making a naughty world a nice one, and so perhaps my poem somewhat obliquely says so.

As to Joe himself, I think your epithets "mocking and affectionate" are just right, taking Joe as an amiable rather than a sinister slob and ridden by vanity more than by the darker prides; sort of like me, indeed. And it should be remarked, quietly and only once, that what poets have always and only found in disaster and suffering is an occasion; a little heartless, as in Dante, Shakespeare, Milton and the rest, but there it is: Joe Blow taking his place among these.

Now as to the poet as mover and shaker. The movie of *Henry the Fifth,* when seen in London a little before D-Day, felt mighty inspiring to many, and a boost in morale, but it inspired only to what had to be done anyhow, and its effect on that great occasion can scarcely have been among Shakespeare's intentions however far foreseeing.

Maybe the very mythological type of the successful political poem is Lillibullero. Written by a marquis and not by a member of the suffering proletariat, set to an available tune of Purcell's, it was ostensibly about the appointment of a new Lord-Lieutenant over Ireland—

> Hey, Brother Teague, hast heard t'decree?
> We're going to have a new depitee—

but owed its immense popularity to its being taken to be about William of Orange's coming from The Netherlands to be England's King, an event upon which it had no effect whatsoever. Two hundred and fifty years later, though, as the perky little tune that introduced the BBC news in the darkest times of the war, it was immensely heartening to millions; but by then, of course, it had lost its words.

Without being especially lace-like, the poet is there to give pleasure (dirty word). When we read, for example, "Avenge, O Lord, thy slaughtered saints . . ." we do it because we like the poem. It will not inspire us to protest marches against the late massacres in the Piedmont, about which it is unlikely we know more than what Milton tells us.

The widespread tendency of modern poets to write apocalyptic poems, and to preoccupy themselves with theories of history determining the instant end of civilization, has its ludicrous as well as its pretentious side. It's rather odd, at least, to write poems on this mighty theme if their predictive accuracy means that they abolish themselves because the civilization to which they are directed is no more. Even a poem about so awesome an event as the invasion of Normandy would have to be assumed to be readable and interesting to generations who would remember no more than that, as Southey's old gentleman says of Blenheim, "twas a famous victory," meaning he could no longer remember who won.

2. *Are you writing primarily for poets? The reference to Shakespeare's line as a model, a scale exercise; the ironic reference to what Homer and Wordsworth could not do and even the great New York Times could not make Yevtushenko do; the reference to Faulkner's Nobel speech; the parody of the opening invitation to the Muse, traditional to epics; the reference to the Muse's implacable small smile—the goad and support of the poet's sense of holy mission—all imply an audience "fit though few." What is your opinion on a limited or specialized audience for poetry?*

Surely if any poem might justifiably be thought of as written for poets this one might qualify for its subject alone. But in truth and as usual I wasn't writing for, much less primarily for, anyone at all; I was writing a poem, an activity strenuous enough, I have found, as to preclude any thoughts *about* what you are doing.

I missed the Faulkner reference, and will take your word that it's there. You missed one in turn: Yeats's On Being Asked for a War Poem:

> I think it better that in times like these
> A poet's mouth be silent, for in truth
> We have no gift to set a statesman right;
> He has had enough of meddling who can please
> A young girl in the indolence of her youth,
> Or an old man upon a winter's night.

Funny that for forty years I should have misremembered "pleasing" for "meddling" in line four, and funnier that I should remain so unreconstructed as to prefer it still. I suppose it became my (remote) model because it seemed there had been one modest improvement since 1914; we were being asked for peace poems (a genre hard to define) instead of poems that would keep the troops in step.

Relative to the population, the audience for poetry is small. In absolute terms, however, it is exponentially larger than the original audiences for Chaucer, Spenser, Wordsworth, Browning, and all. This is of course chiefly owing to the great generosity of our government when in the aftermath of the Second World War it opened higher(?) education first to returning veterans and then to successively greater numbers of citizens to whom it would not have been available before.

When asked how to teach poetry so as to make it popular, I recommend keeping it a secret.

3. *Unlike so many of your poems that are in the form of one-stanza epigrams or in rhyme, meter, and regular stanza forms, "On Being Asked" is in stanzas of uneven length, iambic pentameter varied by considerable free verse, and its rhymes, which happen only rarely and without regular scheme, are slant. Is this broken song a comment on Joe Blow's skill at the instrument or on the whole tradition's inadequacy at satisfying that "implacable small smile"?*

Never thought of the matter. When I write, certain attitudes to form appear almost without my being conscious of them as appropriate to the thoughts. The poem is scarcely more "free" than what would have been thought free verse in Milton's time, e.g., "Lycidas."

4. *The stanza which is simply an "O" will be read in two, and more than two, ways. How many did you anticipate?*

I must be missing at least one of the ways, and maybe more. I read it simply as "O."

5. *How did the poem start? What revisions did it go through?*

I don't have access to, or for that matter any interest in, the successive drafts. What usually happens is that I don't give up till the bones are in place; after that, I may wake up at three in the morning and enthusiastically revise the details of the diction (loading every rift with or? (not a misprint)), but rarely if ever changing the essential argument and narrative.

6. *What other questions would you have liked me to ask?*

What other questions? In all the foregoing, dear Alberta, I have talked like an English teacher, and as if I knew what I was doing or had done; and as if, even, I knew that my poem was good enough to be worth talking about. All lies, or more charitably fictions, instructors for the use of. The following contraries to these are true:

Writing verses is like your relation with your bowels: first you can't and then you can, and at last you must (that's when you reach for the paper).

The world may be arbitrary but is not capricious. Its possibilities of ordering are flexible and immense, but not infinite nor indefinite. In poetry as in making love, the things that go together should come together.

In poetry as in making love, again, the object is perpetuation to immortality, but it is not what one thinks of at the time.

The point about the value of one's work, and about one's qualification to judge of that, has been got just right, I believe, in the last part of W. S. Merwin's poem "Berryman," where the young poet wants to know and the old poet knows he can't:

> I asked how can you ever be sure
> that what you write is really
> any good at all and he said you can't
>
> you can't you can never be sure
> you die without knowing
> whether anything you wrote was any good
> if you have to be sure don't write

Another authority's testimony is the same: "We work in the dark—we do what we can—we give what we have. Our doubt is our passion and our passion is our task. The rest is the madness of art."

HOWARD NEMEROV is a 1941 graduate of Harvard University, who now teaches at Washington University, St. Louis. He has published eleven books of verse, the most recent of which are *The Collected Poems* of Howard Nemerov, 1977, and *Sentences*, 1980. He has also published five books of fiction and several collections of essays. Awards include Consultant in Poetry to the Library of Congress, the Pulitzer Prize for Poetry, and the National Book Award.

STANLEY PLUMLY

*

After Whistler

In his portrait of Carlyle, Whistler builds
from the color out: he calls it an arrangement
in gray and black and gives it a number in order
to commit us to the composition—to the foreground
first, in profile, before we go on to a wall
that seems to be neutral but is really the weather.
Carlyle is tired, beyond anger, and beautiful,
his white head tilted slightly toward the painter.
He is wearing a long coat and rests his hat on his knees.

When I was born I came out holding my breath, blue.
The cord had somehow rotted at the navel—
I must have lain alone for hours before they would let
my father's mother, the other woman there, give blood.
She still had red hair and four years to live.
The place on my arm where they put the needles in
I call my mortality scar. When I think of my grand-
mother lifting me all the way to the kitchen counter
I think of the weight by which we are doubled or more

through the lives of others. I followed her
everywhere, or tried to. I was her witness.
When I look at Whistler's portrait of Carlyle
I think of how the old survive: we make them up.
In the vegetable garden, therefore, the sun is gold
as qualified in pictures. She is kneeling in front
of the light in such a way I can separate skin from bone.
She is an outline, planting or preparing the ground.
For all I know she will never rise from this green place.

Even the painter's mother is staring into the future,
as if her son could paint her back into her body.
I was lucky. In nineteen thirty-nine they still

believed blood was family. In a room real
with walls the color of buckwheat she would sit out
the afternoon dressed up, rocking me to sleep.
It would be Sunday, slow, no one else at home.
And I would wake that way, small in her small arms,
hers, in the calendar dark, my head against her heart.

Although Whistler claims the title and the first stanza of this poem and is part of the last two stanzas, his function seems to be to distance the speaker from a personal experience in order to contemplate its universal dimensions. Carlyle means here, not the cantankerous, dyspeptic author of Sartor Resartus, but all old men, seen by other men, who are all artists in the way they compose experience (profile against weather) in order to understand and live their own lives. The nub of the poem is the speaker's composition of his own life in relation to that of his father's mother. But because of Whistler, the "mortality scar" is not only the speaker's but ours, and we are set to fill in our own outline against the "calendar dark."

1. *Some teachers of young poets today are warning their students against the pitfalls of "confessional" poetry. The facts of one's being a blue baby and of one's grandmother having red hair are not in themselves interesting. Would you have been willing to convey your theme by autobiographical details alone?*

2. *The theme of the poem seems to be stated directly in line 4, stanza 3. The poems of many beginners consist almost entirely of direct statement. Could you comment briefly on the function of direct statement versus indirection as it works in this poem?*

3. *After Whistler, your poem, is a picture you have made up. What autobiographical details did you select, omit, or alter in your portrait?*

4. *How did you "build from the color out," how did you "commit us to the composition—to the foreground / first, in profile, before we go on to a wall / that seems to be neutral but is really the weather"? Did you wish us to watch for those steps in the painting of your portrait in the poem?*

5. *When you refer to "the weight by which we are doubled or more / / through the lives of others," you imply that the doubling of weight works for both the carried and the carrier. In what way was the child following, and in what way a witness?*

6. *In such a tribute, with the sentimental associations of Whistler's mother in the background, you ran a great risk of being sentimental. What conscious strategies or lucky accidents enabled you to avoid a tone of sentimentality in the last stanza? Again, this is*

a considerable risk for beginners. Have you any advice for them on how to cope with that risk?

7. *What determined the poem's form: the long lines and stanzas, their breaks and run-overs? What determined your use of syntax, rhythm, sound repetitions?*

8. *How did the poem start? How did it change?*

Whistler's portrait of Thomas Carlyle stands out, dramatically, against the preciousness of the Pre-Raphaelites. Its sobriety and solidity communicate a power unavailable to the brocaded and sentimental gestures of painters like Holman Hunt and Ford Madox Brown and Rossetti. Carlyle, seated in a small straight-backed chair, in profile, an old man dignifying an old body, looks like statuary, like a figure sculpted from a larger form. His big black hat rests on one knee, his right hand on a cane close to the wall, the background. He seems to have his eye on an idea, projected into the space just outside the picture. Perhaps he's just bored.

He is dressed, appropriately, in black, which Whistler has taken as a clue to the color code for the rest of the painting—though black is a bit of a misnomer, as the painter seems to have created the depth of his pigment by combining color rather than denying it. To press the point, Whistler calls this portrait "Arrangement in Grey and Black, No. 2." Ironically, in calling attention to the painterly values of his work, the application and ordering of his medium, he has called attention to his real subject, which, however presbyterian, has something to do with nobility of character, longevity of purpose.

But the first time I saw Whistler's portrait of Carlyle at the Gallery in Glasgow, I was not so much moved by the quality of the art as by the content of the subject's face, a face quietly alive with fatigue and a lifetime of quarrel. Washed with age though it might be, it was neither gray nor empty. Years later, when I ran across the painting again, I realized why the face and the gray-white head had so struck me. This was a painting about age itself, about being old, about who the old are in our lives, in memory and as vessels of memory. Carlyle looked tired to me; he also looked beautifully complete, self-contained, beyond the passions and indictments of his prose.

I was born in a small Quaker community in nineteen thirty-nine, at about nine-thirty in the evening. There was a problem with the umbilical cord. I had lost, in baby terms, a lot of blood. The marvelous thing about blood, it turns out, is that it's ageless. The only available donor with my blood type, aside from my mother, was the only other relative there, my father's mother. She must have especially appealed to the doctor, coming from the other side of the bloodline. My survival had, I like to believe, the added importance of making me the first grandchild, and this, along with the vital and unique connection between the old and the newborn, was to give me center attention in the household, where, for economic reasons we were all, parents and children, under one roof.

I remember my grandmother as kind but fierce—Rae Englishe Lyn Plumly. Her remarkable red hair made her look younger than she was. I must have felt tethered to her, for as I was told as a part of family lore, after my first year I followed her everywhere, and often propped myself against her, like a pup. She did all the things grandmothers and mothers do—fed me, picked me up, carried me, taught me to talk, rocked me to sleep—all with the grace and warmth and care of long and deep experience. She'd had six children of her own. Hers was the first death in my life. I was, by then, almost five.

Age represented and respected is difficult enough, but the Whistler portrait of Carlyle, like the painter's famous version of his mother, is, you realize, also a work about mortality, in the monotones of reconciliation. *Tragic* would be too large an assignment for the scale of Whistler's work; there is, however, in Whistler's arrangements, a witness of grief, a rounding of the emotion. When I thought about what I had seen that first time, looking at Carlyle, it brought to life a memory. Grief confused with gratitude. One problem, if I were going to write in response to this experience, was the problem all paintings present to poetry. Besides being among the most familiar of contemporary poetic ploys, it's among the most abused. Too often the poem simpy repets the painting in, naturally, inferior terms. The painting, for me, had to be a point of departure. Compounding this concern was the fact that Whistler's mother, the cliché personified, had been the model for "Arrangement in Grey and Black, No. 1." Degas is right, all good paintings are platitudes.

If I used Carlyle I would have to use the painter's mother, because she was not only the antecedent, she was the paradigm. She was also, I was to find out, the solution to the story of my poem.

When I look at "After Whistler" itself I realize its reference has little to do, finally, with paintings or with grandmothers. It has to do with the way metaphor works, beyond the analogical needs of comparison and equivalency; the way it works to act as go-between between matter and meditation—to act, indeed, as an act. Blood may be thicker than water, but paint is thicker than both. We could, I suppose, make a syllogism in which blood is not only ageless but more or less immortal, if, by some alchemy, it could be changed into paint. And by extension, paint might be made more golden if changed into the best words in their best order. Art could become tautological quickly in the roundhouse of such language.

I would straighten the logic of metaphor in the direction of a line—line and storyline—and suggest that metaphor, beyond its comparative capacities, is a narrative construct. It's consecutive information brought to consequence. It's the way, of course, experience is written, it's also the way experience is plotted. Metaphor proposes an inevitability, a connection in time, a whole which is half cause, half effect, yet greater than the sum of these two parts. Whistler's portrait of Carlyle is obviously more than an arrangement in gray and black; it's a sequence of information for the mind's eye as well as the eye, a sequence, in time, in which a transformation occurs, beginning with an arrangement and ending with the content. Metaphor is that point in the sequence where technique is transcended, when the arrangement becomes a portrait. My problem, in the conception of the poem, was to extend the metaphoric logic of the painting to include my own experience. My mother had borne me, my grandmother saved me. I was hers.

Blood is probably the most obvious motif in the poem, and the color of blood in contrast to the housebound colors of buckwheat and black. Gold and green are blood shades insofar as they reflect the natural, mortal world. The body is likewise essential to the texture: though just a baby, I was given the transfusion in the usual place, the pocket of my elbow. Throughout the poem that is the place of vulnerability, the breaking place. The sequence of chairs is also basic to the "plot," occupied, in order, by Carlyle, Whistler's mother, and my grandmother. At one point, chairless, my grandmother kneels in her vegetable garden. Kneeling and rocking, sitting and thinking, this is the work of the old.

My own presence in the poem is to speak of matters witnessed, remembered, and imagined. I'm the mediator of the text, the survivor. I'm only inadvertently the protagonist. The Carlyle portrait reminded me of something I couldn't put my finger on, and when I did find the association, that connection, by default, led to other discoveries. One discovery, in the tableau of the body, is the mortality scar, a life-saving wound that becomes a birthmark. Another discovery is the emotional force of gravity: "the weight by which we are doubled or more/ / through the lives of others." Another is the power of the providential, the luck of having to use Whistler's mother. Although she has but two lines, she brings the possibilities and speculations of the poem together—as if her son could paint her back into her body.

If the tone of my poem's argument is elegiac, its thrust is, I hope, celebratory. The consistent measure of the line, like the measure and variation of the sentences, is meant to formalize an act of praise—to speak quietly and fully my thanks. In the potential richness of the moment, the story the sentences carry is pictorial, while the implications of its connected meanings are metaphoric. The pattern makes a plot. My arrangement, after Whistler, is built by juxtaposition and timing, in stanzas that wish to be patient but must nevertheless get on. The arrangement, like the single sentences creating it, becomes a sequence. As to the content of the arrangement, I meant to suggest that the emblems of the old are, of course, the emblems of the future; that the body we began in and left is the body we go back to, even when the tether is nothing more than a little blood, and love.

STANLEY PLUMLY was born in 1939 in Barnesville, Ohio, and grew up in the lumber and farming regions of Virginia and Ohio. He has taught at many universities around the country, including Columbia and Princeton and the Universities of Michigan, Washington, and Iowa. He is currently a member of the Creative Writing Faculty at the University of Houston. His *In the Outer Dark* won the Delmore Schwartz Memorial Award, and *Out-of-the-Body Travel* was nominated for a National Book Critics Circle Award in 1978. His most recent volume is *Summer Celestial.* He has held a Guggenheim Fellowship and has been the recipient of a National Endowment for the Arts Fellowship.

GIOVANNI RABONI

*

The Coldest Year of Grace

1.

The feet that we don't have—
the felt boots that have been stolen from us
bring us to the snowy marketplace one morning
to sell turtledoves and rabbits
put together the little cages from stakes
to hide the Siberian cats
in our fur, half-closed like a wound.

2.

Another life,
our friend with his heavy beard, the shy eye-glasses
raises with joy
the fish by the tail
offers it baked to us, or boiled while
he unwraps it from the newspapers
as if it were night or morning, and nothing raw
were to separate us.

3.

From the numbers, from two numbers, now, you claim to understand:
the three albino lion cubs
born yesterday in Australia,
your daughter's albino cat
found dead beneath a tree this morning, in the garden:
those of a short life, they say—this one assassinated.
You give yourself things to do, you multiply, divide
white by white, threat by misfortune.

4.

Once, on the steps, the other time
at a kitchen table
sensing you unthreading life
perhaps (I think of it now) it was
Giorgio and Marzia's death you were trying
to swallow it, spit it out, trying to psychosomatisize it,
robbing it from the future
in two far-off houses . . .

5.

It happened once, it happens to me
in dreams sometimes
from the smoke-covered Franz Joseph
to the great windows of the Südbahnhof
snowed-in city-stretch
impossible coincidence
in the twilight thick with street lamps
before the force of day breaks, forever.

6.

We have friends who take us
to the most famous beer halls,
the waiters going round and round, counting the mugs
by swans, saints, or lions—
there's no better place in Europe, no warmer, to taste
the gray of midday
from the tiny icy panes
beyond which, invisibly, the defenestration
　　　　　　　　　　　　of the apostles goes on.

7.

I love to travel
O how I love to travel
and in the plain, unusual things that can happen
each evening in a different inn
I love to imagine
the small hairy presence

of our household gods
their jumps up against the light, oopsadaisy—
of the cathodic theatre.

8.

We leave the house
at an unlikely hour
to study the ground close-up
everything's in order or nearly so
it's almost impossible to understand
where so much of an uproar comes from
if in this violet light
the pigeons moan only above, on the cornices.

9.

Never seen so much rain in spring.
Above a thousand meters it's snowing, freezing.
But it's not that, I know,
as soon as you come in dripping, you murmur
we mustn't trust the phone, burn
or throw away the flyers, those little flying things,
in the toilet, the letters, the witches' addresses . . .
My friends, I've already written this poem.

10.

This is the road, I haven't
taken the wrong road this time—wavy, rolling
behind the huge fence. Foreigners
are granted a slow quarantine
between waking and sleeping
between sleep and death before
a limpid eye opens, thinking of
the bicycle and the dogs of Lev Nikolaevič.

11.

Looking at a little box
9 × 21 cm.

with a smooth, sliding cover
I feel young and tired
like my father
he walks around Milan too
three, four months after the heart attack, he planned
on taking some amusement, some distraction.

12.

He or others say you have
to study and while studying, from the top,
try to understand when we betrayed . . .
with whom we betrayed . . . ourselves
and which link held
that wasn't supposed to
and which link we didn't understand
could not have held.

13.

What a funny story, I thought
I was in the middle of the bubble, in the heart,
of the map of the ice
but I wasn't, someone was limping in the vestibule
of the old-new synagogue
someone I couldn't make out
murmuring in a tongue I didn't know
In Milan, the other night, nearly a meter of snow.

14.

The tenderness of the eggshell
softly emptied by your mouth
decorated with far-off landscapes
we're many who think there's no
way to wrap it the way we ought to
so fragile an object, so brief, and so
there's little hope
for the salvation of the eggshell.

Translated by Stuart Friebert and Vinio Rossi

1. *Does the poem's title, "The Coldest Year of Grace," announce its theme? Do all the parts of the poem refer to the same year? Is it literally cold or cold in metaphorical ways also? Does Grace refer to Christian Grace? Is it used ironically?*

The theme that binds together and unifies the fourteen poems, despite the variety of the individual subjects, is that of frost, to be understood either in the concrete sense (winter, the snow, ice and, naturally, their color, white) or in a metaphoric sense: the weakening of life, the impoverishment of forms, the clouding up of meanings, the hardening of relations, etc. In this last sense, cold/frost is also, of course, a "political metaphor"; and the central theme can also be described as an intermittent voyage (with which are mixed immobility and dreams) through a Europe threatened with devastation by frost (metaphoric) and death (real). The year to which the title refers is not a unique year; it's a symbolic one, the coldest that you can imagine, one you'd hope would never come (but which perhaps, instead, has already arrived). The phrase "year of grace" comes from archaic Italian and refers to the term *a quo* of the redemption; it is then equivalent to the Latin expressions "anno Domini" or "post Christum natum." In the title I mean it to have at the same time an ironic sense (the redemption is far off and grace impossible or lost) and the sense of a paradoxical, irreducible hope.

2. *At times it is difficult to distinguish the poem's literal images from the metaphorical ones (or perhaps they are both): for instance, the little flying things in the toilet (9). Is the uproar (8) a political allusion? Is "wrong road" (10) literal or metaphorical or both? Is "we" (12) the speaker and the father, or perhaps their society or mankind as a whole? Does the eggshell (14) stand for more than an eggshell?*

In general what I've tried to do in this sequence of poems is precisely to give a strong metaphoric tension to a series of small episodes and real details. Many are episodes of travel in Eastern European countries, that is to say, in one of those places which are delegates of ice. Specifically alluding to Moscow are poems 1, 2, 10; poems 6 and 13 allude to Prague; in poem number 5, I allude to two railroad stations in Vienna, from which depart, respectively, trains for the East and for the South. My answer to this question then is fully affirmative: all the images and all the situations have, at the same time, a literal meaning that's recoverable and a metaphoric meaning that is linked or linkable to the general theme of the sequence. As far as the eggshell of the last poem is concerned, for example, it will be useful to know that to empty and decorate eggshells is an Easter tradition in several countries, among which is Bohemia (I bought some in Prague, which broke on the trip home); but, naturally, the fragility of which we speak is not only the fragility of eggshells, but the fragility of all that which ought to be saved and which the hardness and cold of history menace.

3. *The poem's cluster of parts seems to be connected thematically and emotionally rather than in a narrative or other logical fashion. If so, were the parts written at separate times in a different order? What determined their present sequence?*

The fourteen poems were written in a rather brief period and with the intention and the feeling that they would belong together in a whole. Yet while I was writing them, I didn't yet know how many they would be nor in what order I would finally put them. It was a little like writing in a diary with detached looseleaf pages. The order in which I put the individual pages, then, is the order which seemed to me to add the greatest clarity to the whole. To give only one example, the last poem was the first one written: in a certain sense, everything was born from that, from that idea of fragility and whiteness seen as precious and threatened; and it's precisely for this reason that it seemed to me right to place it in conclusion to the whole.

4. *What specific reference might need explaining to a non-Italian reader? The dogs of Lev Nikolaevič (10), for instance, or the process of emptying an eggshell in order to paint it (14), or the significance of Siberian cats (1)?*

I think that the answer, or answers, to this question are already implicit in the preceding answers. In any case: Lev Nikolaevič is none other than the great Russian writer Tolstoy, and the poem recalls a visit to his old house in Moscow, where are kept, among other things, his bicycles and pictures of his dogs; the famous eggshells are emptied by sucking out the contents through a tiny little hole, and then painted; Siberian cats are a breed that's quite widespread in Russia (I've seen an old lady selling them in an open market, in the snow, and I was struck by the gesture with which she protected them from the cold, hiding them in her fur coat).

5. *In other words, these and the many other questions that come to mind are really one: what would American readers, in order to enable them to perceive this poem most fully, need to know—about you, the geography and social setting you live in, the occasions and emotions that initiated the poem, the particular reader you wished to affect and how you wished to affect him, the theory that determined the poem's structure and form, the process of composing and editing by which it grew, and the ways, if any, by which the poem has been affected by this and other translations?*

Many other examples could be cited, but they'd all be more or less of the same type. If there is a theory that determines the structure of the text I find it difficult to state: maybe, what comes closest to a theory is all I've just said about diaries—a diary in which rememberances, dreams and thoughts are recorded as facts and intertwined; a diary which can be of fourteen days or fourteen months or years. I might add one last thing: all the poems have eight verses; it's a sort of homage to the most typical form in western narrative poetry, the octave, a homage which also suggests how the only possible narrative today is no longer a story of great epic truths, but a story of truths that are banal, microscopic, and almost elusive.

GIOVANNI RABONI was born in Milan, Italy in 1932. He studied in Milan, where he received a degree in jurisprudence. He worked in industry before devoting himself entirely to literature. At present, he is a consultant in a large Milanese publishing house (Mondadori) and literary critic for a Roman daily. From among his books of poetry, the most significant are *Le case della Vetra* (Mondadori, 1966), *Cadenza d'inganno* (Mondadori, 1975), and *Nel grave sogno* (Mondadori, 1982). He has also published a collection of prose narratives and one of critical pieces. He has translated several French authors, including Flaubert, Baudelaire, and Apollinaire; and is currently working on a complete translation of Proust's *À la recherche du temps perdu*.

DAVID ST. JOHN

*

Elegy

If there is any dwelling place
for the spirits of the just;
if, as the wise believe, noble souls
do not perish with the body,
rest thou in peace . . .

TACITUS

Who keeps the owl's breath? Whose eyes desire?
Why do the stars rhyme? Where does
The flush cargo sail? Why does the daybook close?

So sleep and do not sleep.

The opague stroke lost across the mirror,
The clamp turned.
The polished nails begin the curl into your palms.
The opal hammock of rain falls out of its cloud.

I name you, *Gloat-of-*
The-stalks, drowse-my-embers, old-lily-bum.
No matter how well a man sucks praise in the end
He sucks earth. Go ahead, step
Out into that promised, rasp gratitude of night.

Seeds and nerves. Seeds

And nerves. I'll be waiting for you, in some
Obscure and clarifying light:
I will say, Look, there is a ghost ice on the land.

If the page of marble bleeds in the yellow grass,
If the moon-charts glow useless and cold,
If the grains of the lamp outlast you, as they must—
As the tide of black gloss, the marls, and nectar rise

I will understand.

Here are my gifts: *smudges of bud,*
A *blame of lime.* Everything you remember crowds
Away. Stubble memory,
The wallpaper peeling its leaves. Fog. Fog
In the attic; this pod of black milk. Anymore,

Only a road like August approaches.

Sometimes the drawers of the earth close;
Sometimes our stories keep on and on. So listen—

Leave no address. Fold your clothes into a little
Island. Kiss the hinges goodbye. Sand the fire. Bitch
About *time.* Hymn away this reliquary fever.

How the sun stands crossing itself in the cut glass.

How the jonquils and bare orchards fill each morning
In mist. The branches in the distance stiffen,
Again. The city of stars pales.
In my fires the cinders rise like black angels;
The trunks of the olives twist once towards the world.

Once. I will walk out into the day.

1. *The poem "Elegy" seems to function as an expansion of its epigraph, a way of filling out and qualifying the kind of dwelling place and peace that Tacitus hopes the nobler souls might enjoy in an afterlife. The first stanza asks the questions that there is no longer any point in asking once one is out of the body. The italicized paradox, "So sleep and do not sleep" asks that we drop these questions and look for others. No matter how adroitly a man has named or otherwise earned praise, he must step out at the end into an entirely different context, a "rasp gratitude of night." Both the speaker. and his hearer will stand in an "obscure and clarifying light," which both destroys what they perceived before and corrects it to a new understanding. Therefore, whatever we leave can be only a* smudge *or a* blame—a fog. *The stories that persist about us or by us cannot be true; we should not try to preserve such inaccuracies. This seems to be the poem's literal meaning, but the way in which it is spoken conveys such love and tenderness for the mistakes that comprise that fog, such pride in the seeds and nerves, such delight in the chiming sounds of words in "smudges of bud" and "blame of lime," in the angels that rise from the cinders and the olive's twist toward the world and the*

sun's "crossing itself in the cut glass," that the errors of human hope and imagination seem infinitely more like paradise than any amount of eternal clarity. When the last line emphasizes that this clarity will come only once, does it imply a typically Roman dread of the afterlife as a pale echo of the real thing? Can it also be read as saying that the clarifying light is here and now? Is the poem itself an act of hymning "away this reliquary fever"?

Perhaps I should say first that the epigraph from Tacitus is a passage which begins the final section of *The Agricola,* Tacitus's biography/eulogy for his father-in-law, the former governor of Roman Britain, Agricola. Though I can understand that it appears the poem "Elegy" functions as an expansion of the epigraph, to the best of my memory the epigraph was found for the poem (its source was suggested by Norman Dubie, who said, "Look in Tacitus ") some time after the poem's initial drafting.

Rather than its "literal meaning," I'd prefer to call what you offer above "a solid reading" of the poem; certainly, it is a reading which provides a good point of departure for a discussion of the poem and its ambitions. The conclusion of "Elegy" is not meant to imply a typically Roman dread of the afterlife, but to place the speaker most definitely on the earthly world and in its light, however ordinary and simple that light may be. The poem wants to affirm the importance of the world; after all, the speaker must continue to reside there a while longer. However, let me add that I've always felt there is something quite accusatory in the tone of "Elegy." Death is often seen as a betrayal, and it's certainly seen that way, at least in part, here in this poem. In answer to another of the questions above, I feel that the daylight in which the poem concludes is a light which has been clarified, in the way we speak of butter being clarified, by the mourning of the poem and by the poem's anger. It is a light more of resolution meaning "resolute" than of resolution meaning "resolved." In that regard, the poem itself is definitely an act of, or an attempt at, "hymning away" the "reliquary fever" of residual anger, and emptiness and terror, congruent to the mourning. The poem concludes as its mourning becomes the literal morning, the day ("The city of stars pales."). This is, perhaps, something too obvious to need stating.

2. Is the you addressed in the poem a particular person, any reader, the author himself?

To the speaker of "Elegy," the *you* is a particular person. To the poet, the *you* is far more general, even self-inclusive.

3. What determined the use of italics in the poem (other than in the epigraph)?

The use of italics was meant to emphasize and echo the processes of naming and unnaming at work in the poem, as well as to provide a mild indication of the doubleness of the poem's address—by this, I mean simply that the poem is both elegy and accusation.

4. *More than most poets you seem to concentrate on the phrase, the exactly right combination of sense, sound, and rhythm to create a surprisingly accurate juxtaposition of words and sensations not usually used together. Could you comment on how the names in lines 9 and 10 came about? The combination of "rasp" and "gratitude," the "tide of black gloss, the marls and nectar," "smudges of bud," "blame of lime," "kiss the hinges," "sun crossing itself in cut glass?" Others?*

The passage, *"Gloat-of-/The-stalks, drowse-my-embers, old lily bum"* was meant to be an act of naming consistent with what Kenneth Burke calls, in reference to Roethke, a "vegetal madness." There seems to me to be an element of madness in all mourning, and in this particular poem the vegetal, the natural, to which all bodies must return, is an important condition of being. Concerning the other pieces of language and phrases mentioned in this question, let me just say that "Elegy" was written at a time when I'd become dissatisfied with the complacency of the language of my own poems, as well as in those poems I saw around me. I wanted the language in "Elegy" to be highly activated, even provocative. All of the phrases mentioned above seem to me, quite obviously, to have their basis in sound couplings, though my hope was that the rhythms of each particular line (into which these sound clusters had been welded) would give them a bit of extra punch. For me, they are, these mirrorings and twistings of sound against rhythm, the purpose of the poem, its real point. I hope that doesn't sound too perverse. Perhaps I should say they are consistent with the point of the poem, whatever that "point" may be.

5. *What determined your stanza divisions and line breaks?*

As always, they were dictated by my own stubborn sense of what constitutes necessity and grace in a line or a stanza. Also, my ideas of phrasing were in this case influenced a bit by what I saw as the formality of an "elegy" as such; though surely this is an elegy of somewhat corrupted formality.

6. *How did the poem start? What revisions did it go through, in what order, over what period? If you have kept the worksheets, may I see a copy?*

The poem began as an attempt to push myself—out of the confines of my more "available" and literal-minded poems—and to push my ideas of language as much as I possibly could. The poem went through a few dozen revisions; I have no idea how many exactly, perhaps thirty to fifty. This is not said in triumph; I just happen to be an endless revisionist. During the spring of 1977, I read a version of "Elegy" at Oberlin College, where I was then teaching. The version I read was more than twice as long as the final version. Hearing the poem aloud, as I read it to a discerning and sophisticated audience, I was able to note to myself, while reading, those passages and moments which seemed less successful, and also those which seemed to be the core of the poem. Within three weeks of that reading, I had what is now the final version of "Elegy." As far as I know, all copies of the early versions of the poem have been, at my request, destroyed.

7. What other questions would you have liked me to ask?

I would have liked you to ask, "Do you really expect most readers to *understand* a poem like 'Elegy'?" I would have answered, "Yes, if only in the most visceral sense of *understand*."

DAVID ST. JOHN was born in 1949 in California. He is author of *Hush* (1976), *The Olive Grove* (1980), and *The Shore* (1980). He has received grants from the National Endowment for te Arts, the Ingram Merrill Foundation, and the John Simon Guggenheim Memorial Foundation. Mr. St. John teaches in The Writing Seminars of The Johns Hopkins University.

DENNIS SCHMITZ

*

Making Chicago

We cannot take a single step toward heaven. It is not in our power to travel in a vertical direction. If however we look heavenward for a long time, God comes and takes us up. He raises us easily.

SIMONE WEIL

let it end here where the blueprint
shows a doorway,
where it shows all of Chicago
reduced to a hundred prestressed floors,
fifty miles of conduit & ductwork

the nerve-impulse climbs to know God.
every floor we go up is one more down
for the flashy suicide, *for blessèd man who
by thought might lift himself*

to angel. how slowly we become only men!
I lift the torch away, push up the opaque
welder's lens to listen for the thud
& grind as they pour aggregate,

extrapolating the scarred forms resisting
all that weight & think
the years I gave away to reflexive anger,

to bad jobs, do not count
for the steps the suicide
divides & subdivides in order not to reach

the roof's edge. I count the family years
I didn't grow older with the stunted
locust trees in Columbus Park,
the ragweed an indifferent ground crew

couldn't kill, no matter the poison.
now I want to take up death more often

& taste it a little—
by this change I know I am not what I was:
the voice is the voice of Jacob
but the hands are the hands of Esau—
god & antigod mold what I say,

make me sweat inside the welding gloves,
make what I thought true turn heavy.
but there must be names
in its many names the concrete can't take.
what future race in the ruins
will trace out our shape from the bent

template of the soul,
find its orbit in the clouded atmosphere
of the alloy walls we used as a likeness

for the sky? the workmen stagger
under the weight of the window's nuptial
sheet—in its white reflected clouds
the sun leaves a virgin spot

of joy.

When Dennis Schmitz mailed me this essay, he cautioned, "Exegesis sanctifies a text, makes it a museum piece, takes it out of the realm of continuing creation. The exegete develops a halo at the expense of the author—if the exegete and the author are the same person the irony is doubled." Yet a reader needs to risk that irony. If a poem becomes momentarily less liquid under exegesis, its more active readers become more so: they enter into dialog with the author, are pressed to notice, recombine, disagree. They read it again and harder and compare and come to decisions of their own. My questions poked at this poem's allegory. I was reminded of the Great Chain of Being and the Tower of Babel and Plato's Cave; I began to suspect allegory in such literal details as aggregate, alloy, and welding gloves; I was on the way to a theology of suicide. Readers like me need exegesis to tell us whether we are sober or need to sober up.

My reading of the poem here is as a commentator, though I'm sure that I intended most of the effects of the poem as I was writing it (it was written over the period of a year, a long time for me). Correlation of means and meaning during the actual process of composition seems instantaneous.

In the late fifties, early sixties, I did some Chicago construction work of the lift-and-carry sort. The little welding I did was the easy cutting or stick-it-back-together. I've spoken about that in other poems. In those poems and in "Making Chicago," the city is a state of being, a communal limbo.

In *String*, from which "Making Chicago" is taken, I wanted poems which would put down the terms of the world, fix a first place by tactile sense (the images of the hand, and the correspondent tongue, occur all through the book)—sift dirt, close the hand around tools or suitable foods, to stroke one's child—to touch things, and then to touch someone else in order to gradually extend to a world permitted by detailed faith in sensibility.

The narrator takes the welder's gloves from his hands as he thinks of the unifying principles of his life and his present task—to put all of Chicago into one building, a Babel of technology beyond the possibilities of hand or tongue. The self-transcendence, that communal effort a Chicago represents, is delusion. "The collective is the object of all idolatry, this it is which chains us to the earth" (Weil, *Gravity and Grace*).

Simone Weil was a hero of the intellect to my college generation brought up on French philosophy, a discomforting figure like Kierkegaard's Knight of Faith. This poem uses several notions and terms of Weil as analogical sources.

The epigraph is from *Waiting for God*, in which Weil says that God searches for man, not man for God (if the word *God* is not a useful one for you, substitute your favorite term for the Principle of the Universe, though it will not have the terror-of-the-sacred Weil intends). The passage to higher being, to the heavenly city, is not by sublimation, nor is the divine to be reduced or lowered. "The central law of this world, from which God has withdrawn by his very act of creation, is the law of gravity, which is to be found analogically in every stage of existence. Gravity is the force which above all others draws us from God" (*Gravity and Grace*). This force is whatever comfort or systematic intellectual compensation will impede God's search for man. Man "falls upward" when he is free of self-manufactured delusions, the make-shifts which help us survive nothingness. Faith is a kind of peripheral vision, an *attention*, not concentration, in the waiting which is a kind of *zazen*.

I have appropriated some of Weil's figurations to show the contradictory directions to which the spirit tends—man's desire to frustrate his desires, the will to suicide. The poem is built on pairs of opposites; the "directions," to simplify, are *up* and *down*.

Jacob and Esau are the warring selves each of us contains, the "blessèd man" and the "flashy suicide," though I don't want to carry that notion into cliché. Esau's rights as first-born (the motif of the second son has been important to me since my first book) are usurped by Jacob-in-disguise—he receives the father's *blessing* but flees at the guilt for the "hairy" self Esau represents. At what point is Jacob aware of his duality and the danger in the belief in himself as Esau?

"Everything we want contradicts the conditions or the consequences attached to it, every affirmation we put forward involves a contradictory affirmation, all our feelings are mixed up with their opposites" (*Gravity and Grace*). Therefore, the suicide also wishes to save himself, to divide and subdivide the steps to the roof's edge by using whatever ritual method will disassociate the act from his responsibility for it—in this case, counting the steps in the actual distance by using a scale derived from what is real or valid in his life. He will never jump—the logic is the logic of one of Zeno's paradoxes—though he will continue to tease himself.

Tennessee Williams, when asked in an interview how old he was, replied that in order to arrive at the sum of his true age, he had to discount the years he spent doing jobs he didn't want to do, and he had to discount other bad experiences—he turned out to be quite young. The narrator in the poem counts his experiences in the same way.

The ritual counting is also important in the motif of the "flashy suicide" who wants to jump from the highest building (the "Chicago"); every storey added by the self who helps in the constructing is one more storey for the self who will jump. The suicide will go in the direction opposite to that of the one who by *"thought might lift himself/ / to angel."*

The last dozen lines of the poem were taken from an early published version of my poem "Chicago: Near-West Side Renewal" (*Field*, No. 3, Fall, 1970). That section, the third and fourth stanzas, and the Weil quotation were reference points in the evolution of the poem. I discovered the poem as I went along.

A poem should be fluid and dynamic—stanza and line breaks are ways of controlling the pace of the delivery, of controlling the information (this new piece joined to that old). The movement should be rapid, emphatic or muted, as the meaning directs. I used run-on stanzas to cancel the static effects of paragraphing the development of the argument, to work against the anticipated, to "phrase" in a musical sense. If I use alliterative elements to balance a line, I will use another device to cancel that effect. Stanzas and the apparent syntactic integrity of the individual lines give static base to the fluid development of the poem.

The double meanings of words, another kind of counterpoint, are often accentuated by line-breaks, "opaque" in stanza 3, for example. "Scarred forms" (stanza 3) is meant to have a Platonic echo. But, ironically, the wood for forms in pouring concrete is used in job after job by contractors; it is cut and reassembled to suit the needs of a particular job. The "concrete" (in two senses) will assume what form it is given (stanza 7). "Nuptial" and "virgin" in stanza 9 are meant to work in tandem. The "weight" (stanza 9) of meaning which makes the workmen stagger echoes "weight" in stanza 4—the resolution in "joy" counters the despair in the meditation on suicide by the speaker (stanza 4).

In stanza 9 the workmen stagger under the weight of the unplaced window (the window is another version of the doorway, a way out and up or down, in stanza 1) in which the natural world is reflected. The publication of the nuptial sheet (to indicate that a marriage had been consummated, that the new wife had been a virgin) was a practice hundreds of years ago. The point of virginity in the ritual was to be unsullied, that the characters in the ritual were servants of it. Incidentally, of course, in a male-dominated society before the discovery of penicillin, female virginity was important to males.

I wanted the poem to read as allegory, to have extended metaphors. But I also wanted the reader to feel that, if an actual building were not being constructed, the mechanics of the process was tangible.

DENNIS SCHMITZ was born in 1937, Dubuque, Iowa, where he grew up. He studied at Loras College and the University of Chicago. He currently works at California State University, Sacramento. His books are *We Weep for Our Strangeness* (Follett/Big Table, 1969), *Double Exposures* (Triskelion, 1972), *Goodwill, Inc* (Ecco, 1976), and *String* (Ecco, 1980).

JON SILKIN

*

The Child

Something that can be heard
Is a grasping of soft fingers
Behind that door.
Oh come in, please come in
And be seated.

It was hard to be sure,
Because for some time a creature
Had bitten at the wood.
But this was something else; a pure noise
Humanly shaped

That gently insists on
Being present. I am sure you are.
Look: the pots over the fire
On a shelf, just put;
So, and no other way,

Are as you have seen them; and you,
Being visible, make them no different.
No man nor thing shall take
Your place from you; so little,
You would think, to ask for.

I have not denied: you know that.
Do you? Do you see
How you are guttered
At a breath, a flicker from me?
Burn more then.

Move this way with me,
Over the stone. Here are
Your father's utensils on
The kitchen wall; cling
As I lead you.

It seems you have come without speech,
And flesh. If it be love
That moves with smallness through
These rooms, speak to me,
As you move.

You have not come with
Me, but burn on the stone.

If I could pick you up
If I could lift you;
Can a thing be weightless?
I have seen, when I did lift you

How your flesh was casually
Pressed in. You have come
Without bone, or blood.
Is that to be preferred?
A flesh without

Sinew, a bone that has
No hardness, and will not snap.
Hair with no spring; without
Juices, touching, or speech.
What are you?

Or rather, show me, since
You cannot speak, that you are real;
A proper effusion of air,
Not that I doubt, blown by a breath
Into my child;

As if you might grow on that vapour
To thought, or natural movement
That expresses, 'I know where I am.'
Yet that you are here,
I feel.

Though you are different.
The brain being touched lightly,
It was gone. Yet since you live,
As if you were not born,
Strangeness of strangeness, speak.

Or rather, touch my breath
With your breath, steadily
And breathe yourself into me.

The soft huge pulsing comes
And passes through my flesh
Out of my hearing.

1. *The poem opens with a dramatic scene—a voice at the door "humanly shaped // That gently insists on/ Being present." The speaker reassures himself from time to time ("It was hard to be sure," "I am sure you are," "I have not denied; you know that"), but he follows with doubt ("Do you?"). The very act of speaking makes the child's presence gutter like a candle. It will not cling to him and be led through the rooms. He cannot pick it up, as he once did, for now it has no flesh and bone. He feels estranged ("What are you?"). He pleads ("Show me . . . that you are real"), reassures himself again ("Not that I doubt"), but the child dissolves to a "soft huge pulsing." Is the poem a wish embodied in a waking or sleeping dream, a metaphysical experience, a structure invented by the author to give a wish "a local habitation and a name?" A mixture of these? None of these?*

   The poem is drawn neither from a dream during sleep nor from a waking dream. It is not a metaphysical poem—one that denies a palpable external reality so as to engender an abstraction or idea. Nor is it one which seeks to give a wish 'a local habitation and a name.' It is concerned with Adam's paying his father not one but one of several visits, and about the father's finally not wanting him to do so. In that sense, the poem was written to achieve a gentle exorcism.

2. *Does it refer to the same child as the subject of "Death of a Son," in* The Peaceable Kingdom?

I have written several poems about Adam. "Death of a Son," "For a Child, on his being pronounced mentally defective by a committee of the LCC," this poem—"The Child," "Burying," and, from *The People*, all of section III called "Testing."

3. *Is the child's presence another and more acceptable form of the presence that for some time had been biting the wood?*

No, the creature that had "bitten at the wood" is not the same creature as the child. I say *"But this was something else"* (italics of this commentary), implying, I think, a distinction between that biting noise and this "pure" one— the phrasing that involves the words "something else" refers to a similar phrase in "Death of a Son." But of course although my son is "Humanly shaped," he is also a creature, and in that sense the two different noises share the condition of mortality. Both, in different ways, "gnaw" at me.

4. *Though rooted in a single individual experience, the poem implies a good deal about the power of human need to create what it needs. To what extent are you willing to have readers generalize from it in this way?*

It is, as you suggest, probable that much of our creation is made out of need. But conscious choice is also involved, and I intended to convey a sense of Adam's ghostly presence visiting me (yet again) and of my attempting, through the poem, to exorcise him. I believe that a substantial part of the poem's value consists in the reader's understanding the poem to be expressing a real experience and not a symbolic or metaphysical one, or yet a generalized extrapolation from experience intended to set up some elegiac equalizer as a form of consolation.

5. *What led you to choose the form of the dramatic monologue?*

The poem is not intended as a dramatic monologue. I do not speak any other person's voice, or through another's mask, but speak rather with my own voice as the father that I then was. I am not speaking directly to some reader, or number of readers, but to Adam much of the time, and to myself, I suppose, when I'm not directly addressing him.

6. *What determined your choice of sentence structure and diction? Are they more complex and adult than would usually be used to speak to a small child?*

You ask me what determined my choice of sentence structure and diction; do I use diction? Isn't it, rather, speech that I use in this poem?

No, you are right; the poem does not use the language of a child or the speech of an adult talking to a child. But I was not in any sense trying to compose that kind of naturalistic verse. I felt that although Adam might not understand what I was saying, exactly, he would get the gist of it. So would I.

7. *What determined your line and stanza breaks? Your choice of rhythm and sound repetitions?*

You ask how I arrived at the line length and stanza out of which the poem is made. I had been working for three years (and would continue to do so) on a three pulse line as that most appropriate to recreating English speech and its rhythms. On the one hand I had a quite formal and flexible line which was, however, finite; and at the same time the line's flexible pace built up a longer flight of stanza or paragraph which contained both movement and stillness. Each stanza pauses, and each completes its rectangle of meaning, even when meaning and syntax cross the stanza break—like a severe enjambment.

8. *How did the poem start? How many revisions did it undergo?*

The poem got started because, six years later, I could not suffer Adam's presence any more. There are many drafts of the poem—about twenty I believe—and the poem only started to shape after I had discarded from the earlier versions something like the first eight stanzas. What one reads thus starts from what was originally the "middle" of the poem. I cannot honestly remember how long the poem took to write, but I would guess at about two months.

JON SILKIN, born in London in 1930, was educated at Wycliffe and Dulwich Colleges, was conscripted into the army and then spent six years as a manual laborer. He started *Stand* in 1952—a literary quarterly—which he still coedits. He has been the editor of *Penguin Book of First World War Poetry* (1979) and author of *Out of Battle,* a critical study of WWI poetry (Oxford University Press, 1972). He is the author of seven collections of verse, the two most recent being *Selected Poems* (Routledge and Kegan Paul, 1980) and *The Psalms With Their Spoils* (Routledge and Kegan Paul, 1980). His collection *Nature With Man* (Chatto, 1965) was awarded the Faber Memorial Prize in 1966. He has read and lectured widely in the United Kingdom and America.

CHARLES SIMIC

*

Classic Ballroom Dances

Grandmothers who wring the necks
Of chickens; old nuns
With names like Theresa, Marianne,
Who pull schoolboys by the ear;

The intricate steps of pickpockets
Working the crowd of the curious
At the scene of an accident; the slow shuffle
Of the evangelist with a sandwich-board;

The hesitation of the early morning customer
Peeking through the window-grille
Of a pawnshop; the weave of a little kid
Who is walking to school with eyes closed;

And the ancient lovers, cheek to cheek,
On the dancefloor of the Union Hall,
Where they also hold charity raffles
On rainy Monday nights of an eternal November.

1. *I have long been intrigued by the "list" poem. From the "Begats" and the "Catalogue of Ships" to contemporary poems like Robert Francis' "Silent Poem" and Allen Ginsberg's "Howl," it seems the most direct way to involve readers without preaching to them, the way to say "look" and make the reader infer meaning from what he himself sees. The result is weight or irony or a new perception more startling than either. In "Classic Ballroom Dances" the dancers are the old, the crooked, the timid, the tardy. The question raised by this list is, what do we really mean by dance? And the answer the sequence suggests to me is that to dance is to achieve a delicate balance, to cope—with age, poverty, indolence, even fear of death. Is this the direction in which you were nudging me? What other or different inferences did you hope or expect I*

185

would make? Did you mean to invite new inferences that you yourself had not yet made?

2. *Did you consciously have in mind a reply to Yeats' "Among School Children," which implies that to dance is the natural movement of physical and psychological wholeness? Your classic ballroom dances seem to be either compensations for lack of wholeness or wholeness of a different order. Did you wish us to make this or any other literary associations?*

3. *Why do you feel that the last phrase, "of an eternal November," is necessary?*

4. *In composing the poem, did you start with the title or the list? Why did you choose the present order of the list? At what stage did you choose the four-line stanza as your form? What changes did the poem go through from start to finish? In what order? Over what length of time?*

5. *If you have kept the worksheets, could I see a copy?*

I like the crowded canvases of primitive painters. I understand that need to put everything in: humans, domestic animals, beasts of the forest, angels, machines. Everything in the world is going on at the same time and deserves to be included. It's a portrait of an eternal present done with an awkward, "childlike" hand unaware of the conventions of pictorial representation. The "list" poem partakes of the same spirit. It's the poetic equivalent of quilt making. One cuts the patches into signs and symbols of one's own cosmology, then one covers oneself with it on a cold winter night.

I too wanted a crowd in my poem. I got the idea for it while standing on a street corner in New York City and watching people go by. Then I thought of an old girlfriend, how I spent hours waiting for her on street corners, cursing and watching people. Once we went to some sort of dance organized by her parents' labor union. A late autumn evening cold and rainy. That was twenty-five years before the poem. The old people danced the foxtrot, the tango, even the waltz.

Ballroom dances put me in a melancholy mood. I was a small child in their heyday. I still remember the grownups in Yugoslavia executing very properly these exotic and faintly lascivious dances. To dance well, one was told, you have to have a natural flair, of course. But, you also have to know the steps. I remember how they used to roll up the rug and outline steps with chalk on the floor. I don't know when it first occurred to me that so many things we do are like ballroom dances. The world is a ballroom full of mirrors and we are the inspired or awkward dancers.

I didn't have that meaning and its many extensions in mind while I was writing the poem. The particular images and their juxtapositions interested me much more. The meaning of images depends on the company they are in. Meaning is a function of proximity. Like dancing it depends on what partner you have. An archangel is much more interesting in company of a pig than a saint in prayer. I mean, it makes a world of difference that those "ancient lovers" come at the end of the poem. To change the order in which the images appear is to have an entirely different poem.

Which is why the poem took a long time to write. In fact, one does not *write* these poems. One puts them together bit by bit. The problem in every poem is to figure out how to make less suggest more. Obviously, I had many more images but they proved unnecessary. I broke the poem down into stanzas to slow down the reading and thus give each detail more gravity. I also wanted a slightly sentimental ending. After all, most of those melodies were unashamedly romantic, if not just plain corny. Still, how we loved them. They made us feel elegant and tragic.

It's true as you say in your letter: "*to dance* is to achieve a delicate balance, to cope—with age, poverty, indolence, even fear of death." Nevertheless, to dance in the usual way is to perform a gratuitous act. So, the crucial question: How can wringing a neck of a chicken or picking a pocket be seen in the same light? This is what I want the reader to figure out in the poem, for I make the claim that they are one and the same.

Like that virtuoso in Robert Francis' poem "Apple Peeler" who, as he peels the apple in one unbroken spiral, remembers the earth turning just as his apple turns, these *dancers* are making their intricate steps before the great dancing master, Time.

I tried to reply to all your questions, except where I didn't really know or remember. For example, I hardly ever keep drafts, so I'm never in a position to reconstruct exactly every nuance of change. I have never had any interest in retaining such evidence. I like a clean desk every morning. Also, it seems to me that I remember what truly matters.

CHARLES SIMIC, who teaches at the University of New Hampshire, was born in Yugoslavia in 1938. Educated at New York University, he worked at various jobs before turning to teaching in 1970. In addition to several books of translation, he has published seven collections of poetry: *What the Grass Says* (1967), *Somewhere Among Us a Stone is Taking Notes* (1969), *Dismantling the Silence* (1971), *Return to a Place Lit by a Glass of Milk* (1974), *Charon's Cosmology* (1979), *Classic Ballroom Dances* (1980), and *White*, a long poem published in 1972. For these he has received the Edgar Allan Poe Award, a Guggenheim Fellowship, and a National Endowment for the Arts grant.

LOUIS SIMPSON

*

Chocolates

Once some people were visiting Chekhov.
While they made remarks about his genius
the Master fidgeted. Finally
he said, "Do you like chocolates?"

They were astonished, and silent.
He repeated the question,
whereupon one lady plucked up her courage
and murmured shyly, "Yes."

"Tell me," he said, leaning forward,
light glinting from his spectacles,
"what kind? The light, sweet chocolate
or the dark, bitter kind?"

The conversation became general.
They spoke of cherry centers,
of almonds and Brazil nuts.
Losing their inhibitions
they interrupted one another.
For people may not know what they think
about politics in the Balkans,
or the vexed question of men and women,

but everyone has a definite opinion
about the flavor of shredded coconut.
Finally someone spoke of chocolates filled with liqueur,
and everyone, even the author of *Uncle Vanya,*
was at a loss for words.

As they were leaving he stood by the door
and took their hands.
                    In the coach returning to Petersburg
they agreed that it had been a most
unusual conversation.

My questions began, "Chocolates" is an especially fine example of what I call a "tuning-fork" poem. It twangs one deceptively simple note that dies away very slowly in widening circles of meaning and feeling. Nothing could seem at first glance more insignificant, more untransformed by the poet than this anecdote of a visit of literary tourists to a great author, who, instead of discussing with his fans the mysteries of his craft, turns the conversation to a subject they might have discussed in just the same way with anybody. Their disappointment is only thinly disguised by the genteel euphemism "unusual." What range of reactions to this poem have you noticed? Do any of your readers share the visitors' disappointment? Do they consider the poem a critical comment on Chekov? Or do they accept it as your comment and Chekov's on themselves and the clichés of literary lionizing? Is the poem also commenting on the nature of Chekov's work and on the universal relation of experience to literature? Some ears will hear the widening circles of a tuning-fork poem longer than they perhaps should. I was one of those readers: my questions grew from reading the poem as satire and its related style as a movement toward the prose poem. In the following essay Louis Simpson points me in another direction, toward a poem I like even better.

The poem is based on an actual incident. Some women who admired Chekhov paid him a visit. They wanted to talk about his writing, but Chekhov, who probably welcomed the interruption of his work, said to one of them, "Do you like chocolates?" What followed was pretty much as I have it, though I don't know if Chekhov stood by the door and took their hands as they left—I have imagined his doing so, like a character in one of his plays.

The reader will have noticed a difference between this account and my poem. Chekhov's visitors were women—in the poem they are "some people." I had to make this change, for if I had said they were women it might have appeared that Chekhov was condescending to women, talking about a frivolous subject, chocolates, because he thought women were not to be taken seriously. Nothing, of course, could have been further from Chekhov's mind—no one who has read Chekhov could accuse him of holding women in contempt. But there are always those who misunderstand, so I protected Chekhov, and myself, against the charge by changing "women" to "some people." Of course, if a reader wishes to be aggrieved he, or she, can always find a reason.

Reactions to the poem have been very favorable. I recall a letter in the *London Times* praising "Chocolates" because, the letter-writer said, it showed that poetry could be understood. And audiences at poetry readings seem to understand: they laugh at the line, "They spoke of cherry centers," from relief—this is not going to be a serious poem—and laugh again at the lines about shredded coconut and chocolates filled with liqueur. Audiences at poetry reading are grateful for poetry that is at all entertaining—most poetry is deadly dull. They make appreciative noises at the words "*unusual* conversation," right at the end.

"Chocolates" is more serious than some of these listeners think. Superficially it may appear that I am poking fun at the kind of people who would go to see a famous author, but readers who feel superior to these visitors are missing the point. In real life I might find such people absurd, but I would not hold them up to ridicule in a poem—I am more intelligent when I write than I am in person. The desire to see and speak to a great man or woman is not something to poke fun at. Only snobs, who are usually people of no talent, look down at those who have a sincere wish to better themselves.

Then what is the poem about? It is about happiness, the things that make people happy, and the delight we feel when we are able to express our happiness to another person. This may be the closest we get to heaven. Chekhov knew that people have preferences, though they may not be aware that they have them and may think that they should talk about philosophy instead. As Schopenhauer pointed out, we live according to our instincts and fashion our ideas accordingly—not the other way round, as Plato has it. A taste for chocolates may run deep—deeper than the wish to discuss *The Cherry Orchard* or politics in the Balkans.

And yet, though they like chocolates, people will talk about the things they think are expected. How boring for everyone!

This was why Chekhov brought up the subject of chocolates. It didn't have to be chocolates—anything they liked would have done, birthdays, for instance, or picnics—but chocolates were a happy choice. The visitors were relieved—like the audience at a poetry-reading when the solemnity is broken. The visitors gave their opinions, tentatively at first, then in a torrent, "interrupting one another." This was what Chekhov wanted, to have them express their enthusiasm. It is the conversation that matters, not the subject.

What happened that day was nothing grand—nothing as holy as what might have taken place in Tolstoy's house, but far more enjoyable all around.

Chekhov's poems and stories are about people who are prevented by character or circumstance from being happy. "My holy of holies," Chekhov said, "is the human body, health, intelligence, talent, inspiration, love and the most absolute freedom—freedom from violence and lying, whatever forms they may take."

So he asked his visitors to tell him if they liked chocolates, and when they said they did, the barriers were broken down. What followed was a communion of souls, and as they were talking about something they liked it was a happy communion.

Writers like Chekhov—but is there any writer like Chekhov?—through their sympathy and humor show that it is possible to live in the world. There is poverty, sickness and old age. There is bureaucracy; still, we can understand and love one another. Since the world will never be any different from what it is—not as long as it is inhabited by human beings—Chekhov's is the ultimate wisdom.

About the writing of "Chocolates . . ." I had heard this story about Chekhov some years before I wrote the poem. I was staying at a friend's house in the country. On Sunday he and his wife went to church, and I didn't feel like going. I was left behind with the *New York Times* and the *Boston Globe.* Perhaps

"Chocolates" was triggered by something he and I had been talking about, some remark about poetry, I don't recall. I picked up my notebook and started writing. The poem was written in a few minutes. I may have changed one or two words afterwards, or changed a line-break, but nothing important.

"This poem," one reader observes, "generally uses the rhythms, syntax and diction of prose fiction." I don't think so—to my ear the poem moves in lines of verse. If "Chocolates" were printed not in lines but as prose, the reader would soon be aware that lines of verse were struggling to break free.

(Incidentally, I have a low opinion of prose poems, unless they are written by Baudelaire. They don't have the absolute rhythm that you get from lines of verse; the rhythms are arbitrary, and so the work as a whole falls short of poetry. Poetry is absolute—it could not be other than it is. The prose poem could be written several different ways and the effect would be more or less the same. Prose may be very well written, of course, but it can never have the power of poetry written in lines.)

Are the syntax and diction of verse different from the syntax and diction of prose? I don't think so. A long time ago Ezra Pound remarked that poetry must be as well written as prose. That is to say, verse must sound as though the writer meant it. Verse is not a convention of style but an expression of mind. If the language of verse differs from prose it is not because the style was fetched from a distance but because verse is more highly charged with meaning, requiring more complex expression.

All good writing is experimental, but readers are listening for the rhythms and diction of poems they already know, so a new kind of poetry is said to be "anti-poetic." Wordsworth in his time was said to be writing prose. So were Whitman, Frost, Eliot and, of course, William Carlos Williams.

For twenty years I have been developing a kind of writing in verse that would accommodate my thoughts as easily as prose yet have a lyric flow. Coleridge said that the poet "diffuses a tone and spirit of unity, that blends, and (as it were) *fuses*, each into each, by that synthetic and magical power, to which we have exclusively appropriated the name of imagination." In poems such as "Chocolates" I have attempted to enter into a situation and imagine it strongly so that everything—words, phrases and sentences—would fall into place with no seeming effort on my part.

LOUIS SIMPSON was born in Jamaica. At seventeen he came to the United States and studied at Columbia University. He served in the U.S. Army, worked in publishing, and then went into university teaching. Since 1967 he has been teaching at the State University of New York at Stony Brook. He is the author of several books of verse, works of literary criticism, a novel, and an autobiography. His most recent publications are *The Best Hour of the Night* (poems) and *People Live Here: Selected Poems 1949–1983*.

DAVE SMITH

*

In the House of the Judge

All of them asleep, the suspiring everywhere is audible weight
   in the winter-shadowed house where I have dreamed
      night after night and stand now trying
   to believe it is only dust, no more than vent-spew
      risen from the idiotically huffing
grandfather of a furnace in the coal room's heart of darkness.

Haven't I touched the flesh-gray sift on bookshelves, on framed
   dim photographs of ancestors, on the clotted arms
      of the banjo clock that tolls past
   all resemblance to time and clicks like a musket's
steel hammer? And every day I wipe my glasses but still it comes,
   as now, at the top of the whining stairs, I am

come to wait with my hand laid light on the moon-slicked railing.
   I hear the house-heave of sleepers, and go jittery
      with no fear I can name. I feel myself
   shaped by the mica-fine motes that once were one
      body in earth until gouged, cracked,
left tumbled apart and scarcely glowing in a draft-fanned pit.

Pipes clank and gargle like years in the ashen veins of the Judge
   when they came to his house, the dung-heeled, some
      drunk, all with stuttered pleas to free
   their young, who could make it given a chance, just
one more good chance, so they said. Impassive, in skin-folds thick
   as a lizard, he stared at the great one for a sign,

the dog across the room, who kept a wary eye and was a one-man dog.
   Overhead do the same unbearable stars yet wheel
      in bright, ubiquitous malice, and what
   am I, wiping my glasses, certain this house walks
      in nail-clicking threat, going to plead?
I look out through warped Civil War glass buffed by men now ash

192

where the small park he gave in civic pride lies snow-blistered.
  Sub-zero then, as now, sent fire in the opening
    throat, but they came: tethered horses,
  striding shadows, and women who shrieked nightlong
until even gone they continued in his head. He heard them breathing.
  He painted his house a perfectly sneering white.

I stare at that snow as at a scaffold. Whose lightening footprints
  could soften my fear or say why I sniff like a
    dog, seem to taste a skim of black air
  upsweeping the maple stairwell, and feel my hair
    go slowly white? How many hours must
a man watch snow shift the world before he sees it is only a dream

of useless hope stamped and restamped by the ash-steps of those we
  can do no justice to except in loving them? But
    what could he do before the raw facts
  of men cleaving flesh like boys hacking ice?
I think how he must have thought of his barking teacher of law:
  There is only truth and law! He had learned the law.

But what was the truth to leave him trembling like a child in prayer?
  In late years he kept the monster by his side, two shades
    walking alone in the ice, the nail-raker, one
  who howled without reason and clawed at the heart
    of door after door. In the end he was known
inseparable from his beast who, it was said, kept the Judge alive.

Until he was not. Until his house emptied. Until we came who I hear
  breathing, those heads warm as banked ash under my hand
    laid light as I have laid it on this railing.
  But are we only this upfloating and self-clinging ash
that loops freely through dark houses? Those enigmatic fissures
  I see circling the snow? Are those only the tracks

of the dog I locked out, those black steps no more than a gleaming
  ice, or the face of some brother in the dirt betrayed,
    pleading, accusing? The moon, far off and dim,
  plays tricks with my eyes and the snow path turns dark as
a line of men marched into the earth. Whitely, my breath floats
  back at me, crying *I did not do this,* when the shuddering

courthouse clock across the square booms me back to myself. Dream's
  aftershock, the heirloom banjo starts to thud and drum
    so I turn and hustle downstairs to halt it.

Even with my hands laid on its hands it wants to thump
        its malicious heart out, but I can do this
at least: I can hold on to help them sleep through another night.

I can sit for a while with love's ice-flickering darkness where ash
        is heavily filling my house. I can sit with my own
                nailed walker in the snow, one whistled
        under my hand without question or answer. If I sleep
he will pad the floors above the fire-pit. He will claw me awake
        to hear breathing in the still house of the Judge

                where I live.

*The poem appears to be a true experience that gradually expands into metaphor. The
speaker (and by implication the reader) is living in the house of the judge (the self); the dust
of the past is sifting down on him; winter (the raw facts of injustice) is outside; the nailed
walker (truth) is pacing inside and clawing him awake to do justice, but the only justice
possible to him is to stop one small clock from striking off one small part of the lives of his
loved ones, to protect their breathing for a short time.*

1. *Did the poem begin as a conscious metaphor, or was the metaphor suggested by one or
    more of the narrative details and gradually took over their selection?*

2. *How much of the poem is actually historical and/or autobiographical? The dog? The
    banjo clock? The winter scene? The judge's reverence for the law and his trembling
    before the truth?*

3. *The poem's speaker says that he is writing out of fear: "no fear I can name," "Whose
    lightening footprints/could soften my fear?" But the rhythms and diction seem less to
    reflect terror than to reflect on it. Was this a conscious device to distance the reader
    from the intense emotion of the experience?*

4. *How did the poem's form, its sound and appearance on the page, develop?*

5. *The poem's style seems to move away from some fairly general recent poetic prefer-
    ences (single-syllable Anglo Saxon words, extremely concise syntax, avoidance of
    adjectives, adverbs, and prepositional phrases) and to prefer long sentences, poly-
    syllabic words of Latin origin, compound nouns and adjectives reminiscent of Homeric
    epithets or Anglo-Saxon kennings (ice-flickering darkness, moon-slicked railing,
    nail-raker, ash-steps). Was this a deliberate choice on your part of a "higher" style
    suitable for a serious subject, in the sense of classical and Renaissance "decorum?"*

6. *I have noted allusions to Conrad's "The Heart of Darkness" and to classical and heroic-age epic. What other use of allusion does the poem rely on to create its meaning and tone?*

In June of 1980, undertaking a year as a Visiting Professor at the State University of New York at Binghamton, I moved my family into a rental house in the rural town of Montrose, Pennsylvania. It was called the Judge's house because its late owner, father of our landlord Sue Smith, had been a local judge. A looming white Victorian house with stained glass windows, a rear view of cows in pastoral fields, its front porch faced the Susquehanna County Courthouse, built in 1855. In between was a sort of village green. Some houses are only places to live, indifferent, but this had the nearest thing I have ever known to a ghostly presence. Call it a sustaining spirit. I loved the claw marks of the judge's dog on the inside of every door. I loved to watch the life of the county streaming in and out of the courthouse. I loved the living fact of history in Montrose. To feel continuous with a past is to feel an imminent order in the future. To live in the Judge's house was, inevitably, to become something of a judge oneself.

Fall came grandly as a multicolor calendar. I didn't seem to notice because I was teaching, commuting, and writing hard. Sometimes a writer simply waits, his mind like a net fixed for whatever comes; sometimes he can't set the words down fast enough. I had both experiences with my poem "In the House of the Judge" and I am not certain which accounts for the poem's genesis. But two events seem to me significant.

The Judge's house had not, as real estate people say, been updated. It was heated by an ancient coal furnace in the basement, a furnace whose only modification was the replacement of vents for rising hot air with a system of steam heat that circulated through radiators. The furnace had to be stoked and stripped of ash daily, a task performed for the Judge by an old black man. I rented this man with the house, aware of his existence only by his banging below us each morning. Somewhere in that fall Sue Smith informed me this man had died. His brother, however, had assumed all duties. I paid no more conscious attention to that black man in his death than I had in his life, nor to the furnace. Except that with the onset of hard winter I began to notice a constant sift of ashen coal dust on my books and typewriter.

I am a creature of habit. It was my habit, while writing at night, to let out my dog and to stand on a second floor landing before tall windows where I might watch him a while. I watched because a dog might freeze to death in a country where I have seen days at forty below. I watched because I liked to look down on the snow-laden green before us and liked the postcard tranquility of that village. When I watched I stood with my back to the five bedrooms where my children slept and my wife slept, I listened to them breathing. Sometimes, hearing the courthouse clock strike and our own zany antique clock strike double and more, alone like that, I felt peaceful and in control. But often I felt helpless before the beautiful mortality of those I loved. Death, I often thought, was all that we added up to. Perhaps this was reinforced by a subconscious awareness of that black man's death, one who seemed to be sifting up from our furnace; perhaps I felt keenly the presence of the dead Judge. We all seemed to be breathing those bodies.

That fall there was a sensational murder trial at the courthouse. A teenage girl, pregnant, had run off with her lover to North Carolina. Her father had followed later, returning with his daughter and her illegitimate infant. In due course, the lover returned. He and the girl then bludgeoned and shot, while they slept, her father, mother, and brother, leaving one brother barely alive. With no attempts to hide their movements, they went back to North Carolina. When apprehended, they readily confessed. Their public demeanor seemed to make clear their belief that everyone would accept their outraged love as sufficient justification. They were as poignant as Romeo and Juliet, though each was subsequently tried, convicted, and sentenced to execution.

I am not particularly interested in violence, nor especially sympathetic to murderers. There was, however, no way of ignoring what took place over several months in our front yard: squadrons of police, the guilty marched in and out in chains, television trucks, wailing kin, spectators. Once we watched our dog on the local evening news. The more I watched, the more I felt the killers were, in appearance, indistinguishable from my students. The whole affair was outrageous and confusing. When I pitied them for an overreaction in ignorance, despair, and anger, I recalled the bloody butchery, felt the ache of the girl's parents, and thought of my growing children. In the end, I felt they had surrendered to a chaos in all of us. What order of resistance made any of us different? I began to fear a world in which innocence, guilt, accusation, and judgment seemed merely words. But they had not been mere words to Judge Edward Little, these concepts which set civilized order against chaos and death, and I was imaginatively, imperceptibly becoming the Judge by virtue of living in his house. I was increasingly preoccupied with the mysteries of morality, ethics, and the self's powers of resistance to surrender, and all this in the face of life's one implacable and constant enemy: Death.

I wrote my poem without a conscious awareness of either of the two events I have described, and offer the description as background, not explanation. The writing of the poem is the product of work, experience, and habits of assimilation. It is the product of what Flannery O'Connor called the writer's gift, meaning something like talent or vision or, perhaps, susceptibility. The gift and the habit constitute the force for art which pushes through the literal to an apprehension of the metaphysical. The result of habit, or considered selection, is form; the result of the gift, with luck, is truth. About these I shall speak briefly later on, but first here is my poem's initial draft:

Dog Tracks

All, all asleep, the suspiring seeps out of each
room like dust from the old coal

furnace, the vent—spew
I find on bookshelves,
framed pictures of ancestors,
even, for God's sake, on my glasses
every morning I see the sun grayer.

But now I stand at the top of the moon—slick stairs,
hearing breath, hearing the house—heave
of my family and those who were
here before us, and think
it is dust I hear,
the mica—fine ash of earth's
body, bodies circling audibly
so I am suddenly light in arm,
in leg, as if my heart has lifted.

Who is it? I ask. Pipes clank, coal enflamed.
Like a dog I sniff what I hear.

Then I remember an absence, something left out.
Through the window of warped, civil—war glass
the upsweeping blue flare of snowlight
spills on me like a sticking shine.
Blinded, I lift my hands
to wipe the double lens again,
then see the looping orbit
of tracks in the small park
where horses once were
tethered for court. I live
in the house of the judge.

Odd as a question unanswered, the track looms
blacker before me, deep—gouged, that
almost holy glow everywhere
split by this fissure
where the earth answers the sky.
I think how he must have stood alone
with the brute facts of neighbors,
their flesh cleaved in dark rows,
the face before him frank,
of a soldier, and a good one,
and no answer. There was none.
Had there been, he would offer
mercy, good God, do anything . . .

He had a monster in this house, the nails
raked doors so deeply paint in clots
could not conceal the wounds.
I think of him staring
into padded tracks, unable to see
what he could not remember
letting out the door, his
uncertainty mounting
into terror, self—hatred.
He was the judge, he was fair.

The dust flies up and I breathe it, feeling
it only in my mind, and I want to know
what shape is in it, what good.
I hear the breath of family
taking it in around me.
I place my hand on the rail
and look once down the funnel
of darkness I have climbed up,
then once more at his tracks.

I will go down into the ice—light
to find him waiting, dark—eyed,
shivering as if I would not
return, after his love.
He will be inside or out
and this will not matter.
I will let him stand beside me
who has walked the darkness
under the white fury,
who will claw me awake
to hear them all softly breathing.

Any intelligent reader can see that this draft makes no true poem. Its details do not cohere, its attention is unfocused, action is blurred, there is no necessary resolution, and worst of all nothing much is at stake. My speaker is trying to look at dog tracks and the judge simultaneously, but until that speaker can fuse the particulars into a unity greater than the sum of the parts, a super-image, he is right to say "this will not matter." The metaphysical and literal movements, that is to say, are not in a clarity and congruence of mutual reinforcement. The poem is more than half blind. The plain fact is that I did not know what the poem was about.

I thought I was writing about the fear of losing my dog to the weather. I would discover that fear was the context, not the issue. I would find my fear was for my family, myself, and by extension for what little order I believed my world to have. The value of this draft lay in realizing I wanted to write about the

Judge's resistance and power. While I felt powerless and alone, a stranger in this village, I saw that the Judge was also a stranger to all by virtue of being a man. We were, I imagined, one and the same. He offered me the opportunity to dramatize my fear which, if simply confessed, would appear to the reader as vague, unmotivated, a weakness of character, little more than a personal problem. Such confession would not be made substantial by any pronouncements about law, ethics, time, death, fear, truth, or justice. Yet the reader would confront, in the Judge, one who had lived these abstractions, whose authoritative *knowing* had already been paid for with his death. He was not a speculator but was a historical, immediate bearer of experience. The speaker could, therefore, ask what the Judge had done, to what effect, and with what rightness; the speaker could credibly examine himself and his comprehension of issues through his proximity to the Judge, his analogue.

To me, any poem successfully lives according to the presence of its implied or literal action, assuming as I do that action generates tension. The reader will see that my speaker's only true action is his attempt to silence a malfunctioning antique clock, by which he hopes to protect his family's peaceful sleep. But he is aware this act is a metaphorical attempt to stop time—and Death. He is aware of his act's futility. Yet he acts because he will not surrender unconditionally to Death or to poetic despair, which is only a death-imitation. If the little courage of holding a clock's hand is all he can manage, it is still courage and that is something. The action of the poem, like the action of my speaker, consists in the attempt to muster courage to confront illusions which, if they prove to be valueless, impotent, or sham, must leave him—and us—with greater, not less, fear and despair. Joseph Conrad suggests, in Robert Penn Warren's description, what I mean:

> Conrad's skepticism is ultimately but a "reasonable" recognition of the fact that man is a natural creature who can rest on no revealed values and can look forward to neither individual immortality nor racial survival. But reason, in this case, is the denial of life and energy, for against all reason man insists, as man, on creating and trying to live by certain values. These values are, to use Conrad's words, "illusions," but the last wisdom is for man to realize that though his values are illusions, the illusion is infinitely precious, is the work of his human achievement, and is, in the end, his only truth.

The action of the poem, then, would be a search for, through, and beyond illusions—for the truth. The truth by which men might live.

Action, of course, demands form. The form of my poem is that which came to seem right to my eye and my ear. Anything else I might say is largely supposition in hindsight, probably revisionist, and properly suspect. But I will point out that I have no story to tell and do not write a narrative poem: there is no dramatic or mimetic sequence with defined beginning, middle, and end. If the form is inclined toward epic reaching in language and a quasi-exalted personage in the Judge, it is not an epic. Neither is it a lyric. Perhaps it is closest to a psychological monologue, an attention to a mind jumping from one particular act of witness to another while the speaker is entirely fixed and static in time and space. For this speaker, all action is an internal shuffling of mysterious pieces. The reader sees only the movement of his consciousness, a movement of feeling rather than thought. Because the mind's movement in feeling does not proceed linearly or selectively, I felt I had to arrange an order of composition which would suggest the disorder of the consciousness but also bring into perceivable meaning the barrage of fragmented, disparate, and repeated images that have, inherently, neither shape nor meaning. That verbal composition which accepts mirrored chaos as sufficient is not art. Poetry is art. Poetry is particularly the art of repetition and resistance.

In the draft called "Dog Tracks" I write a variable but essentially short line, a line which traditional prosody would identify as normative three-stress. By the final draft of "In the House of the Judge" I wasn't paying much attention to ordinary repetitions. I did pay attention to a rigorous visual and rhythmic symmetry. This was a decision in service of resistance to verbal and emotional chaos. It was a decision in favor of patterns whereby I hoped to gradually make clear the particulars, to make them cohere in an emotional and logical resolution of the poem's forces of inertia and momentum. I wanted to control the forward movement so that the reader would feel the rush and pressure of narrative-like experience but would at the same time feel the countering pressure of sentence, line, phrase, and stanza—the collective function of which is to stabilize matters for the emergence and observation of meaning. The rhythmic principle of surge and stop, containment and release, is operative—I hope—in the design of line lengths. I formed them visually, though with stress patterns agreeable to my ear. I did not form them by counting syllables or stresses. The repetition of symmetrical line lengths, with some alteration, is intended to imitate the mind's movement, not precisely but loosely—as an illusion of movement. This form seemed to me appropriate to the internal, subjective experience of my speaker. Lacking narrative drive, the chaining of the stanzas is intended to establish a compensatory rhythmic order which might "tease" the reader forward, both vertically and horizontally, so that he is affected by emotional and sonic pressures which, with luck, push beyond the rhythmic experience of the poem. The phrase, for example, should give concrete detail to the eye; the line should give rhythmic ordering (and control); the stanza should give accrued shape to the chaos of the literal; the poem should arrive at the resonance of a sustained symbol, which is the apprehension of meaning. I am, of course, well aware that I may be constructing a scaffold for what exists in my eye only.

Unless a poem is a simple image, in which I have temperamentally little interest, it is a manifestation of the principles of repetition and resistance. These principles create selection. Many readers are prepared for the repetitions of traditional verse which are signalled by symmetrical line lengths, stanza regularity, and rhyme schemes. Many expect a predictable syllable count, a pattern of stressed and unstressed syllables, a poem whose surface, or mechanical aspects, are repeated. I have been faithful in part to such expectations. I have leaned, however, toward repetitions which are less obvious and less expected, but which are to me more important. Among these is the recurrence of certain images which carry common connotative values: ash, snow, footprints, dissonant sounds (pipes clanking), fire, clocks, skin, dogs, breath, and darkness. These are—some anyway—characteristic of gothic novels and horror movies whose common context is fear and psychological disorientation. In one aspect, my poem is a ghost story. That is also true of fairy tales, *Macbeth*, and the parables humans compose to remind themselves of finity in an infinite and scary world. I consider the evocation of literary and visual art forms which work initially on a visceral level—and the employment of their devices and strategies—to be an organizing repetition. I imagine that the speaker's attempt to hold disorder at bay in himself is a minor imitation, hence repetition, of the Judge's lifelong resistance to social disorder. Indeed, if the poem is successful it is so because of the parallels drawn to fuse the living and the dead into one witnessing. All repetitions, it hardly needs to be said, exist to establish unity, to reform chaos: each part must function within the whole and echo the whole. The principle upon which I hope to build my poem is that everything must connect and serve, either by repetition or resistance.

As writers are often asked, I have been asked whether this poem's style reflects a movement away from current trends in poetry. Perhaps it does in some sense, though I think the movement may be more a return than a departure. The diction and syntactical construction of "In the House of the Judge" probably has more in common with traditions of the epic and the monologue than with the personal lyric that seems the mainstay poem now. I mean to point at a certain Latinate syntax, Anglo-Saxon sonic echoes, a spatially carved and dramatic stanza, a willingness to confront and employ didactic strategies, and a seeking after grand certainties or truths. It may be that my poem has more in common with prose fiction than with contemporary poetic style, though I don't believe there is anything like a monolithic style. The influence of fiction would neither surprise nor displease me. I do not want a pure poetry, but a poetry that walks in the common world with the fullness of ordinary experience. I want the poem that is a superior entertainment. I am certain others look at matters differently. As one who loves poetry, I would be woefully bored if all poets wrote or thought as I do.

I asked of "In the House of the Judge" what I ask of every poem I write, what I have failed in every poem, total experience and total enlightenment and total pleasure. I want the poem to say everything at once. I am ambitious for the poem which will find, know, and express the truths—or the illusions—by which we may live completely. In the last line of the first stanza of my poem I allude to Joseph Conrad's magnificent story "The Heart of Darkness." I wrote that line almost automatically and immediately felt unworthy of his words. I excised the words, altered them, returned them—many times. In the end I used them because I thought this poem a descent into my own heart of darkness. Behind my Judge, I think, stand Conrad's Kurtz and Marlow, men who had "illusions" and who put them to the test of action in a world governed only by the law of the beast. This test consists in determining that despite malice and horror and emptiness a responsible and significant order, a life, is possible if a man pursues with courage the civilizing of his nature, a pursuit which is unblinking commitment to *knowing*. Conrad's Stein says: "The way is to the destructive element submit yourself, and with the exertions of your hands and feet in the water make the deep, deep sea keep you up." For me the poem, any poem, is such a test, a submission. But the reader, who becomes the poem's judge, must also take this test. It will require him to become an *other* in order to become a *self*. The poem is the house where reader and poet come to resist unconditional surrender, where repetitions and brave resistances continue until, with patience and forebearance and fortune, they become one self. This, of course, is an answer to life, not death. Neither I nor my poem know what to make of that, though it consumes us.

DAVE SMITH was born in 1942 in Portsmouth, Virginia. He holds degrees from the University of Virginia, Southern Illinois University, and Ohio University. He teaches at Virginia Commonwealth University. His books include a novel, *Onliness* (Louisiana State University Press, 1981), his seventh collection of poems, *In the House of the Judge* (Harper & Row, 1983), and *The Morrow Book of Younger American Poets*, which he has edited with the poet David Bottoms.

GARY SNYDER

*

Song of the Taste

Eating the living germs of grasses
Eating the ova of large birds

    the fleshy sweetness packed
    around the sperm of swaying trees

The muscles of the flanks and thighs of
        soft-voiced cows
    the bounce in the lamb's leap
    the swish in the ox's tail

Eating roots grown swoll
      inside the soil

Drawing on life of living
    clustered points of light spun
        out of space
hidden in the grape.

Eating each other's seed
      eating
    ah, each other.

Kissing the lover in the mouth of bread:
      lip to lip.

1. *The poem begins with a seemingly accusing grocery list, reminding us that much of what we eat is the germinal stages of some lives (eggs, nuts, seeds) and the expressive parts of others (muscles of flank, sweetness of grape). Just before the end you remind us that we are cannibals. The last two lines, however, equate this killing and eating*

with love. For most of its length the poem has stung readers who expected to be made ashamed for being members of the race that is making whole races of plants, animals, and even other human beings extinct. Then at the end it denies them even the comfort of that shame. Though I doubt that you mean to lessen their guilt, in what sense do you mean them to read the terms kissing and lover? Where would you consider the act of love to stop? Are vegetarians denying themselves love? Are armies at war for a strip of desert performing an act of love?

2. *The poem states facts that are such common knowledge that they are taken for granted, in words that are equally common and familiar. The juxtaposition, however, is unexpected (not grotesque or surrealistic), but nonetheless surprising: The expected nut becomes the equally familiar sperm; potatoes or turnips become the slightly archaic roots grown swoll; muscles become the bounce and leap that are the acts of muscles; the usual phrase bread in the mouth becomes in the mouth of bread; and the reader's notice is attracted to these changes and his attention reinforced by sound repetitions: Sweetness/ sperm/ swaying/ trees; swoll/ soil; seed/ eating/ each; lover/ lip/ lip; and many others. Would you comment on the habits, strategies, or accidents that transformed the common and expected into the surprising?*

3. *The poem has nineteen separate lines: eight begin on the left margin; six others are indented slightly; and five are indented considerably more. The lines occur in six unevenly sized and shaped groups that suggest stanzas. Each of these begins with a capital in the left margin and ends, with one exception, on a line that starts with the first or second indentation. The overall effect is that of starting at the left and drifting toward the right, starting again at the left and drifting again toward the right. Why do you want the reader to move in that manner? Do you want the idea to dawn on the reader gradually, as it would on a person who was in the process of discovering the idea for himself?*

Note: I am hoping you will use the questions as a jumping-off point for a brief essay on how this particular poem developed.

The primary ethical teaching of all times and places is "cause no unnecessary harm." The Hindus, Jains, and Buddhists use the Sanskrit term "*ahimsa*" "nonharming." They commonly interpret this to mean "don't take life" with varying degrees of latitude allowed for special situations. In the eastern traditions "cause no unnecessary harm" is the precept behind vegetarianism.

Nonvegetarians, too, try to understand and practice the teaching of "nonharming." People who live entirely by hunting, such as the Eskimo, know that taking life is an act requiring a spirit of gratitude and care, and rigorous mindfulness. They say "all our food is souls." Plants are alive too. All of nature is a gift-exchange, a potluck banquet, and there is no death that is not somebody's food, no life that is not somebody's death.

Is this a flaw in the universe? A sign of a sullied condition of being? "Nature red in tooth and claw?" Some people read it this way, leading to a disgust with self, with humanity, and with life itself. They are on the wrong fork of the path. Otherworldly philosophies end up doing more damage to the planet (and human psyches) than the existential conditions they seek to transcend.

So again to the beginning. We all take life to live. Weston LaBarre says, "The first religion is to kill god and eat him" or her. The shimmering food-chain, food-web, is the scary, beautiful, condition of the biosphere. Nonharming must be understood as an approach to all of living and being, not just a one-dimensional moral injunction. Eating is truly a sacrament.

How to accomplish this? We can start by saying Grace. Grace is the first and last poem, the few words we say to clear our hearts and teach the children and welcome the guest, all at the same time. To say a good grace you must be conscious of what you're doing, not guilt-ridden and evasive. So we look at the nature of eggs, apples, and ox-tail ragoût. What we see is plenitude, even excess, a great sexual exuberance. Millions of grains of grass-seed to become flour, millions of codfish fry that will never—and *must* never—grow to maturity: sacrifices to the food-chain. And if we eat meat it is the life, the bounce, the swish, that we eat, let us not deceive ourselves. Americans should know that cows stand up to their hocks in feed-lot manure waiting to be transported to their table, that virgin forests in the Amazon are clearcut to make pasture to raise beef for the American market. Even a root in the ground is a marvel of living chemistry, making sugars and flavors from earth, air, water.

Looking closer at this world of oneness, we see all these beings as of our own flesh, as our children, our lovers. We see ourselves too as an offering to the continuation of life.

This is strong stuff. Such truth is not easy. But hang on: if we eat each other, is it not a giant act of love we live within? Christ's blood and body becomes clear: the bread blesses you, as you bless it.

So at our house we say a Buddhist verse of Grace:

> We venerate the Three Treasures
> [Buddha, Dharma, Sangha]
> And are thankful for this meal
> The work of many people
> And the sharing of other forms of life.

Anyone can use a Grace from their tradition, if they have one, and infuse it with deeper feeling and understanding, or make up their own, from the heart. But saying Grace is not fashionable in much of America now, and often even when said is mechanical and flat, with no sense of the deep chasm that lies under the dining table. My poem "Song of the Taste" is a grace for graces, a model for anyone's thought, verse, song, on "the meal" that the fortunate ones on earth partake of three times a day.

GARY SNYDER born San Francisco 1930, grew up Pacific NW—Reed College—Forestry and logging and snowpeak ascents—Linguistics at Indiana—Chinese and Japanese at Berkeley—San Francisco docks—Sierra Trail crews—wiper & fireman in the engine room. Buddhist studies in Japan 1956–1968. Guggenheim & Bollingen. Pulitzer (poetry) 1975. Sierra pine forest melon patch with two sons; wife Masa Uehara. Calif. Arts Council member; San Juan Ridge Study Group. *Books:* Riprap / Myths and Texts / Six Sections / Earth House Hold / Regarding Wave / The Fudo Trilogy / Turtle Island / The Old Ways / He Who Hunted Birds in His Father's Village / The Real Work / The Back Country / Axe Handles.

WILLIAM STAFFORD

*

Yellow Cars

Some of the cars are yellow, that go
by. Those you look at, so glimmering
when light glances at their passing. Think
of that hope: "Someone will
like me, maybe." The tan ones
don't care, the blue have made
a mistake, the white haven't tried.
But the yellow—you turn your head:
hope lasts a long time if you're happy.

William Stafford wrote two essays in answer to my questions. The first floats the reader into the poem; the second is the guided tour. After teetering between them, I decided that both are needed.

1. *To me this is an example of Stafford at his slyest, a stated concern so childlike and obvious (" 'Someone will/like me, maybe' ") that it seems blandly amusing, evoking an "aw, so there" kind of warm sympathy, but nothing darker. But then we notice emphases: the suspension of hope caused by putting* go *at the end of line 1 and by* at *the beginning of line 2, much like the turning of a head; the return to that turning head in the next-to-last line; and the undercutting of the final* happy *by the realization that even the longest hope can last only as long as it takes a car to pass. Am I overreading? Is that the sequence of awarenesses you were consciously inviting your reader to make? Were you also inviting your reader to make others? Or hoping for some you hadn't thought of yet?*

2. *Did you wish us to associate the yellow cars with taxis? The other colors with things of those colors? The colors with moods? Why did you pick yellow for the major color (you do the same in "Yellow Flowers")? Is it the association with the sun?*

3. *If one called the tone wistful, would that be too weak a word? Would several words be needed?*

4. *Does* you *in the poem mean* I *or everyone? How do you feel about disguising the* I *in a poem? Do you prefer to speak directly as yourself (or one of your selves) or to use a persona or an impersonal point of view?*

5. *I have long noticed that you use a great deal of assonance in your poems, usually between words inside the lines or between end-line words and inside ones, rather than arranging end-line words to emphasize each other. For instance, the similarities be- tween* glimmering, think, *and* will; *and between* made, tried, *and* head *are less conspicuous than those between* go *and* yellow, *those,* so, hope, *and again* yellow *and* hope; *or between* by *and* light, like, white, *and* time. *Does this interplay of sounds happen automatically when you write or instinctively at first and consciously later, when you revise?*

6. *What determined the line breaks in this poem?*

7. *How did the poem begin? How many changes did it undergo and in what order? How long did it take to finish it? If you still have the worksheets, could I see a copy?*

Where "Yellow Cars" Comes From

Writing a poem is easy, like swimming into a fish trap. Analyzing a poem is hard, like swimming out of a fish trap. In casting back through the experience of having "Yellow Cars," I would like to find my way into what happened along in the writing, the easy part, the process that finds its way by accommodating emerging experiences. And then I'd like to try to account for the fish trap pattern that one can reconstruct, rationally, the hard way, swimming out.

In early April of 1980 I was on a reading circuit, and of course kept on writing a little each day. The pages from that time give me little hints of a current that turned out to be on the way to this poem. On April 4 I find two stray jottings:

My room has light, and I
    am for the light, but when
that light goes wandering, my
    thought makes another room
where light can lead me home.

My vial of anti-light pours a path
for my shadow.

On April 8, among many jottings, I find this:

Some time you look from your window
into storm, cold, dark. It is warm
where you are. Some day it will be home out there.

On April 10, strangely positioned amid another kind of sequence, is this:

> Mostly it is right, when a word goes by,
> to turn my head and watch it go into
> someone else's ear and let them answer.

Then, on April 12, I find, sprung amid other jottings, an essentially complete passage that became "Yellow Cars," with spooks of phrases from earlier passages in April:

> Some of the cars are yellow, that go
> by. Those I follow, so hurried are they
> when light allows their passing. Think
> of that optimism: "Some one will
> like me, maybe." The black ones
> don't care, the blue have made
> a mistake, the white haven't entered.
> But the yellow—I turn my head:
> hope lasts a long time, if you're happy.

Now, was this poem written in a few minutes—the version above—on April 12? Or was it written, jerkily, blunderingly, but with never-faltering direction, by means of writing experiences (and other experiences) that were happening along to me all during several weeks of April, 1980? Either way, I could live with the choice, but the second way is the one that seems to me more helpful in considering how a piece of art *arrives*.

It would be endless to prowl through the influences and the characteristic turns I feel in this poem; but staying a long way short of that kind of excursion I want to consider certain perceptible trends as the poem unfolded. And then will come my turn toward considering the poem as a set of strategies.

About this poem, from the inside, how it feels to me, small and quiet as it is—it reverberates mightily with many of my most strongly held life commitments. It starts so easily, with a ridiculously quiet, and insultingly clear but slowly developing relevance. It offers readers or hearers something that can be tossed aside, if they are dumb enough—they get what they deserve, and there is a mean part of me that likes to let people have what they impetuously claim for themselves. The poem continues to assert undeniable, but perhaps trivial, observations—but perhaps not trivial. And the experience of reading the poem is itself not an experience of attaining or not attaining worthy statements, but an experience of taking a roller coaster of offerings, withholdings, little giddy turns, and then a closure that suddenly welds together what the whole poem has been tending toward.

Or so I see it. Small as it is, quiet as it is, I'll take my stand with the sound it makes when struck to test its completeness and tone after it is finished.

Now, to swim out of the fish trap—to seek patterns or tactics that seem to carry this little package out of ordinary *message* and into poetry—I stare at the finished poem. It doesn't spin its wheels, make claims for itself, overrun its demonstrations; that is, it eases the reader into an experience that does not require giving credit to the writer or bracing oneself to admire. But it does begin at once to have various little bonuses in the telling.

It spills along, line by line, roving downward, till it gets to the last, three, end-stopped lines, where conclusions begin to happen. The trajectory of the poem is smooth-onward, then staccato as it drives home. I believe I was led to this pattern from just following opportunities that came to me; but once the opportunities come along, they are embraced. The "revision" process is largely a process of accepting what one can, from the given, and then of politely declining and selecting among alternatives when it feels right to do so.

The persona in this poem, it seems to me, begins to be easy and a little deprecatory—and then stays that way. There is sympathy for our humanness, a general participation feeling; but the power that inheres in being a participant in humanness is enjoyed by the speaker: by the end of the poem what is claimed is not much, but it is undeniable; and something as natural as choosing a color one likes becomes like a banner for the life force.

Why yellow? It occurred to me. And after it occurred, I could maybe understand why—the sun, April (and the poem was written in April), flowers and spring in general, gold, preciousness. Why do people value gold? I do not need to know why, but they do. And I am there with them. . . .

Though the poem ends with "happy," I perceive in it not a frivolous but a solid and realistic human position: "maybe" is in the poem, "go by" is in the poem, "someone" is in the poem. The conditional is in the poem, all the way through it, as it is through life.

As for sound, I live in one great bell of sound when doing a poem; and I like how the syllables do-si-do along. I am not after rhyme—so limited, so mechanical. No, I want all the syllables to be in there like a school of fish, flashing, relating to other syllables in other words (even words not in this poem, of course), fluently carrying the reader by subliminal felicities, all the way to the limber last line.

And I find that up to the last I was tinkering there, putting in a comma before "if you're happy," and taking it out so as to let readers coast to the end, either noticing how drastic that last phrase is, or not, thus getting just what they deserve, in the infinitely rewarding but absolutely justice-rendering world of art.

The World and "Yellow Cars"

An attitude prevalent today—and a kind of poem all but universal today—frames us into a false pair of alternatives: you can be bland, simple, innocent, a little bit dumb, and be happy; or you can be intense, profound, and smart, and realize how grim and serious life is.

The first choice, people are indulgent about; the second, though, is of course the valid one, say significant people today.

But "Yellow Cars" won't accept that formulation; it, and many poems that come to me, come from an attitude that assumes and lives in light of a different perception, one that accepts what comes and is not surprised by chance, but does not give up a tough, sustained, gusto about living.

It is not my intention to defend happiness at great length here, but I do know it is possible without evasion and that considering a poem like this one calls for early and decisive positioning: this poem embraces extremes—innocence and experience both. This poem's quirks come clear only with acceptance of its kind of being.

From the first line, a minimum experience is accepted gratefully—*some* of the cars, and they just go by—that is, they go/by. And you look at them, the yellow ones. You don't own them, and even those who do own them have a quaint wistfulness about it (but they keep on trying). Then comes a whimsically judgmental (but not assessing blame exactly) part about the mistakes and indecisiveness of people not using yellow cars. And then, a sharp last line of allegiance to the speaker's kind of lifestyle.

I mean every nuance of the poem, every time a line breaks with suspense or a roving of tentativeness, every word or syllable that acknowledges limits—glimmering, glances, passing, hope, maybe, care, mistake—and all hints in the language that sustain the attitude of leaning forward even while knowing the odds; I mean all of these: *some*one, *if*, and the length, but also the terminal implication, of *lasts*. I hope the reader will get lost in a series of glimpses, and retain a sense of going on from the poem into more glimpses, with a sense of there being many such, now and later, in art and in life.

Yellow is the color for many reasons—the sun, gold, light, spring flowers. But I do not make the choice by realizing the literary or worldly justifications for my choice, but by making my choice from the same set of human feelings that have given yellow its value and gold its cost.

This could be called a wistful poem, and I would not object. But the wistfulness is as tenacious as life is; the stance in the poem is powerful by being realistic and at the same time hopeful, like a healthy being, alive, vital.

The poem is about everyone, or, anyone *could* be in the poem; so it says "you" look, "you" turn your head. I consciously made that wording, to be general, not just about myself. I even revised that way, after starting by being the person inside the poem. I get tired of the centrality of "I" in current writing: that pronoun is often there just from habit on the writer's part—not that it happens to me, but that it happens, is usually the real point. Changes in sentence structure, so that central intentions get main-clause treatment, can help many poems. Or, changes of person—as this poem does it.

In this poem, and throughout my writing when I am in a flourishing phase, sounds make a continuous difference, in the first encounter while dreaming/writing along, and later when revising. It is not that attention is called to similar sounds (a rhyme in the first line—cars-are—is so much disguised that only looking back do you see it), but I want, and I feel, the sounds homogenized all the way through an utterance. I would have every "l" in this poem recognize every other "l." So many skipping, intermittent touches occur to me that I despair of identifying and claiming them. Even the syncopation of a sentence, the thought-rhyme of having a series that proceeds by sinking through a sequence of predicates (don't care, made a mistake, haven't tried)—I live by these little universes.

Many congenialities of sound happen automatically when we write (when we talk, too?); they come as volunteers, and they are kept if they continue to please. I find options in successive rewritings, but I find them as the first ones came—by chance encounters and then recognition, or it seems chance.

And line breaks, too, happen along. By now, in my writing, many considerations occur to me in jotting down even first hints of a poem. I like to feel patterns—number of stresses, multi-unstressed, or few-unstressed sound units, lines that carry over and make a reader reach a bit, pauses in the line that come at varying, helpful places, early in the line, middle of the line, later in the line. But I make the lines the way they are by welcoming opportunities that come to me, not by having a pattern in mind.

Often a poem crystalizes fast, during my daily writing; that is, it flows along in a sustained burst of jotting things down. This poem was like that—one swirl of writing. But in another sense it came on very slowly, like a plant underground, becoming itself for days till it came out into full consciousness, by means of my cultivating of the ground on the day it found its light.

Looking back over jottings of a week or so before it happened, I find phrases and attitudes that reach out for each other and came on together, till I recognized a poem, and welcomed it as mine.

WILLIAM STAFFORD was born in 1914 in Hutchinson, Kansas, and earned his B.A. and M.A. from the University of Kansas, and his Ph.D. from the University of Iowa. He has taught high school in California, taught college in Iowa, California, Kansas, Indiana, Washington, Alaska, Ohio, and Oregon, and lectured on literature throughout the world. He has published many collections of poetry, including *Stories That Could Be True* (Harper and Row, 1977) and *A Glass Face in the Rain* (Harper and Row, 1982), and several books of prose, including *Writing the Australian Crawl,* views on the writer's vocation (University of Michigan Press), *Friends to This Ground* (National Council of Teachers of English), and *Down in My Heart* (Church of the Brethren Press).

GERALD STERN

*

For Night to Come

I am giving instructions to my monkey
on how to plant a pine tree. I am telling
him to water the ground for hours before
he starts to dig and I am showing him
how to twist the roots so the limbs will bend
in the right direction.
                              He is weeping
because of the sweet air, and remembering
our canoe trip, and how we went swimming
on Mother's Day. And I am remembering
the holiness and how we stopped talking
after we left Route 30. I show him the tree
with the two forks and the one with the
stubs and the one with the orange moss
underneath, and we make our nest in a clearing
where the wind makes hissing noises and the sun
goes through our heavy clothes.
                              All morning we lie
on our backs, holding hands, listening to birds,
and making little ant hills in the sand.
He shakes a little, maybe from the cold,
maybe a little from memory,
maybe from dread. I think we are lost,
only a hundred yards from the highway,
and we will have to walk around in fear,
or separate and look for signs before
we find it again.
                              We pick a small green tree,
thick with needles and cones and dangling roots,
and put it in the trunk on top of the blanket,
and straighten the branches out, and smooth the hairs.
All the way back we will be teary and helpless,
loving each other in the late afternoon,

213

and only when we have made the first cut
and done the dance
and poured in the two bushels of humus
and the four buckets of water
and mixed it in with dirt and tramped it all down
and arranged and rearranged the branches
will we lie back and listen to the chimes
and stop our shaking
and close our eyes a little
and wait for night to come
so we can watch the stars together,
like the good souls we are,
a hairy man and a beast
hugging each other in the white grass.

1. *The story of how I taught a monkey to transplant a pine tree is both absurd and sentimental, yet after we have smiled we suspect that the monkey and the I are one and the same. The monkey is the speaker's more vulnerable and primitive part, and their clinging together is a way of shoring a self (any self) against outer darkness. The I tells this monkey all his wisdom, which is about the care of small trees, and about this he is very wise. They love each other tenderly and share nostalgic experiences. The monkey, the more physical of the two, remembers swimming and shivers with cold, memory, dread. The I, the wise one, remembers holiness, but both are lost "only a hundred yards from the highway," and both are afraid. Only after they have performed the ritual of the tree together do they stop shaking, "like the good souls we are." At this distance the reader too sees himself as "a hairy man and a beast/ hugging each other in the white grass." Did you expect (hope) your reader would read this poem so close to allegory? Or am I closing the poem more than you want and in ways that make you squirm?*

2. *Do you feel an ambivalence of love, pity, scorn and admiration for the pair?*

3. *Does the monkey indeed stand for the primitive part of the I, rather than another and contrasting character?*

4. *Your most frequent way of distancing self in your poems is this cartooning of your personae into lovable clowns, foolish but for the right, or at least not ignoble, reasons. Any influence of Berryman here? I detect none of his self-hate, no real self-pity.*

5. *The form of the poem seems to me to insist far less than most free verse poems do, yet to be as inevitable as only a good ear and conscious control of rhythm and sound can make it. What determined your line breaks? Why do the paragraphs begin when and*

where they do? What determined your choice of rhythms, such as that of the last
paragraph? How conscious were you of assonance? Could the poem do what you want
if it were in prose-poem form?

6. *How did the poem start? How long did it take you to finish it? What revisions did it go*
through?

"For Night to Come" is one of the three or four poems I have written that
seem to carry a meaning independent of, and beyond, my own attempt at
explanation, either to myself or to others, and I am always surprised, when I
return to it, how simple and literal it is on the one hand and how difficult and
elusive it is, at least for me, on the other. I wrote the poem, I must confess,
without tongue in cheek or any sense of irony, let alone cuteness. I *was* teaching
my monkey how to plant a pine tree; we *were* visiting a woods—it was in the
heart of the Pine Barrens of southern New Jersey—and we *were* stealing a tree, a
pitch pine, from a state preserve so I could plant it in my back yard. Moreover,
the event was so real to me, and so natural, that I am surprised when it is
viewed figuratively in any sense of the word. I have to remind myself not only
that I don't have a monkey but that monkeys don't weep and sigh the way this
one did. It is, in a way, sad to have to acknowledge that. Certainly it is true that
the monkey seems to be my more primitive, or at least less educated or more
innocent, part, and certainly we did cling together to protect ourselves against
cruelty and indifference, but it was a real being I was with there, not a figment
or a fragment or an idea. And I loved him then, and I love him now. The poem
seems allegorical—it is allegorical—but I had no allegory in mind. I was the
subject of a moving and overwhelming experience in the middle of a heavenly
woods a few dozen yards from route 539 where I went to rest, and feel the sun,
and listen to the birds and take a tree, so I could remember that place forever,
and I hope that what I did will help the reader re-enter his own sweet place, and
stop his shaking.

I don't remember exactly how this poem came to be written, whether I
started with a few words or a little conceit and tapped into an underground
spring, or whether I started with the experience itself and discovered the "device" to represent it. I'm not sure about other poets, but I tend to start with a
few words or a phrase, although recently I have been experimenting with
"ideas," or at least tentative ones. I obtained the formal elements of "For Night
to Come" from an old Chinese drawing I saw ten, twelve, years ago in the
Metropolitan. It showed an old man and a monkey sitting on a high mountain,
with mist rising around them. The man had thin hair and loose dugs and he
was explaining something to the monkey, who was listening attentively, with
downcast eyes. The title, as I recall, explained the drawing: "Poet giving instructions to his monkey." It was part of a series and, my guess is, part of a tradition.
I bought a post card of that drawing and kept it with me for years, although I
must confess that the poem itself probably colors my memory of the original

drawing. It made a deep impression on me—it haunted me—and it may have done so because it stirred or awakened in me certain feelings and ideas. I don't think I "derived" the poem itself from the drawing. I think I had my own monkey, so to speak, waiting in the wings and the drawing helped not only to unearth but to focus it. I wrote the poem, finally, when either circumstances or feelings allowed me, or forced me, to make my connections with *my* monkey.

It is interesting that there is little or no monkey mythology in Europe and North America, but a great deal of it in Africa and Asia. It may have to do simply with the literal presence of monkeys and their availability to the imagination. The monkeys we have in America are in zoos, or in Hollywood, and they are amusing to us, and sweet, and childlike. The only monkeys I remember from my own childhood are the organ grinder's little assistant, with his hat and his tin cup, or the Lou Lehr special on Saturday afternoon, "Monkies iz the cwaziest people." Apes are different. They are a little awesome, a little brutal, a little pathetic, and somehow available for myth—and literature—even if they are not close by. I am thinking of the King Kongs. And writers like O'Neill and Orlovitz. In our culture, it is more likely to be the ape that stands for the primitive part of the self; the monkey is too cunning, too successful, maybe even too dear. And yet it is the monkey I invoke in this poem, it is not an ape. I have never thought about it till this minute, but maybe the monkey, in its delicacy and its intelligence, is more of an equal or comrade to the human than the ape is. Maybe, as in the poem, we can hold hands and suffer together. Maybe the monkey is not exactly the "animal" in us; maybe he is the true us, stripped of pretenses and pride and science; maybe his presence forces us not into an encounter with the "dark unconscious" but with our own pure and honest selves. He is much more human than the ape. And he is less a shadow, whatever the line of evolution.

I am not absolutely sure what the monkey was to the Chinese poet. As I recall, he was quite small and off to one side, and though there was affection between them it was affection that class and age and education and relative size would permit and encourage. The affection between my monkey and me—I am taking myself as the speaker in the poem—has more equality to it, which may say something either about education in America or my own philosophy and habits. I love the monkey, as I would a brother. He is my soul. He is open, and tender and loving and helpless, an utterly trusting and believing "student." I am teaching him something quite simple, and even technical, but it has a tremendously important overtone, something out of all keeping with the matter at hand. It is as if we were talking about life and death and love and survival, and not how to plant, or replant, a little stolen pitch pine. The silence and beauty of the forest may have had something to do with it. And, of course, the fact that this forest, a million-and-a-half-acre tract in southern New Jersey, is at the very fringe, on the edge, of the "unconscious," as it were, on the border of our cities and farms, and that a few yards away from route 539, or 70 or 30 or the Atlantic City Expressway, we are reunited with the awesome woods that preceded our culture, and it is very very easy to get dislocated there. This *woods* is the unconscious; *it* is the primitive, the other; the monkey is of *my* culture, and we build a nest together and a refuge against the wilderness.

We have experienced something important together, and something frightening. We went through a descent together and re-emerged a little wiser, maybe a little happier, and we are closer than ever and, at the end of the poem, more equal than before. Really true equals, even if I was once the teacher, the father. The poem ends on a return, to hearth and home,—in this case to back yard and side porch—reminiscent of many other returns in myth and literature, from *The Odyssey* to *Gulliver's Travels* to "Song of Myself." It is probably appropriate that such a momentous voyage, such great distance and such great undertaking, be taken with a funny little animal. Only a canary or a mongrel would have done as well. I think whatever irony I do display has to do with the voyage itself, its absurdity, its slightly mock seriousness, its secure terror, its simple goal. But there is not a lot of irony. I mean the trip to be taken literally. I mean to say that this is the kind of adventure given to our age. I mean to say that true significance can be found here, that is, there, not in the Himalayas or the Amazon, or not less than in those places. And just as I do not denigrate this quest, neither do I denigrate these heroes. They are not mock heroes or anti-heroes, and they are not out of the pages of Berryman or Beckett. I know the situation is crazy; I know the tone is unusual, even weird. But I am, frankly, so far gone (I mean in the poem) that I hardly realize that. I start at the edge, maybe at the end; I start where comedy leaves off, though my characters may seem comic. Nor do I have any distance from my pain. Not in this poem. As far as the particulars of the poem, the images and objects and events, they are not at all out of some dream reservoir. They are hard and literal and technical. They are realistic and accurate. What gives them their strangeness is their order and mixture and the manner in which they are presented and accepted. It is the context. It is a man and a monkey doing this. It is a man and monkey doing it earnestly, even desperately. And it is they doing it comfortably, and for an unknown, or unstated reason. The reader observes them with the same wonder he would observe any such pair, who are doing something unusual or preposterous, and are absorbed by it.

There are four stanzas. I don't remember now what determined my line breaks. My guess is that the first stanza ended as it did according to sense and syntax, and I ordered the second and third. Or perhaps I made the separation after the poem was written, to see what I had, and what I was giving to the reader. Most of the lines—until the "Making of the cut" in line seven of stanza four—are five-stressed; after that there is an urgency and speed and the mood and rhythm change and the lines are shorter, and end strictly according to content, each one describing a separate action or condition. The two of them, the two of us, are overcome by ritual here, are carried away, though, as always; the *poesy* was unconscious, or almost so, and the language and the experience and the emotion took over, and determined, the technique. I wrote this poem, I remember, quickly and easily. The issue was survival. And peace. And understanding. Forever and ever. Through love and identity. A hairy man and a beast.

GERALD STERN was born in 1925 in Pittsburgh, Pennsylvania, and educated at the University of Pittsburgh and Columbia University. His books are *Rejoicings*, Poems 1966–72 (Metro Books, 1984), *Lucky Life* (Houghton-Mifflin, 1977), winner of the Lamont Award, *The Red Coal* (Houghton Mifflin, 1981) winner of the Melville Caine Award, and *Paradise* Poems (Random House, 1984). He is on the faculty of the Writers' Workshop at the University of Iowa.

MARK STRAND

*

Where Are the Waters of Childhood?

See where the windows are boarded up,
where the gray siding shines in the sun and salt air
and the asphalt shingles on the roof have peeled or fallen off,
where tiers of oxeye daisies float on a sea of grass?
That's the place to begin.

Enter the kingdom of rot,
smell the damp plaster, step over the shattered glass,
the pockets of dust, the rags, the soiled remains of a mattress,
look at the rusted stove and sink, at the rectangular stain
on the wall where Winslow Homer's *Gulf Stream* hung.

Go to the room where your father and mother
would let themselves go in the drift and pitch of love,
and hear, if you can, the creak of their bed,
then go to the place where you hid.

Go to your room, to all the rooms whose cold, damp air you
    breathed,
to all the unwanted places where summer, fall, winter,
    spring,
seem the same unwanted season, where the trees you knew
    have died
and other trees have risen. Visit that other place
you barely recall, that other house half hidden.

See the two dogs burst into sight. When you leave,
they will cease, snuffed out in the glare of an earlier light.
Visit the neighbors down the block; he waters his lawn,

219

she sits on her porch, but not for long.
When you look again they are gone.

Keep going back, back to the field, flat and sealed in mist.
On the other side, a man and a woman are waiting;
they have come back, your mother before she was gray,
your father before he was white.

Now look at the North West Arm, how it glows a deep
    cerulean blue.
See the light on the grass, the one leaf burning, the cloud
that flares. You're almost there, in a moment your parents
will disappear, leaving you under the light of a vanished star,
under the dark of a star newly born. Now is the time.

Now you invent the boat of your flesh and set it upon the
    waters
and drift in the gradual swell, in the laboring salt.
Now you look down. The waters of childhood are there.

1. *The poem works a child back through childhood to the time before conception. The child (the* you *of one and everyone) invents the "boat of his flesh," and the sea that boat rides on is all that he perceives. Literally this is how a child develops in the womb, the first speck of awareness beginning in a sea of amniotic fluid in which the fetus floats. It can also imply the gradual particularization of a person's consciousness, concern, speech, and habits, which will continue from first childhood to the gradual blurring and letting go of second childhood. It also implies current theories of the evolution of life on this planet: from undifferentiated to specialized to extinct. Am I overreading?*

2. *The last stanza suggests that the self is responsible for what it is and what it sees; from inception "you invent," "you look down." Do you mean to suggest free will or just biological exuberance or necessity?*

3. *It is literally true that the light of many of the stars we see takes so long to reach us that its source is already extinct and, conversely, that the light of many newer stars must have not reached us yet. Do you extend time backward in this way in order to intensify the tone of loss: the reversal of growth to decay, emptiness, and finally to intergalactic unconsciousness?*

4. *What determined your choice of a title that recalls Villon's "Ou Sont les Nieges d'Antan"?*

5. *Are the house and ton described here the place where you grew up? Is "that other house half hidden" a graveyard or another neighbor's house?*

6. *What started the poem? How did it develop, over what period?*

7. *What determined the poem's structure? Its sounds and rhythms?*

8. *Have readers interpreted the poem as you hoped or expected?*

9. *What other questions do you wish I had asked?*

Dear Alberta:

I shall answer your questions in a fairly methodical, plodding way, the only way, alas, at this distance from the poem, that it is possible for me. The poem was written in 1977, so my interest in it, the excitement I experienced writing it, are long since gone.

1. Yes, the poem works back through childhood to the time of conception. Things are given up or lost on the journey back and yes, the sea by poem's end is the amniotic fluid. But I was not aware of anything having to do with ''the particularization of a person's consciousness, etc.'' Nor was I aware of current theories of evolution.

2. Your second question strikes me as a little grand for my intent. Since the poem has been a series of instructions as well as observations, I urge the listener (myself) to invent what he could not have known. From the boat of his flesh he looks down into the waters of childhood. I think that the journey backwards has not been a mere relinquishing, but a history of relinquishment that paradoxically has created a self.

3. What you say about the stars was what I had in mind and I suppose I intended some enlargement or intensification by bringing in the heavens. I think I tried to consider birth in the largest of contexts. I also tried to make it as absolute as possible.

4. Oh the title just came. It is easy to see how Villon's title could suggest a melted down version of itself, given the subject of this poem.

5. The places and things in the poem—the houses, the dogs, the trees, the North West Arm—are places and things from my childhood. Most of them are Nova Scotian (French Village, Glen Margaret, Seabright), a few are remembered from Philadelphia. The house was a neighbor's house, but I don't recall which one or where.

6. I don't know what started the poem. Perhaps it was an attempt to write directly about my childhood, perhaps a try at getting more of the concrete world into my poetry.

7. The regressive movement of the poem determined its structure, a backward narrative. Its sounds are the result of a self-conscious striving after greater density. Its rhythms are the result of what I can only describe as a sense of musical rightness.

8. In general I don't know how readers have interpreted my poems; I don't read reviews or critical articles of my books unless their authors send them to me. Sometimes—as in the case of Linda Gregerson—the reading I get is way beyond anything I could have hoped for. The reading on which the questions sent to me were based struck me as extremely insightful, and for that I am grateful.

9. None.

Yours,

Mark Strand

MARK STRAND was born in Summerside, Prince Edward Island, Canada of American parents, but he has spent most of his life in the United States. He has taught at a number of colleges and universities, including Harvard, Virginia, and

Yale. His books of poetry are: *Sleeping with One Eye Open* (1964), *Reasons for Moving* (1968), *Darker* (1970), *The Story of Our Lives* (1973), *The Late Hour* (1978), *Selected Poems* (1980). He has been the recipient of numerous fellowships and awards; most recently, in 1979, the fellowship of the Academy of American Poets.

JEAN VALENTINE

*

December 21st

for Fr. Michael Perry

How will I think of you
"God-with-us"
a name: a word

and trees paths stars this earth
how will I think of them

and the dead I love   and all absent friends
here-with-me

and table: hand: white coffee mug:
a northern still life:

and you   with-us
without a body

quietness

and the infant's red-brown mouth   a star
at the star of a girl's nipple . . .

It is especially risky to talk about a Valentine poem, because each poem itself is the only way to express exactly what it has said, yet since most poems intend to do just that, it is more than ever important for students of poetry to ask how such a success could happen.

224

"December 21st" asks a question that is grammatically incomplete (a series of how clauses ending in three dots) and unanswered, yet it is so phrased that it is its own answer. The "deep structure" seems to be, "How shall a human creature perceive God?" But by saying how shall one "think of" a word, the physical universe, absent loved ones, near and present physical objects, the sensation of quiet, and the connection among them (the star of the sky become the star of the mouth at the star of the nipple), the answer is implied: we shall perceive them all as one, with wonder and worship. The word perceive is not used; the perception takes place in the reader. Since this perception is the kind that most often occurs as a wordless suffusion of feeling, I should guess that the poem was a long time developing its present spareness of image, exactness of structure, and its gradually intensifying reverence of tone, which starts with reflection and ends in worship. So, I'd like you to talk in some detail about how the poem took form. Could you comment on what made you begin the poem; when, in relation to Christmas, you started it; why you used so few concrete, specific images until the last two lines; why you said God-with-us instead of Emmanuel; whether the you in "you . . . /without a body" refers to God-with-us or to quietness or to a specific loved one or to all these; why you used the line and stanza breaks you did; why you used or omitted or added which kinds of punctuation; how long all these decisions took and in what order they occurred. It would be especially valuable in the case of this poem to see the worksheets. Do you still have them? And finally, how have your readers reacted to this poem? Have they taken it as far as you hoped? Farther?

After sitting down to a few more formal efforts, these last weeks, I see I'll do best by talking to you in a letter about this poem, "December 21st." So, here are the most particular responses I come up with, to what you ask and say about the poem. What you say seems the best that could be said about the poem, and alongside what I can say from the inside, it may make something interesting or companionable to your readers.

I wrote the poem in December 1977, at The MacDowell Colony in New Hampshire. As you say, worksheets might be valuable, but I don't have them; so I'm looking at the poem now, and in memory. This poem itself wasn't in the works a long time; maybe three or four weeks. But I'd been on leave for seven months, and at MacDowell for two months, by the time I wrote it. I'd been slowly working on what would turn out to be the sequence "Solitudes" (in the book *The Messenger*); when it got finished, the sequence began with "December 21st" and ended with a piece called "March 21st," but I didn't know anything about that when I wrote this December poem. I did know that December 21st marked the winter solstice—I was more conscious of that, living there in the country—and in the weeks before Christmas, a church nearby was playing Christmas carols on bells that we could hear in our studios. One of them that goes "O come, o come, Emmanuel" reminded me of that word, and its meaning, God with us. I used "God-with-us" in the poem because it had more immediacy for me than "Emmanuel," more sense of physical fact.

You ask what made me begin the poem. It's a good question, but I don't know if there's ever a complete true answer to it! It reminds me of Elizabeth

Bishop saying, "And how do they know? It takes probably hundreds of things coming together at the right moment to make a poem and no one can ever really separate them out and say this did this, that did that." But, sometime I suppose towards the beginning of writing the poem, I was conscious of not knowing at all how to see God or how to knowingly be seen by God, and at the same time I knew that this seeing was simple fact. So the "inside" of the poem was bewildered but peaceful. I remember thinking, "But I don't know how to look at this path, this table, etc., either"; but it was a warm, almost restful ignorance, if I can put it that way. I didn't feel that the answer was implied; more that the question wasn't *agitated*, I could let it be.

About why I use so few concrete specific images until the last two lines: well, I don't know. Looking at the poem now, I see what you mean. At the time, right from the second line on I thought I *was* with specific concrete images. The "quietness" for instance felt filled, not empty, a *positive* quietness; another thing I remember trying to get at was that no one, nothing, seemed away, or gone, though I was in fact sitting there alone in the studio. So the unconcreteness is nothing more interesting than a mistake; but mistakes have their own interest.

A few years ago I changed "and you/ without a body" to "and you with-us/ without a body." My hope was to make it more clear that the "you" I'm talking to is the same "God-with-us" as in the first stanza. "Quietness" is meant to be another way of saying "you"; and although a single specific loved one wasn't in my mind, I don't see any harm in it! I did mean to bring "the dead I love and all absent friends" along in to that "you."

About the line and stanza breaks, and the present and missing punctuation: it's all for timing, the wish to have someone else hear it the way I hear it; likewise the grammatical incompleteness of the poem. I needed a certain amount of space and time on the page to let the thing float, or rest; that seems familiar in some kinds of poetry. I don't remember how long all these decisions took, or in what order they occurred, except that, as I said, the poem didn't take long.

"And finally," you ask, how have readers reacted to the poem? One old friend and one-time mentor liked it best of the poems in that book. And a good friend, a young priest, whose chosen name is Emmanuel, likes it. When I found that out, I dedicated the poem to him; so I'm sending it now with the new "with-us," and with that dedication, both added since the book got printed.

JEAN VALENTINE was born in Chicago in 1934, and graduated from Radcliffe College in 1956. She has published four books of poetry: *Dream Barker and other poems*, Yale University Press, New Haven, 1965; *Pilgrims* (1969), *Ordinary Things* (1974), and *The Messenger* (1979), all published by Farrar, Straus & Giroux, New York City. She lives in New York City, and teaches at Sarah Lawrence College.

RICHARD WILBUR

*

Cottage Street, 1953

Framed in her phoenix fire-screen, Edna Ward
Bends to the tray of Canton, pouring tea
For frightened Mrs. Plath; then, turning toward
The pale, slumped daughter, and my wife, and me,

Asks if we would prefer it weak or strong.
Will we have milk or lemon, she enquires?
The visit seems already strained and long.
Each in his turn, we tell her our desires.

It is my office to exemplify
The published poet in his happiness,
Thus cheering Sylvia, who has wished to die;
But half-ashamed, and impotent to bless,

I am a stupid life-guard who has found,
Swept to his shallows by the tide, a girl
Who, far from shore, has been immensely drowned,
And stares through water now with eyes of pearl.

How large is her refusal; and how slight
The genteel chat whereby we recommend
Life, of a summer afternoon, despite
The brewing dusk which hints that it may end.

And Edna Ward shall die in fifteen years,
After her eight-and-eighty summers of
Such grace and courage as permit no tears,
The thin hand reaching out, the last word *love*,

Outliving Sylvia who, condemned to live,
Shall study for a decade, as she must,
To state at last her brilliant negative
In poems free and helpless and unjust.

1. *Is this poem the record of an actual visit with the Plaths and Edna Ward? Did you know Sylvia only by means of this meeting? How long after the event did you write the poem? Had Sylvia and her work become a "cult" by the time you wrote it?*

   In my book *The Mind-Reader*, I offered this little note on the poem: "Edna Ward was Mrs. Herbert D. Ward, my wife's mother. The poet Sylvia Plath (1932–1963) was the daughter of one of Mrs. Ward's Wellesley friends. The recollection is probably composite, but it is true in essentials." I keep no diary, and have a rotten memory, but would swear to this in court: that Mrs. Ward did telephone us in 1953, when we were living nearby in Lincoln, asking us to tea with Mrs. Plath and with her troubled and talented daughter. My wife and I were expected to be sympathetic and encouraging presences, and presumably we accepted the assignment, though our teas with Mrs. Ward and her guests were so many that specific memories elude us. In my mind's eye there is a clear image of the undergraduate Sylvia, "pale, slumped," fearfully withdrawn, and looking, as I later wrote in my notebook, like a *gisant* on a cathedral tomb. That image could have two possible sources: either it derives from Mrs. Ward's tea, or it comes from another occasion on which Sylvia Plath interviewed me for *Mademoiselle*. I met her once again, after her marriage to Ted Hughes, at the house of John Holmes, and found her animated and engaging.

   The poem was written in the seventies, when Sylvia (as I shall call her, despite our slight acquaintance) had been established in the canon, and the "confessional" in poetry was an issue. My poem, however, was not conceived as a comment on her reputation or as a consideration, by way of her, of the confessional mode in general.

2. *Could the last line be read as reproof, not only of Sylvia and the excesses of her followers, but of all the self-indulgences of the romantics? Those who are helpless cannot be free; unjust can mean not only unfair but deformed, untrue, not plumb. Am I overreading?*

   The last lines are not intended as reproof. The constellation *brilliant-free-helpless-unjust* is an effort to be fair and downright. The poems of Sylvia's last days were brilliant, and they were free in the sense that they came fast and well; they were helpless and unjust because she was writing out of an ill condition of mind in which she could not do justice to anything but her own feelings. There is a limit to the utility of a poetry so skewed and so personal, but I say that with regret and in no spirit of blame.

"Cottage Street" is sympathetic to Sylvia throughout. It does, however, potentially quarrel with those who glamorize emotional illness and regard suicide as honorific.

3. *Though the poem seems ostensibly to be about Sylvia and about poetry, it also raises such questions as, what is genius for? Is it a tool for fashioning civilization or a means of escape? Is it better to be immensely drowned or a life-guard in the shallows? Is it better to be an Edna Ward, making living your work of art? Do you wish the reader to resolve the questions you raise or to keep asking them?*

The poem does indeed raise such questions. Discussing them apart from the poem, I'd take the general position that life is more important than art (though in the greater sense of art the two are not separable), and that usable orderings of the world are more valuable than eccentric subjective intensities. Within the poem, these questions are so weighted, I trust, as not to make a case against Sylvia; I should like them to add up to a feeling of regret that a remarkable talent could not have survived to embrace more of common experience. It is not seriously assumed that poetry unlike Sylvia's must be shallow.

4. *The form of the poem exemplifies the restrained, balanced, gracious Edna Ward point of view, the acceptance and shaping of existence rather than a brilliant refusal. The stanzas are complete thoughts, the meter regular, the rhymes exact, the syntax and diction formal. Yet in them the winds of disorder churn: "frightened Mrs. Plath," "pale, slumped daughter," the strained atmosphere, the shame and impotence of the published poet, the possible choices between milk and lemon, weak and strong tea, life and death, and the shallows of the life-guard compared to the immensities of Sylvia's sea. To what extent did you consciously select and shape the poem's form to emphasize this irony in the situation?*

The pentameter quatrain is a familiar form in which definite rhythmic meanings may be conveyed to people who still have the hang of reading metrical verse. For example, the second quatrain of "Cottage Street" contains four end-stopped lines of no great rhythmic élan, which together with such subverted words as "strong" and "desires" give a sense of confinement, tedium, and tepidity. All of this contrasts with the free movement and wrenched, complex grammar of lines 12–16, which speak of Sylvia's having been "immensely drowned." I believe that this contrast of movement (and of words) may operate in three ways. First, it sets the intensity of Sylvia's suffering against a background which is low keyed and comfortably routine. Second, it may imply the nullity of the everyday as perceived by someone painfully self-absorbed. Third, it prepares, as "slight" and "genteel chat" continue to prepare, for a species of counter-statement in stanza six. I am better acquainted with depression and alienation than some who romanticize them, and I know that mental anguish can be "immense"; but there is also magnitude in a long life well lived in the world of others, and stanza six, without chiding Sylvia, laments that she was deprived of those dimensions. For those with whom the poem potentially quarrels, stanza six amounts to a reminder that the world is dull only to the dull or ill, and that mental illness entails a shrinkage of awareness and sensibility.

5. *How was the poem started? What changes did you make and in what order? Would you change the poem in any way if you were doing it now? If you have saved the worksheets, could I see copies of them?*

My worksheets have been given to a library. I daresay that the poem was written, as is usual with me, very slowly from beginning to end, with much tinkering in the process but no revision thereafter. At some time not long after Edna Ward's death, I wrote a few words in my notebook amounting to a suggestion that I might be able to make, out of my sketchy memories of a tea in Wellesley, a poem which would, in a short space, and with some atmospheric and emotional force, say all the things mentioned in 2, 3, and 4 above. I imagine that I got 'round to writing the poem when a good first line occurred to me.

6. *What other questions would you have liked me to ask?*

You might have asked, in view of my testimony, whether my poem has generally been taken as I meant it. I recall that one malign reviewer, perhaps in the *New Republic*, took it for an attack on Sylvia, and that two young women, fresh from some course in "American Women's Poetry from Phyllis Wheatley to the Present," once came to me for reassurances. But on the whole, those who have testified about "Cottage Street" seem to have understood what sort of balancing act I intended. I am glad of that, because I feel that a poem which doesn't largely control the responses of a trained reader has not done the job.

RICHARD WILBUR was born in 1921 in New York City and was brought up on a farm in New Jersey. He went to Amherst, served with the 36th (Texas) Infantry during World War II, and was then a junior fellow at Harvard. He has taught at Harvard, Wellesley, and Wesleyan, and is now writer-in-residence at Smith. He is a poet, translator, critic, editor, writer and illustrator of children's books, Broadway lyricist, and recipient of various prizes. Recent books are *Responses* (prose, 1976) and two books of verse, *The Mind-Reader* (1976) and *Seven Poems* (1981). In 1982 he published three volumes of translation: *Molière: Four Plays* (PEN Translation Prize), *The Whale*, and Racine's *Andromache*. He is a former president and chancellor of the American Academy of Arts and Letters.

NANCY WILLARD

*

Night Light

The moon is not green cheese.
It is china and stands in this room.
It has a ten-watt bulb and a motto:
made in Japan.

Whey-faced, doll-faced,
it's closed as a tooth
and cold as the dead are cold
till I touch the switch.

Then the moon performs
its one trick:
it turns into a banana.
It warms to its subjects,

it draws us into its light,
just as I knew it would
when I gave ten dollars
to the pale clerk

in the store that sold
everything.
She asked, did I have a car?
She shrouded the moon in tissue

and laid it to rest in a box.
The box did not say *moon*.
It said *This side up*.
I tucked the moon into my basket

and bicycled into the world.
By the light of the sun
I could not see the
moon under my sack of apples,

moon under slab of salmon,
moon under clean laundry,
under milk its sister
and bread its brother,

moon under meat.
Now supper is eaten.
Now laundry is folded away.
I shake out the old comforters.

My nine cats find their places
and go on dreaming where they left off.
My son snuggles under the heap.
His father loses his way in a book.

It is time to turn on the moon.
It is time to live by a different light.

1. *"Night Light" is to me a typical Willard poem because it transforms an absolutely
literal domestic object, in this case, a tasteless, mass-produced china nursery lamp in
the shape of a crescent moon, back into a real moon, with all its primitive mystery and
power. This transformation implies the broader transformation of the modern routines
of living into the original meaning of ritual: a response to the same compulsion that
would make a cat bring a mouse to her kittens, then lick them clean and curl around
them to sleep. This reinvesting of cliché with its full meaning seems so inevitable that it
looks easy. Just take any breakfast table: bread, poached egg, cup of coffee, knife and
fork, and arrange them so that hens flock and wheat fields wave and donkeys carry
panniers through mist-filled valleys. But most people and poets don't do that or don't
know that they can. Has this way of seeing been a lifelong habit of yours? Did your
parents or early reading encourage it? Do (can) you teach it to beginning poets?*

When I was a child, my mother used to amuse me during long train trips by
letting me play with whatever objects she was carrying in her purse. Her compact was a clam with a mirrored mouth, or a porthole opening onto another
country—and how could I get into that country? Her lipstick, hooded in its
jeweled case, was secret, dangerous, and alive. The metal curler she carried (to
liven up her bangs before walking into church) was a silver giraffe, long of leg
and elastic of neck.

So now a china moon is a modest banana—or a real moon. And instead of
acting out the game, I'm writing down the poem.

A good many of the poems I write for children come from toys I have
made—and almost always I have made these toys out of "found" material. The

poems in *A Visit to William Blake's Inn* evolved, in part, from the model of an inn (six feet tall) I was making around the time my editor at Harcourt Brace Jovanovich asked me to write a book of poems for children. The characters who inhabit the inn were stitched, glued, and painted from odds and ends—a ping-pong ball is the moon, false teeth are Druid shrines (a ring of blessed stones); stick pins, postcards, postage stamps, all became part of the life of the inn. The Wise Cow, the Sun and Moon Circus, the Marmalade Man—I made them with my hands before I made them in the poems.

I suppose turning a china moon into a real one is part of this process.

2. *In this poem you make no attempt to disguise the I or use other than personal experience, although the current reaction against so-called confessional poetry frowns on both. To what extent are you willing to follow this or other poetic fashions?*

I don't write confessional poetry; I have nothing very interesting to confess. The following excerpt from a lecture I gave on becoming a writer will explain why I don't—can't—follow poetic fashions.

> When I was growing up, ours was the only family I knew that did not buy its clothes in a department store. Spring and fall, an ancient lady would arrive at our house in a car nearly as weathered as herself. Her name was Ella. She came from Owosso, Michigan, and she stayed for a week. She would set up her portable sewing machine in our sunroom and plug in her radio and ask us, what clothes did we want her to make us this season?
>
> My mother and my sister prudently chose ready-made patterns from the big pattern books at Muehlig's. My aunt sent Ella an assortment of dresses she'd bought on sale, with instructions to "fix them so I look like I have a little more on top and a little less in the behind." I drew pictures of the dresses I wanted, leaning heavily on third-rate Victorian novels illustrated with consumptive young women in long skirts and blouses that ballooned at the shoulder and pinched at the wrist. To my girlfriends, who read *Seventeen* and wore cashmere sweaters and tailored skirts, I must have looked like the victim of a time warp. But Ella's business was to sew, not to criticize. She would study my sketch, draw up a pattern, and send me forth to select the material.
>
> Velvet, wool, muslin, corduroy, heaped on tables and folded on chairs, flooded the sunroom with promises of better things to come. One by one the fabrics, ample as flags, submitted to Ella's shears and took shape. She snipped, she basted.
>
> "Try it on," she said.
>
> Whatever I tried on was always full of pins. Whichever way I turned, the dress bit me, needled me. I stood with my arms straight out, as if directing the invisible traffic of needles and threads, while Ella crept round me on her knees, taking the measure of the hem, her tape measure dangling around her neck like a stole, her mouth so full of pins that she seemed to have grown whiskers. I turned, she pinned, and her radio told us its troubles. We listened to *Portia Faces Life*, *Ma Perkins*, *Stella Dallas*, *Backstage*

Wife, we listened to ads for Oxydol and Rinso, we heard how many boxtops of both you needed to send for your free recipe file and earrings. To this day when I read the story of creation in the book of *Genesis*, when I hear God commanding the light to come out of hiding and the earth to bring forth grass and creeping things and every beast after its own kind, I see them all falling from Ella's shears, waking to life under her needle. And behind God's voice, I hear the still, small voices of Portia and Stella Dallas and Ma Perkins, making it through.

On the day of Ella's departure, which was always after lunch, she would intone a long blessing over our food, in which she thanked God for my mother's cooking and implored Him to keep her car from breaking down. As she drove away, we could see her sewing machine and her radio and our half-finished garments piled high in the backseat, watching over her. Three weeks later a large box would arrive in which we found all we'd asked for and more. The dresses were folded and pressed. Attached to each were the scraps, rolled neat as a prayer rug. Years of sewing had taught Ella never to throw anything away.

One day my mother reminded me that Ella would not be around forever, and she bought me a sewing machine for Christmas and hired Ella to instruct me in its use. What Ella taught me about sewing has passed into my hands and become as automatic to me as tying my shoe. But more important than what she taught me about sewing was what she taught me about craft. An indifference to fashion. A respect for what is well-designed and well-made. Save all your scraps. Throw nothing away. If you don't get it right the first time, take it apart and try again. Revise. Anything well done takes patience, experience, and a lot of time. *"Becoming a Writer," Angel in The Parlor*, Harcourt Brace Jovanovich, 1983.

3. *In this poem you do not explain your meaning, but trust your reader to infer it from the title, which at first means department-store junk, but by the last line means a point of view, the light of primitive wisdom and worship. Would it bother you if readers made various interpretations of "different light"—if they read it as wholly comforting, unrealistic rather than more real, slightly sinister, or as the easy refuge of fantasy?*

The interpretations that readers make of this poem don't bother me, as long as they remember that good fantasy is not an easy refuge. It's a bridge that leads us back to our ancestors, the way dreams do. That's the kind of fantasy I'd like to write.

4. *To what extent do you (and have you here) modified actual details to shape the progress of the poem? If, for example, your bicycle basket contained a slab of salt pork instead of salmon, would you have mentioned the pork? Why? Or if there had been eight cats instead of nine, would you have said eight?*

A number of actual details were changed for the sake of the poem. We have only two cats. (I wish we had nine.) Why nine, in the poem? Perhaps I've addled my brain with a surfeit of Anglo-Saxon charms, like "Lay of the Nine Herbs" or "Lay of the Nine Twigs of Woden," or "Lay of the Magic Blasts":

I alone know the running streams,
And the nine adders now they guard.

I do not think my bicycle basket has ever carried salt pork or salmon, though it often carries groceries. But salmon seems more at home in this poem than salt pork. It was the Salmon of Knowledge and the nuts of the Nine Hazels of Wisdom that made Kionn so wise a poet in the old Irish tales. So the list of things I really do carry—meat, bread, milk, laundry—includes one that I'd like to carry: the magic fish, the feast that makes wise singers out of foolish poets.

5. *What determined your choice of a four-line stanza form with a final closing couplet?*

Ear and eye.

6. *How did this poem start? How did it grow? What did you change? When? Would you change anything now? Is this poem's development typical of the ways you work? If you have kept the worksheets of this poem, could I see copies?*

In the beginning was the light, an electric moon that my son liked to have lit in his room at night when he was small. You can't turn on the moon every night without asking yourself a few questions about what you are really doing.

NANCY WILLARD lives with her husband, Eric, and their son, James, in Poughkeepsie, New York, where she is a lecturer in the English Department at Vassar College. Her published writings include volumes of short stories, books of poetry, a collection of essays, and several children's books. A *Visit to William Blake's Inn* won the Newbery Medal in 1982.

Her most recent books include *Household Tales of Moon and Water* (poems), *Angel in the Parlor: Five Stories and Eight Essays,* and a novel, *Things Invisible to See.*

CHARLES WRIGHT

*

Nightdream

Each day is an iceberg,
Dragging its chill paunch underfoot;
Each night is a tree to hang from.
The wooden knife, the mud rope
You scratch your initials on—
Panoply, panoply.

Up and up from his green grave, your father
Wheels in the wind, split scrap of smoke;
Under him stretch, in one file, Bob's Valley, Bald Knob,
The infinite rectitude
Of all that is past: Ouachita,
Ocoee, the slow slide of the Arkansas.

Listen, the old roads are taking flight;
Like bits of string, they, too,
Rise in the pendulous sky,
Whispering, whispering:
Echo has turned a deaf ear,
The wayside is full of leaves.

Your mother floats from her bed
In slow-motion, her loose gown like a fog
Approaching, offering
Meat; across the room, a hand
Again and again
Rises and falls back, clenching, unclenching.

The chambers you've reached, the stones touched,
All stall and worm to a dot;
Sirens drain through the night; lights
Flick and release; the fields, the wet stumps,
Shed their hair and retire;
The bedroom becomes a rose:

(In Kingsport, beneath the trees,
A Captain is singing Dixie; sons
Dance in their gold suits, clapping their hands;
And mothers and fathers, each
In a soft hat, fill
With dust-dolls their long boxes).

1. *"Nightdream" especially interests me because it uses the apparent randomness and
    surrealism of one individual's dream to imply the attitudes and relationships that
    program the days of most individuals without their realizing it. Without dissolving the
    reader into this apparent randomness, the author might have to state such conclusions
    as, our actions compensate for our deep sense of guilt or lack, our need for pattern,
    purpose, ownership, beauty, symmetry. Consciousness of these stick through the
    dreams ("Panoply, panoply," "Each day is an iceberg . . . each night is a tree to
    hang from," "The infinite rectitude/of all that's past"), but most of the conclusions
    are implied in the series of dream details ("the wooden knife, the mud rope," "Under
    him stretch . . .", "a hand/ . . . clenching and unclenching," "The bedroom be-
    comes a rose"). Which came first, bits of real sleep dreams and/or awake dreams (free
    association) or the mood they invoke? Did they all occur at once? In this order? Or are
    they a later assemblage?*

    Like most of my poems—even those I still like (and this is one I still like
parts of)—I remember little, if anything, about its composition. I remember
the time: late spring or early summer 1972 (almost 11 years ago, today being
March 1983), my father having died in early May 1972. My mother had died
some eight years earlier, in 1964. I remember we lived in a small house on Oak
Street in Laguna Beach, California then, with an even smaller "cottage" out
back I used as a writing room (it had been a tool shed and surfboard storage
area before I converted it). Our son was quite young then, two, and it was
during the period—free time being at a premium—when I worked very consciously in stanzas in all my poems. Which is to say that for a period of several
years, due to family exigencies, I purposefully wrote poems in patterned
stanzas, that usually being the length of time allowable for concentrated attention. It began as a physical necessity, and evolved through the books *Hard
Freight* and *Bloodlines*, into a technical mystique and prosodic base for me.
Which ultimately, I suppose, along with other considerations, devolved into the
highly compressed "chapters" of my long poem, "China Trace." All this is just
to say that the stanza was, conceptually, the normal length of any given "run"
in a poem, the final poem, whatever its length, being merely a compilation, or
placing together, of these runs into some kind of melodic and overall whole.
And even though I don't work—or think—that way now (the runs are shorter
and more synaptical), I still find it an interesting idea, and can see how it
helped me in learning how to organize and squeeze down. *Ut filius poesis. . . .*

So the poem is an assemblage, finally put together from six blocks of material, which in turn were put together out of smaller bits and pieces. The blocks were originally in a different order (as they were written individually, remember), although the first and last stanzas were always first and last, it appears. It's called "Nightdream," but is, in fact, mostly a day dream. The only "dream" sequence is in the fourth stanza, which is taken from a sequence in a Luis Buñuel movie, "Los Olvidados," a story of Mexican street children. I called it "Nightdream" as I wanted that whole, rather slow motion quality to move the poem, as though it were underwater, and drifting back and forth in the currents, in focus and out, in and out. Waters of oblivion, and whatnot.

The first stanza states facts: what the mood is after a parent's death, the futility of things and their apparent proliferation, the inability of anything except the poem to rescue what once was. The second and third stanzas again state facts: what is missing, what is gone now for good. The fourth stanza brings in the other parent, also dead, whose sustenance in the material world is also gone, and cannot be reached ever again. The fifth stanza shows where the speaker is now, at a still, small point. The sixth stanza, in its putting away of childish things, allows the speaker to get on with it, the business at hand, the business of living. A gloss of the poem, of the emotional quotient of the poem, would include these lines from *Canto LXXVI* by Ezra Pound:

> nothing matters but the quality
> of the affection –
> in the end – that has carved the trace in the mind
> dove sta memoria

2. *What determined your selection and sequencing of the names in stanza two? Your father's history? Sound? Something else? Is the name "Kingsport" real, symbolic, both?*

Bob's Valley is next to Carter's Valley, and both can be seen, looking south toward the Smokies, from the ridge our house was on, Chestnut Ridge. Bald Knob is a combination of two terms given to hills without much timber on them, a bald or a knob. It's imaginary, beyond Bob's Valley, in the distant mountains. Ouachita is a river in Arkansas my father used to fish. Ocoee is a lake in Tennessee, but I also remember it as a river in western North Carolina and a series of dams on that river, Ocoee #1 and Ocoee #2. The Arkansas is, of course, the Arkansas River. He was from Little Rock. So sound and history both. Kingsport, Tennessee is where he lived the last 25 years of his life, where he died and where he is buried.

3. *Why is the last stanza in parentheses? Is it to indicate that it's not a night dream but an actual description of daytime events which drift into a dream interpretation at the end in order to merge the exposed and hidden parts of the iceberg and extend one individual's dream sequence to make it universal?*

Yes, something like that, if you leave off the last four words of the question. It's also in parenthesis because a poem I admire very much, Eugenio Montale's "6th Motet," has a last stanza in parenthesis as an enigmatic addition to the body of the poem that explains and extends the emotional quality of the poem at the same time. He does it with one image. I try to do it with an imagistic scene.

4. *Does the last line's reference to "long boxes" refer both to coffins and the florists' boxes used for long-stemmed roses? A combination of natural futility and the fragile beauty of human accomplishment—hence a tone of both cynicism and celebration?*

I had no notion of floral boxes, but perhaps subliminally there was something there. For the last 20 years of his life my father raised roses, raised them very seriously, planning the beds all winter and working them all summer. The last line of the fifth stanza has that as background. But I had thought of the long boxes only as coffins, which the dolls of my parents now inhabit, as I, as the doll of my son, will do as well. One is no longer a child when one's parents are no longer alive. So it is celebration in that sense (though that's not much cause for celebration). I never thought it cynical in any way. My father's father, and his grandfather were both captains: one in the Confederate army, one in the American army in the Spanish-American War. I was a captain in the U.S. army. Out of four generations, he alone escaped the military (although he did spend three years in Oak Ridge during World War II in "related" activity). And sons always wear gold suits.

5. *I detect in the poem a great deal of conscious craftsmanship. Could you comment on why you chose the six-line stanza, how you chose your line breaks, to what extent luck or searching produced the sound echoes of, for example, fathers, fill (and by implication fall), doll and boxes in the last line or what determined the doublings of sound, meaning, and rhythm of "Panoply, panoply," "whispering, whispering," "Again and again," and the same effect in "approaching, offering" and "clenching, unclenching"?*

I was working in seven- and nine-syllable lines for the most part back then (with sixes and eights and tens scattered about). The swing was three/four stress lines, an occasional two and the odd five. But the base line, the background line, was seven syllables and everything branched out from that. If the line broke better with eight, then I'd eight it. And so on. I probably chose the six line stanza because the first stanza I finished had six lines in it. And that would be the guiding block. I see that on the first page of the six work pages I have for the poem (It seems to have come out fairly whole and quickly—grief will sometimes make that happen, a terrible controller and organizer), I have managed three lines in one spurt, most of which stayed in the poem, two lines that were an assumption I then made an image from, and one additional line that became part of the second stanza. Then the writing stops and there is a ridiculous-looking drawing of a pig, complete with "oink," and a hard pencil line down the center of the page. I can only assume I got as far as those disparate six lines, Luke came in, I tried to draw him a pig, he then tried his hand at it (the one line down the center of the page) and that was that for poems that day. The next page of the notebook is more complete.

There is, of course, always the element of luck in sound and sound echoes, but *father* and *fill* and *doll* and *boxes* weren't luck only. There is, I hope, the thought toward quantity in that stanza, the heft and length of syllable, the sound it makes in the ear, the shape it makes in the ear, the patterning of sound that weaves in and out and through the doubling and repetition, the total articulation of the stanza. All the sound values are conscious. If we don't make music, how can our voices rise to the primal chord?

6. *How many and what revisions did the poem go through? In what order, over what period? If you saved the worksheets, may I see a copy?*

As I said, it seems to have come out amazingly clean. The poem following it was still-born. The one preceding it went on for 16 pages. You never know. There seem to be three run-throughs for this one. An unusually small number.

7. *What other questions do you wish I had asked?*

No more, please.

CHARLES WRIGHT was born in Pickwick Dam, Tennessee, in 1935 and was educated at Davidson College and the University of Iowa. He lives in Charlottesville, Va. He has published six books of poems, the most recent being *The Other Side of the River,* and two volumes of translations, *The Storm,* by Eugenio Montale, and *Orphic Songs,* by Dino Campana. His *Country Music/Selected Early Poems,* was a winner of the 1983 American Book Award in poetry.

DAVID YOUNG

*

October Couplets

1.
Again the cold: shot bolt, blue shackle,
oxalic acid bleaching a rubber cuff,

a cow-eyed giantess burning roots and brush,
the streak and smash of clouds, loud settling jays,

crows roosting closer—my older-by-one-year bones
have their own dull hum, a blues: it's all plod,

but they want to go on, above timberline,
to boulders, florets, ozone, then go free

in the old mill that the wind and the frost run
all day all night under the gauze and gaze of stars.

2.
Somewhere between sperm cell and clam shell
this space cruiser takes me places I'd rather

stay clear of: a planet all graveyard, mowed,
graveled and paved, bride-light and parson-shade,

or a milkweed, bitter, about to burst, or a dropped
acorn even a squirrel didn't want, browning to black,

and I have to learn to relax with it all, to sing
"Where the bee sucks, there suck I," though the lily

is sticky and choking, bees don't suck, and the sting
is a greeting you never recover from.

3.
"Steam of consciousness," a student's fluke,
makes me see a lake, linen-white at evening,

some amnesia-happy poet all curled up
sucking a rock at its black bottom;

oblivion tempts everyone, but I
would miss too much—whales and ticks,

the weather's subtle bustle, blue crab clouds,
my kite rising, paper and sticks, a silver ember,

while the poem's ghost waits by the empty band shell,
does a little tango, taps out its own last line.

4.
But this fall rain, somehow both thread and button,
sewing itself to the malachite grass,

beading the clubs and brushes of the spruce —
all day I have sat as if gazing over water,

wind feathering the reservoir, stupid as a church,
and thought of summer: all those burst horizons,

mineral cities, rosy meat, clean seas and shaggy islands,
the wine cork popping in the grape arbor,

these things seem better and clearer than gods just now,
raspberries hung like lamps among their brambles.

5.
These leaves, these paper cutouts drifting the yard,
stars, fish, mittens, saddles: the badges and epaulets

of emptiness—last night in my dream
I was the killer, the guard who failed to stop him,

and the child who froze and was spared: Nothing lasts,
sang the crowd, and I answered, It sure does;

is nothing sacred, roared the statesman—I do
believe it is, said I . . . I wake and shave,

still full of my dreamflood—oh skim milk sky,
oh brown star curling in my hand. . . .

1. *In North America we tend to think of October as a crisp month: colors bright, air bracing, an assertion of finality, yet a stimulation of resolve. And we think of the couplet form as crisp, the form of firm assertions. In "October Couplets" you recall this expectation by your title, but the poem makes the finality less final and the resolve uncertain. The wind and frost still run the old mill under "gauze and gaze"; the poem's ghost taps out its own last line; raspberries hang like lamps; and the resolve takes place in a dream that is countered, but not at once destroyed, by a sky gone to "skim milk" and a star to a "curling" leaf. The couplet form too becomes much more tentative than we might expect. Rhythm, sound and thought are not boxed in matched pairs of lines; the slant rhymes occur between couplets or within them rather than at the ends of the lines; and only an occasional line scans. But each of the five groups ends on a statement which clearly concludes it, and the last couplet sounds suspiciously like iambic pentameter. I should much like to know how and why you came to use this traditional form and genre for coming to terms with your own mortality.*

While I'm accustomed to analyzing poems in my teaching, I always feel a bit tongue-tied in talking about my own work, as if I had been caught on the wrong side of a fence. Last spring, visiting a class that had been reading my poems, I found myself saying, "Well, the speaker in this poem," and then laughing because while that is the useful caution we urge on students—distinguishing the poet from the voice that speaks in the poem—it seemed odd to be using that kind of distinction with my own poem. It was right, but it felt funny. Can one be the speaker *of* a poem, *in* a poem, and then turn round and speak *about* the poem without getting roles mixed up? It's tricky, but I'll try.

Your question certainly makes my task easier, because it points me toward my answer. Yes, I was working with a tension, exciting to me but heretofore scarcely acknowledged consciously, between tidy form and messy content. Something symmetrical seems to be going on—five sections, five couplets each, strict variations on a theme—and yet the content belies that, since the poem constantly seems to be turning corners and coming upon the unexpected, with the speaker (there's that funny feeling, but it's true, the speaker isn't exactly me) growing confused and uncertain, at the mercy of his experiences rather than, as the form would suggest, in brisk command of them. Often in Yeats there is an almost comical discrepancy between the "Yeats" inside the poem, failing and confused, and the Yeats outside, confident maker. I don't mean to compare myself with this master, but to point out that the tension I speak of has good precedent. My "postmodern" version of it takes the matter more for granted, while searching for a music very different, I would think, from that of Yeats.

2. *The poem's tone seems at once sober and amused, rueful rather than appalled, very understated, very complex. I find it hard to frame a question about it without over-simplifying. Could you talk about the poem's tone: just what do you consider it to be; was it consciously chosen before you started writing, or did it grow gradually out of the poem's images as you went along; did it change?*

If you find it hard to frame the question, pity my struggle for an answer! I would say that the poem's consciousness is weighted by a sense that the subject is too familiar: we all face death, we all think of autumn as a time when consciousness of mortality is not only apt to weigh on the individual but to provoke the poet to poetry. The persona's melancholy may be increased by the consciousness of all those other autumn poems, and the reader, perhaps, is invited to find that mildly amusing. I suppose I believe that even when we seem to be in command of our experience (see above) we are more likely to be at the mercy of it. So the speaker of this poem responds to accidents. A student typo reveals to us that the speaker's a teacher and that his mind can be set off on a course of associations by the strangest or slightest chance, a fact that he is at no pains to conceal from us. Jaques, in *As You Like It*, is a professional melancholic, which means he really enjoys it. So too my speaker's *weltschmerz* is qualified by his delight in finding figures for it. A planet all graveyard (as ours, alas, may someday be) makes this one a bit more habitable for the moment. The fact that the color of grass can sometimes be compared to malachite is an appetizing counterpoint to the glum mood produced by rain. All the things that leaves resemble in their desiccation makes contemplating them—not to mention rak-ing them—less tedious. And so the improvisation goes. The poem covertly celebrates invention, I suspect, as an antidote to autumn gloom, so that its tone is more than a little at odds with itself. This may be most openly acknowledged in the very middle of the poem, the middle couplet of section three. The speak-er's love affair with the world continues, his "steam of consciousness" continues to cast up patterns that please him and make his short life something more than simply nasty and brutish. The climb into the ozone goes on.

3. *What was the sequence of the poem's development: was it planned or discovered? In what order were the parts composed? Over what period? With what kinds of revisions? Which lines came hardest? Which are your favorites? Have you saved the worksheets?*

I'm writing this in Vermont, and the worksheets that would enable me to answer this question fully are in Oberlin. I recall writing this poem in a matter of two or three weeks, in the sequence in which it now stands. I recall revising it, but not, I think, very substantially. I don't date worksheets, but I'm pretty sure the poem was started in late October, 1979, and finished in November. Coming up was a Wallace Stevens 100th birthday celebration. Stevens's late, long-line couplet meditations may well have partly inspired me, but I also know that I like Sylvia Plath's use of couplets, and I think I was teaching *Ariel* that fall. Readers may make what comparisons they like among these models.

As for favorite lines or passages, I feel a kind of skeptical affection for the whole thing. After I've finished a poem I find it acquires what interest it has through the eyes of others. A friend wrote to say he found the "planet all graveyard" image unforgettable, so I am fond of it for his sake. "Sperm cell and clam shell" tickled a couple of listeners when I read the poem out loud, so it became a phrase I like by the same token. Other associations are more private. "The weather's subtle bustle" amuses me because of the anagram. The raspberries "hung like lamps" make me think of Italy, where we had been that summer, picking berries where we were staying and learning their name, *lamponi*, from the gardener. The passage in which there's equivocation about "nothing" makes me a little nervous because I am concious of not being there first, but that is where the poem wanted to go. Finally, I'm fond of the image of the giantess (a sort of Juno) burning roots and brush because I had been carrying the image around for years without successfully putting it in a poem. It's something that farmers do a lot in my area, a sort of leaf-burning on a grand scale. These are the sorts of reactions one is apt to have about one's own work, I believe: detached, professional, eccentric.

4. *What do you expect from your readers: a recognition of Hopkins' "Windhover" in "it's all plod" (line 6); a knowledge of the context of "Where the bee sucks. . ."; a smile at noticing that the slant rhyme of "gauze and gaze" don't end the couplet's lines; an ability to paraphrase and explain the syntax of the first two lines of Part Five; an awareness of the symbolic value of sky as it changes from the first stanza to the last? In other words, if you had your druthers, just who would be your ideal reader, and how would he go about reading this poem?*

Another hard question, but I'm glad you asked it. I would be deeply chagrined if any reader thought the point of the poem was to uncover allusions. Writing a poem that is partly about the activity of writing a fall poem, I can't avoid them. They are part of the music, part of the method of letting the poem accumulate itself by association. They probably enrich the reading if you know them. But they have the same value as anything else, no more or less, and they won't mean to the reader, necessarily, what they mean to me. I have tried not to put in anything that would *depend* for its meaning on the reader's knowing exactly what it was and where it came from. I have rules! The ghosts who flit around section three, for example, include Sylvia Plath and Samuel Beckett and Charles Dickens and Fred Astaire. But they are just ghosts, and they keep company with my own history, unknown to the reader, and my predilection for certain sounds and combinations of sounds. I keep coming back to the notion of music because I think it is the truest thing to say about the composition of the poem. To call it a pure musical exercise sounds excessive. Some readers will think it has no music whatsoever. But music is what I was after. Is that a technical interest? Well, yes and no. Doesn't music, when it works, express all we know and feel, and in a way which we are helpless to explain? "October Couplets" isn't *all* anyone knows or feels, but it does try to add a little music to the world. No wonder my tongue ties up at the thought of explaining it. Now, if it were just by somebody else. . . .

DAVID YOUNG's poem, "October Couplets," is from his new collection, *Foraging*, which Wesleyan will publish early in 1986. His other books include *The Names of a Hare in English* (Pittsburgh, 1979), *Work Lights: Thirty-two Prose Poems* (Cleveland State, 1977), *Boxcars* (Ecco, 1973), and *Sweating Out the Winter* (Pittsburgh, 1969). He has also published two critical studies of Shakespeare, and translations from several languages, most notably Rilke's *Duino Elegies* (Norton, 1978) and *Four T'ang Poets* (*Field* Translation Series, 1980). He teaches at Oberlin College and coedits *Field*, a semiannual poetry magazine. He has also coedited two anthologies: *The Longman Anthology of Contemporary American Poetry*, and *Magical Realist Fiction: An Anthology*.